Six Modernist Moments in Poetry

Six Modernist Moments in Poetry

by David Young

University of Iowa Press   Iowa City

University of Iowa Press, Iowa City 52242

http://www.uiowa.edu/uiowapress

Copyright © 2006 by the University of Iowa Press

All rights reserved

Printed in the United States of America

Design by Wendy Stevenson

The University of Iowa Press is a member of Green Press
Initiative and is committed to preserving natural resources.

Printed on acid-free paper

Library of Congress Cataloging-in-Publication Data

Young, David, 1936–.

Six modernist moments in poetry / by David Young.

p.   cm.

Includes bibliographical references and index.

ISBN 0-87745-954-1 (cloth)

1. Poetry, Modern—20th century—History and criticism.

2. Modernism (Literature).   I. Title.

PN1271.Y68 2005   2005043913

809.1'9112—dc22

06 07 08 09 10 C 5 4 3 2 1

CONTENTS

ACKNOWLEDGMENTS

I would like to thank the following for permission to quote:

"The Bowl of Roses," "The Panther," and "Archaic Torso of Apollo" from *The Book of Fresh Beginnings* by Rainer Maria Rilke, translated by David Young. Copyright 1994 by Oberlin College. Reprinted by permission of Oberlin College Press.

"Among School Children" from *The Collected Works of W. B. Yeats*, vol. 1: *The Poems*, revised and edited by Richard J. Finneran. Copyright 1928 by the Macmillan Company; copyright renewed 1956 by Georgie Yeats. Reprinted with the permission of Scribner, an imprint of Simon and Schuster Adult Publishing Group.

"Sunday Morning" and "Earthy Anecdote" from *Collected Poems* by Wallace Stevens. Copyright 1954 by Wallace Stevens. Reprinted by permission of Alfred A. Knopf, Inc.

"January Morning" and "Danse Russe" from *The Collected Poems of William Carlos Williams*, vol. 1: *1909–1939*, edited by A. Walton Litz and Christopher MacGowan. Copyright 1938 by New Directions Publishing Corporation. Reprinted by permission of New Directions Publishing Corporation.

"An Octopus" from *The Collected Poems of Marianne Moore*. Copyright 1935 by Marianne Moore; copyright renewed 1963 by Marianne Moore and T. S. Eliot. Reprinted with the permission of Scribner, an imprint of Simon and Schuster Adult Publishing Group.

"Mediterranean" and "To Spend the Afternoon" from *Selected Poems* by Eugenio Montale, translated by Jonathan Galassi, Charles Wright, and David Young. Copyright 2004 by Jonathan Galassi, Charles Wright, and David Young. Reprinted by permission of Oberlin College Press.

The Rilke chapter grew out of a shorter piece written for a Rilke symposium in *FIELD* 63 (Fall 2000). The Yeats chapter was presented as a lecture, "'Man

Can Embody Truth, But He Cannot Know It': Yeats's 'Among School Children,'" in the Oberlin College winter term series "Truth," January 2003.

I owe a considerable debt of gratitude to friends who read chapters of this manuscript at various stages of its completion: John Hobbs, James Longenbach, Peter Schmidt, and David Walker. Their suggestions and encouragement were invaluable.

INTRODUCTION

DURING MY freshman year in college I happened to pull a book off a library shelf that turned out to be the work of a modernist poet. The poet was Wallace Stevens, and the book was *The Auroras of Autumn.* It was a momentous occasion. The sun stood still, and the world began to rearrange itself. I could scarcely make heads or tails of what Stevens was saying, but I knew by my excited response to his language, his playful titles, and the mysteries of subject and speaker that I was in the presence of something important and that I was going to need some time to figure it all out.

That wasn't really my first encounter with modernist poetry. I had had a high school infatuation with the introspective self-dramatizings of T. S. Eliot and a merry old time with the savagery and sentimentality of e. e. cummings, who was then my favorite poet. But this was different. There was something uncompromising in the Stevens poems, something truly new that both challenged my worldview and piqued my curiosity. There would be no turning back from that moment when I found myself walking into the brilliant light and profound shadow of the modernist poet's world.

That day in that college library in Minnesota was the beginning of my introduction to a reconfigured universe, and this book marks an outcome of that encounter. Years of studying and teaching, writing poems myself, translating poetry, and thinking hard and lovingly about the modernist poets have all led me to assemble this composite portrait. I have concluded that the modernist narrative is really many narratives at once and that modernist poetic practice as I understand and value it can best be demonstrated through close attention to six exemplary poems: Rainer Maria Rilke's "The Bowl of Roses," W. B. Yeats's "Among School Children," Wallace Stevens's "Sunday Morning," William Carlos Williams's "January Morning," Marianne Moore's "An Octopus," and Eugenio Montale's "Mediterranean."

These are six rooms in my gallery of modernist poetry. It takes both time and patience to explore them fully. It has certainly taken me the better part of a lifetime. Yeats and Stevens were my first discoveries. It took me longer to learn how to hear William Carlos Williams's music and longer still to tune in successfully to Marianne Moore's. Rilke and Montale, meanwhile, were poets I had to discover by means of translation; caring enough for their poems to bring them over into English finally gave me a familiarity with their worlds and sensibilities that I do not think I could have achieved in any other way.

All six of my "moments" are poems that ask a good deal of their readers. I would not call them willfully obscure, but in the process of acting out their revolutionary discoveries, they take some extraordinary twists and turns. They are full of risky behavior, especially in relation to traditional notions of what poems ought to do and be. It's my hope that grouping them together and examining them in the company of someone who has spent a lot of time with them will prove a helpful experience for the reader.

What might readers expect along the way? In the first instance, perhaps, we can say that these are all poems that are in part about poetry, implicitly and sometimes explicitly. Modernist poems are notoriously reflexive. They are about themselves, the creative process, and the problems of their linguistic medium. They tend to make us participate in the experiences and struggles that brought them into existence. Their creators do not pass themselves off as wise experts, packaging the truth for you, but rather as fallible fellow humans, struggling with large questions and unsure of definite answers. We join these workers in their workshops, "putting dirigibles together," as Richard Wilbur once put it.[1]

But what if you've never seen a dirigible? Having one put together in front of you, then cruising in it, is going to change your view of everything. And you find, to your astonishment, that your own role is crucial. The thing won't fly without you. Modernist poems posit an indispensable role for the reader, usually a remarkably creative one. Such a poem, as one critic notes, "remains hypothetical until the reader enacts it" (Walker, 1984, 17), and it thereby acknowledges the act of reading as a necessary element in the creative process.

Thus we have the apparent contradiction of an art that is announcing its own limits and exploring its own boundaries, even as it tries to open up new kinds of knowledge and new areas of experience. Modernist poems tend to put us in an imaginary space (see Reynolds) where we see the world in new terms. We're aware of the flimsy construction of the dirigible, you might say, but we're also delighted to realize that it can rise above its own beginnings, giving us a larger view of the world we live in. Reading these poems, we hover over our lives, re-creating our sense of their meaning and location.

In recent years attention to modernist works of art has shifted from an emphasis on their surface characteristics (the lower case of cummings, the Baudelairean love affair with urban squalor in Eliot) to a consideration of their innermost impulses and ultimate motives. It is as if we finally began to listen to Mallarmé, who said as long ago as 1861 that artists should be concerned less with the object represented in a work of art "than with the effect it produces" (Hamilton 157). That relocation of aesthetic focus from verisimilitude of representation to expression by the artist and to complex response in the reader or spectator was really a revolution, the advent of a "postrealism" that is still playing out its full possibilities.

Modernist poems also tend by their very nature to be both fragmentary and dynamic. They like to multiply perspectives on a subject and to include different and even contradictory responses; hence the fragmentary aspect. But multiplication also involves process, which introduces the dynamic element as well. Painters did a similar thing; Cézanne's paintings, as an art historian has put it, offer us multiple sightings of their subjects that introduce change and process—to still lifes as well as to landscapes and portraits. The result is a picture that "becomes a record of the continuous present, of the experience of space in the mode of time" (Hamilton 44). The playing with space and time is a modernist constant (Kern); the ways in which it can be done differ tremendously, which is why we are better off with six poets and six poems than just one poet, such as Pound, or a single work, such as the *Cantos*.

The modernist aesthetic's immediate predecessor was the late-nineteenth-century movement called symbolism. The symbolist view of art, which made the artist a kind of priest and art's subject matter mostly a spiritual longing for escape and transcendence, had conferred upon the imagination a tremendous new authority and validity. The new understanding of imagination's role was quite comparable to the ideas being worked out by the then contemporary philosophers eventually known as phenomenologists. Their reconfigured philosophy argued that imagination is *always* involved in perception. The old way of thinking about imagination had been to see it as an irrelevant warehouse of unreliable images. The new way recognized it as "a *sui generis* activity of our intentional relation to the world" (Kearney 16). In other words, human consciousness, which is a constant interrogation of the meaning of things, cannot operate without imagination. We construct reality as we go about our daily living and perceiving, and that fact validates the artistic imagination as a heightened form of ordinary human thought and consciousness.[2]

Tying imagination back into the activities of perception and conscious-ness helped heal the great split between art and life that the Symbolists had encountered. We will see that process of healing being enacted in the first two of our poets, Rilke and Yeats, both of whom grew up in the midst of the Symbolist movement and turned themselves gradually into modernists as they matured. Both were anxious about art's relevance to life and about the artist's relation to the experience of ordinary people. Both saw their poetry as a struggle to resolve the art/life differences. The generation that followed them, represented here by Stevens, Williams, Moore, and Montale, was much more confident that art speaks to life and from life's midst and is inti-mately connected to everyday objects and experiences. As a consequence, they reside more squarely and fully in the modernist and phenomenological consciousness.

Three of the four poets in that "second generation" are American, and, more to the point, they are Americans who stayed home, as opposed to exiles like Stein, Pound, and Eliot. Their connection to international mod-ernism meant that they had to formulate their aesthetics and practice their art in circumstances that must sometimes have seemed especially difficult. It was one thing to be in Paris or London or Zurich in these years; it was another thing to be in Rutherford or Hartford or Brooklyn. But if modernist art was to be truly valid, applicable to every place and every culture, then it could and should be naturalized and practiced on American soil. Stevens, Williams, and Moore all found different and fascinating ways of making good on that possibility. American modernists are more often examined these days along the nationalist lines pursued by American Studies. Yet their connection to the aesthetics and experiments of their European counter-parts is one we cannot neglect if we are to understand them fully.

For my final modernist I return to Europe and to an Italian master, Euge-nio Montale, who, like the three Americans, found that his own native locale, in this case the coast of Liguria, could become the crucible in which his modernist art was forged. He confirms the international character of modernism and its transportability to different languages, cultures, and locales. He also affirms its determination to make art in the here and now out of simple materials at hand.

The loving study of the everyday world produces some of modernism's finest moments. The prolonged and empathic engagement with things such as a bowl of roses, a children's classroom, a Sunday in spring, a ferry trip from New Jersey to Manhattan, a wilderness mountain, and a rugged sea-coast produces an exhilarated sense of connection to the nonhuman world and its inner vitality. It is the excitement connected with "being aware of being." When we add the reflexivity and self-examination of modernist poems we add a layer of awareness, a new dimension in which the text itself becomes continuous both with our selves and our outer world. It is "being aware of being aware of being."[3]

Modernist poetic practice tended to challenge orthodox ways of thinking, including the old binaries of mind and body, subject and object, inner and outer, human and nonhuman. The binaries have tended to reinforce false assumptions about the human place in the world. Thus it is that, again and again, these modernist poems move toward a critique of our long-standing anthropocentrism. In that sense they continue a tradition whereby poetry has often presented a sort of minority report to the official culture, including its notions, sometimes reinforced both by religion and science, of the primacy and exclusiveness of human needs and desires. Turning to the nonhuman world with a new respect and interest, modernist poets challenged old assumptions about it. Their insights prefigured positions that would eventually be outlined by deep ecologists and ecofeminists. In six quite different ways, each of my chosen poets reflects a sensitivity to issues that are currently embraced by environmentalists; together they mount a substantial critique of what one critic calls "Lord Man" (Oelschlager 69).

If emergent phenomenology gives these poems common ground, so do a number of other factors. Darkness plays a powerful role in their visual emphasis in quite varied ways. Experimentation with poetic form, involving a sometimes contentious dialogue with the past, takes them in different directions while giving them a common purpose. Suspicious of finality, they eschew definitive resolutions and emphatic endings. Meanwhile, skepticism about firm truths and received orthodoxies helps them forge their new models of being and, indeed, makes them as diverse as they finally become. I document these features as I go along and survey them again briefly in my concluding remarks.

Writing this book for the general reader is a challenge I have willingly embraced. An additional challenge stems from the fact that Montale and Rilke must be presented in translation, and I am well aware that any "close reading" of poetic texts in other languages is problematic. In both cases, I have chosen poems that seem to me highly accessible despite their first existence in another language. Readers who can read the Rilke and Montale texts in their original form will, of course, have an advantage, and those texts are readily available in bilingual editions. I have addressed specific issues of translation quite often along the way. Meanwhile, I think the expanded horizon for modernist poetry is worth the difficulty involved in negotiating between languages.

Each poem in its entirety precedes the chapter that discusses it. That both allows and presumes an initial acquaintance with the poem before the reader embarks on the discussion, although I also cite lines and passages frequently during the course of each account so that readers will not have to shuttle back and forth.

An entire century now lies between our own time and the beginnings of modernist poetic practice. The distance has not lessened the power of these poems to alter the world in the way that I first found it altered in that college library some half a century ago. They retain their magic, their daring, and their profundity. Readers can still thrill to their newness and the changed awareness they offer. These dirigibles, we might say, still fly!

Six Modernist Moments in Poetry

1

Rainer Maria Rilke writes

THE BOWL OF ROSES

Angry ones: you saw them flare up, saw two boys
ball themselves into a something
that was all hatred, tumbling on the ground
like an animal attacked by bees;
actors, towering overstaters,
raging horses, crashing to collapse,
eyes rolling, baring their teeth
as if the skull was going to peel itself,
starting from the mouth.

But now you know how that's forgotten:
this full bowl of roses stands before you,
unforgettable, filled to the brim
with the utmost expression of being, bending,
yielding, unable to give, simply existing,
that could ever be ours: utmost for us too.

Soundless life, opening and opening, no end in sight,
a use of space that takes no space away
from space that things around it need,
an existence with almost no outlines, all background
and pure inwardness, and much strange softness
and self-illuminated—right to the rim:
do we know anything, anywhere, that's like this?

Then like this: that emotion is born
from the touch of petal to petal?
And this: that a petal comes open like an eyelid
and underneath are just more eyelids, nothing else,
closed, as though they had to be asleep

ten times deeper to shut down visionary power.
And this above all: that through these petals
light somehow has to pass. From a thousand bright skies
they slowly filter each drop of darkness
within whose fiery luster the tangled group
of stamens stirs and rears erect.

And the movement in the roses—look:
gestures from such small angles of eruption
they'd never be noticed if not for the way
their rays fan out to the cosmos.

Look at that white one; it has opened in bliss
and stands there in its great splayed petals
like a Venus erect in her shell;
and the blushing one, that turns and leans
as if embarrassed, toward the one that's cool,
and how that cool one won't respond, withdraws,
and how a cold one stands, wrapped in itself,
among the opening ones, that shed everything.
And *what* they shed: how it is light or heavy,
how it can be a cloak, a load, a wing
and then a mask, now this, now that,
and *how* they shed it: as if before a lover.

Is there anything they can't become? Wasn't
that yellow one, lying there hollow and open,
the rind of a fruit where the very same color
more concentrated, orangey-red, was juice?
And was unfurling just too much for this one,
because in the air its anonymous pink
has picked up a bitter aftertaste of violet?
And the one made of cambric, isn't it a dress
to which the soft and breath-warm slip still clings,
both of them tossed aside in morning shadows
near an old pool in the forest?
And this one, opalescent porcelain,
easily shattered, a shallow china cup

filled with small, lit butterflies,—
and that one, which holds nothing but itself.

Aren't all of us like that, containing just ourselves,
if self-containment means: transforming the outside world
and wind and rain and spring's great patience
and guilt and restlessness and masquerading fate
and the darkening of the earth at evening
and even the clouds that change and flow and vanish,
and even the vague command of the distant stars
all changed to a handful of inwardness.

It now lies carefree in these open roses.

(Tr. David Young, *The Book of Fresh Beginnings*)

THIS POEM of some seventy-two lines must have felt very new in 1907 and still retains the capacity to startle and unsettle us. It begins disconcertingly, creating an emphatic discrepancy between its title and opening lines, then switches tone and returns, with what proves to be a surprising amplitude, to the title's promise. Its speaker, whom we more or less take to be the poet, brims with urgency and passion, addressing a "you" whose identity is never fully revealed. The poem is divided into stanzas, which helps us follow the shifts of subject and thought, but only two of the nine stanzas are the same length, and they do not follow any particular pattern (the sequence is 9-6-7-11-4-12-15-8-1). We get the impression that their changing sizes are governed by the subject, the bowl of roses, rather than by a commitment to any traditional pattern.

The poem is somewhat daunting, not so much because it feels obscure—it is quite clear compared to many modernist texts, in fact—but because of its length and evident intensity. That so much passion should be expended on a simple flower arrangement or a still life painting of such an arrangement may make us wary. Sentimentality is usually understood to mean an emotional response in excess of the occasion or subject, and this poem seems to be risking that charge. The subject does not seem to match the treatment. Why write about a bowl of roses at length and so passionately? We may wonder what in the world occasioned this poem. How did the speaker manage to muster so much excitement about a relatively simple subject?

As it happens, we know quite a bit about the circumstances of the poem's composition. "The Bowl of Roses" was written in January, 1907, while Rilke was using a cottage in Capri, part of the estate of a wealthy German family. He had just turned thirty-one and had been invited to winter there. When he was not working, he enjoyed the company of the three women who were wintering there, too, and who admired him greatly. These circumstances suggest a certain amount of luxury and pampering, and readers suspicious of Rilke's taste for aristocrats and patronage may bristle at this information. They will also not find it especially inspiring to learn that he wrote the poem in part to acknowledge indebtedness to another friend who had been his hostess, a countess.[1] Does the sentimentality the poem risks reflect the wealth and indulgence of the company he was keeping or the personal favor he was acknowledging?

These background facts, as it turns out, are mostly incidental to the poem's originality and success, which can be said to stem much more from Rilke's time in Paris, studying art and seeking a new poetic style, than from any inspiration provided by Capri and aristocrats. They are the sorts of facts that we typically encounter when we are trying to discover the ways in which Rilke's work was and was not grounded in his life. That he liked to move in such social circles is interesting and not particularly flattering, but it was his association with other writers and with visual artists like Auguste Rodin and Paula Modersohn-Becker that proved to be truly crucial to his innovations as a poet.

Rilke's life, on the whole, does not offer us an especially gratifying story. Restless and often impoverished—he had no regular income much of the time and was never able to manage his finances sensibly—he moved around a great deal, often depending on the hospitality of wealthy and aristocratic friends for whom he liked to act as a kind of pet or "court poet." The incessant relocating mirrored the fact that he was also incapable of sustaining intimate relationships. This recurrent pattern not only left his lovers unhappy, but depressed him as well. His life, even when well told by biographers such as Leppmann and Freedman, makes for rather melancholy reading.[2]

Rilke's artistic maturation, however, is quite a different story. Most of his vacillation about where to live and whom to love is replaced in this narrative by a portrait of steady ambition, hard work, acute self-criticism, and a canny sense of what would best serve his needs at each stage of his development. In his early years he had explored and discarded the attractions of two nineteenth-century aesthetic practices, romanticism and naturalism.

He had experimented with theater and fiction as well as writing lyric poems. He also came to the realization that journalism, publishing, and university teaching, while they might support him, would tend to interfere with his vocation as a poet. That vocation, as it became more and more central to him, partly under the early guidance and encouragement of his first lover and lifelong confidante, Lou Andreas-Salomé, took on a dimension and dedication that crowded out other things and people. The artist as a priestly or saintly figure, apart from the crowd and isolated in utter consecration to the cause of creativity, was much in fashion at the turn of the century, though not everyone who was a practicing artist found it convenient or attractive to live by it consistently. In Rilke's case, however, it became the center and raison d'être, the one constant in a life that was otherwise characterized by confusion, vacillation, and depression.

Early in his development Rilke identified spiritual issues as central to his art, and his early poetry, fiction, and drama all borrow heavily from the Christian tradition, recasting stories and images involving monks and saints, Mary and Jesus, icons and ecstasies. He journeyed to Russia twice, with Lou Andreas-Salomé, searching for a less decadent and more immediate spiritual life than the one he had encountered in contemporary Europe. In Russia, he felt, religion and art still interpenetrated significantly. What that meant was not so much the possibility of a conversion or an attachment to a faith such as Orthodox Christianity, but rather an infusion of purpose for the artist. A poet could hope to draw clarity and purpose from revisiting a society in which art still had the meaning it had had in the Middle Ages, a vehicle for direct contact with the divine, a source of transcendence, and an accessing of divine energy. This was the same attraction that drew Yeats and Lady Gregory into contact with the Irish peasantry, drove Gauguin to spend time among the Breton peasants and then later among the Tahitians, and made Picasso draw on the raw energy he took to be expressing itself in African masks. Societies that were excessively literate, sophisticated, hierarchic, and materialistic were condemned by both symbolists and modernists as deadly to art. A return to a simpler life—a form of the pastoral, really—promised a renewal of creative energies and a spiritual rebirth for both artist and audience.

Rilke retained this religious strain throughout his career. Even as he was struggling to articulate the group of late poems that would eventually become *The Duino Elegies*, an exploration of alternatives to the Christian religious tradition, he traveled to Spain to study the paintings of El Greco, still much preoccupied with saints and with mannerist and baroque images of religious ecstasy conjoined with sexual rapture. In his set of religious and spiritual preoccupations, he was of course in perfect accord with the reigning symbolist aesthetic. Plays like Wilde's *Salomé* and poems like Mallarmé's *Herodiade* confirm the preference for religious subjects, for issues of faith and spiritual crisis, and for a somewhat decadent view of religion that uncovers submerged sexual meanings and retells biblical stories and classical myths to exploit their more unsettling possibilities. Rilke's fiction, in *Stories of God* (1898–1899), and early poetic sequences, such as *Visions of Christ* (1896–1897), put him very much in the intellectual and artistic currents of the time. Add to that an interest in the musicality of language and a somewhat overripe poetic style, and you have a card-carrying young German symbolist, moving from Prague to Vienna to Munich to Berlin, searching out kindred spirits and soaking up the artistic milieu of the century's close. One need go no further than the working titles of his maturing verse collections—*The Book of Monkish Life*, *The Book of Pilgrimage*, *The Book of Hours*— to see how readily his poetic themes are attuned to the fashionable aesthetic bent.

Within these activities, however, one senses that Rilke is already dissatisfied, already searching for alternatives. Spiritual yearning needed a counterbalance, a rediscovery of the world of objects and the realm of the senses. Rilke's expanding tendency to associate with visual artists provided an increasingly significant alternative to the symbolist haze of poetry that aspired to pure music, transcendent escape, and orgiastic religiosity. Painters, he could readily note, worked with canvases and oils and charcoals. Sculptors carved blocks of stone, chiseled reliefs, and poured molten metal. They all needed to represent even spiritual subjects—angels, Madonnas, saintly goodness, the torments of the damned—in terms of objects and people, the things of this world. The very materiality of the visual arts was in itself a kind of challenge to symbolism at its dimmest and dreamiest, and while symbolism clearly had a great impact on contemporary artists like Rodin, Gauguin, Matisse, Munch, Klimt, Van Gogh, and Picasso, other terminologies were already being devised to describe the artistic innovations they represented. Retaining the symbolist emphasis on art's independence and power and its refusal to serve existing values, they brought it back to bear on the world of daily life, immersing it in the mundane and abandoning the yearning for transcendence and escape that had so often characterized both romanticism and symbolism. That shift, which marks the profoundest change from the symbolist aesthetic to the modernist one, was first enacted in the visual arts, and it became the wave that Rilke rode into the new century, partly because he had cast his lot with the painters and the sculptors.

By the fall of 1900, Rilke had found his way to the German art colony at Worpswede, where he could associate with young artists such as Heinrich Vogeler, Paula Becker (the most gifted of the group), and Clara Westhoff (whom he soon married) and with more established artists like Otto Modersohn.[3] His monograph on that artists' colony was fairly inept as art criticism, but it was the beginning of a commitment that was to flower in his productive relationship with Rodin, whose secretary he was for a time and whose work was the subject of his second, and more successful, monograph. His growing visual sophistication was channeled into his lifelong pursuit of a poetry that would reflect the robust expressiveness that he found appealing in the visual arts—their plasticity and energy, their profound engagement with the world of objects, and their ties to sense phenomena.

The move to Paris, which became his aesthetic home base, was surely inevitable given the city's centrality not only for symbolist theory and practice but also for all the new forms of modernism that were hatching, in effect, from the original symbolist aesthetic. Rodin, as an older master, could provide a kind of mentoring stability. Masters like Cézanne were coming fully into view through exhibitions and discussions. Younger artists, like Paula Modersohn Becker, who developed side by side with Rilke during the crucial period of the *New Poems* and whose early death he felt especially deeply, could show him newer possibilities in still lifes and portraits.[4] Thus, while suffering uncertainties in his personal life, Rilke was able to develop into a deeply innovative modernist, especially through his emulation of the new developments in the visual arts.

One commentator has recently argued that Rilke's subjects never really changed, merely his artistic treatments.[5] That is both true and false. There is indeed a spiritual continuity throughout Rilke's early, middle, and late preoccupations, one that profoundly reflects both German romanticism and French symbolism. But shifts in artistic treatment, whether they involve form, style, or subject matter, are substantive, not incidental. If you are writing about a panther instead of a monk, your shift of subject matter will do much to determine your meaning, even if you think you are seeking the same qualities in each. And if you move away from religion as a subject to art as a subject, even if you are emphasizing art's religious power, then you have entered more fully the curious and complex realm of aesthetic discourse, art about art. Rilke's responses to the visual arts in his *Neue Gedichte* (New Poems) which fill two volumes, completed and published in 1907 and 1908, move him away from both self-preoccupation and picturesque but overfamiliar representations of spirituality. They also reinforce his art's authority and independence by exploring, explicitly and implicitly, art's power to rival metaphysics and theology.

Just previous to the *New Poems* Rilke had assembled a collection called *Das Buch der Bilder* (The Book of Pictures; the term *bilder* can also be translated as "images"), a series of poems that already represents an attempt to replicate in language some of the things that painters accomplish. That this was a stage and that Rilke intended to move beyond it seem clear from the next title, *New Poems*, and from the manner of the poems that followed. If the lyrics in *The Book of Pictures* seemed at times to suffer from their obligation to the visual arts and to feel two-dimensional and picturesque, Rilke was determined that his new poems would be equivalents to painting and sculpture, not derivatives of them.

One thing that helped him do this was a stronger interest in sculpture. Three-dimensional art, which objectifies subject matter in a way that allows us to move around it, viewing it from many angles, seems to propose an antidote to flatness in representation. As soon as one recognizes this, one can return to certain painters, not least of all Cézanne and the cubists, who were inspired by him, with the recognition that they are exploring the same insight. However, wandering around Rodin's studio and watching the way that torsos and body parts grew in meaning as they expressed themselves in space and changing light were profoundly instructive to the young poet, who was also visiting the zoo, rereading the Bible, watching the carousel, studying the cathedral's windows and sculptures, revisiting the museum, and examining numerous human types and individuals. He could reveal many facets of a subject in one treatment, and he could deliberately confuse inner and outer worlds, the so-called subjective and objective realms, allowing them to interpenetrate, a practice that argued implicitly for their essential identity.[6] Thus, the observer of the famous panther goes out of himself to study and empathize with the caged animal. He observes its outward behavior closely, while speculating simultaneously on its inward world. So rapt does he become that he endangers his own inner world, the panther threatening, in effect, to swallow him with its powerful gaze:

His gaze, from passing all those bars,
Is too tired for anything more.
It seems to him there are a thousand bars
And past those thousand bars no world.

The soft gait of supple flex and power
That pads around the smallest circle here
Is like a dance of strength around a point
In which a mighty will stands dazed.

Once in a while the curtain of the pupil
Parts silently—. An image goes in then,
Runs through the trembling stillness of the limbs
And vanishes inside the heart.

(Tr. David Young, *The Book of Fresh Beginnings*)

The poem does not fill out a picture but moves restlessly into shifting perspectives and insights. We begin with the blank gaze of the bored and pacing animal. It has been caged too long to have any interest in seeing beyond the bars that enclose it. We then move on to study the endless circling that, like the bored gaze, calls attention to the unnatural treatment of a wild animal, caged and with its "mighty will" thwarted. In the final stanza, however, the speaker recognizes that the animal's gaze, usually blank, is still capable of powerful activity. The implication, it seems to me, is that the speaker, who has been complacently observing the caged animal, is suddenly noticed and seen by it. His image is taken in through the animal's limbs and to its heart, almost as though he were its prey. The devouring is of course metaphorical, but it still proposes a revolution in perspective. In effect, the beast leaps, and the safety and complacency of the observer are shattered by the sudden eye contact.[7] The effect is that much more powerful given the animal's subjugation. A panther in the wild would produce mainly physical responses and physical issues. The interchange here is decidedly psychological and spiritual because, given the bars, that is the only possibility.

This matter of the gaze, its power and full meaning, is vital to an adequate understanding of the new world of Rilke's middle lyrics. Thinking about the visual arts and their peculiar power led Rilke to innovative characterizations of the very act of looking. He compares the gaze to touch, to a hand; he objectifies it as powerful and dangerous, as well as creative; most of all he reverses its apparent one-way meaning. In "The Panther" there are two gazes, that of the speaker and that of the panther, and the moment when they interlock is the moment of danger and insight that the poem impels us toward.

But what about an object? Can that gaze back at you, too? The idea that something you look at might affect you is of course not difficult to entertain; it still preserves the subject/object dichotomy. To grant the thing gazed at equivalency—of being, awareness, even volition—is one more step, small in one sense, but a huge leap in terms of traditional boundaries of logic and categories, even in terms of common sense. It is partly a return to the way preliterate peoples thought, and it is partly an advance toward relativity and quantum mechanics. Rilke proposes this leap, aided by traditional ideas of divinity and godhead, in "Archaic Torso of Apollo," which replicates some features of "The Panther" and opens the second volume of the *New Poems*. That a piece of stone, ancient and fragmented, displayed in a museum, might suddenly decide to look back at you is powerfully conveyed in this famous sonnet:

ARCHAIC TORSO OF APOLLO

We've never known the legendary head
where the eye-apples ripened. But
his torso glows still, like a candelabrum
in which his gaze, turned down,

contains itself and shines. Otherwise
the breast-curve wouldn't blind you so, nor would
the hips and groin form toward that smile
whose center held the seeds of procreation.

And then this stone would stand here, short and broken,
under the shoulders' clear, cascading plunge
and wouldn't ripple like a wild beast's fur

and break with light from every surface
like a star: because there is no place
that doesn't see you. You must change your life.

(Tr. David Young, *The Book of Fresh Beginnings*)

Here the gazer, a casual museum visitor imagining the missing head and glancing at the break just above the genitals, is abruptly exposed to the glare of the sun god's regard. The looker is looked at and seen so irrevocably that that person's life must change. There is no going back from this moment when apparently dead stone returns to its godhead and godhood, locking us into its gaze. Light breaks from every surface of the statue, but light is also everywhere around us, like sunlight, and in it we are illuminated and visible to everything. Our being seen is universal.[8] Even more than with the panther, the result feels ego-shattering. The transformation resembles the kinds of transformations the symbolists explored and longed for. It also of course echoes the reverence, instituted by the Renaissance, for the power and independence of sculpture from the classical world. However, the ways in which it is mundane, rooted in physical being, set in a familiar place, a daylight world and not some symbolist twilight, escapist and subjective, takes us beyond symbolism and into modernism. Mallarmé would clutch and cherish this insight as his own or as one to be shared with a tiny coterie. Rilke hands it to the reader, any reader, who is left at the end of the poem with an injunction to an action that must postdate the poem itself.

The implications of these poems in which the gazer is gazed back at by animal or by object are deeply philosophical, related to the phenomenological insights that were beginning to emerge from the work of Edmund Husserl and his pupil Martin Heidegger.[9] They suggest that perception always involves reciprocity and that you can't, in effect, gaze at the world without a meaningful interchange. The world will gaze back at you, and the interaction will affect you both. This insight breaks up the old Cartesian model of subject and object, undermining it irrevocably. All of the familiar binary distinctions involving self and nonself, inner and outer, mind and body, spirit and matter, and even life and death are now subject to re-vision and re-view. Rather than remaining an isolated observer of a reality that surrounds it, the self is continually implicated in that reality and its being. The self's borders shift constantly, and there is a steady commerce through the senses that affects both "self" and "other." Reality is fluid and unstable, and the reciprocity of existence is continuous and inevitable. If I fail to recognize that, I will desolate and isolate my natural sense of being. If I accept and understand it, I can demystify both self-consciousness and mortality. Indeed such terms are themselves now suspect because both imply stable borders and separable states that this new insight dissolves and challenges. I must change my life.

Language's role in all of this is most ambiguous. It can unconsciously reinforce the old ways of understanding the world, even as terms like *self-consciousness* and *mortality* and even *thing* tend to do. But it can also be a tool with which to mediate, explore, and reopen the consciousness to reciprocity of being, a way to live the new knowledge. That is what Rilke saw happening in the arts. Rodin's sculptures and Cézanne's paintings gazed back at him, ripening his senses and telling him he needed a new form of understanding to see them and be seen by them. That was the task he proposed that poetry undertake with language: undermining its tendencies to reinforce the old borders, categories, and binaries, leaping forward through verbal innovation into new realms of understanding and interaction. To encourage that subversion of language's normal tendencies, he needed the help of arts that did not employ language as their expressive medium. Most symbolists, recognizing the dilemmas of language, gravitated toward the abstract and apparently disembodied attractions of music; Rilke connected instead with what painters and sculptors were doing.

If the reciprocity idea applies to works of art and if paintings look at us, too, then it is natural that Rilke would turn to their wordless ways of accomplishing such reversals. Since a painting is intended to be looked at, it carries that intention into the interaction with the gazer. It looks back at you and alters your way of seeing; if it does this radically enough, challenging your notions of subject and object, person and thing, it can startle you out of complacent assumptions about hierarchy and about spirit and matter. That is precisely what many modernist canvases were accomplishing in Paris in the first decade of the new century. Cézanne, Rilke recognized, had somehow refashioned the inward life so that it was external to the conscious self, embodied in paintings—portraits, landscapes, still lifes—that forced the spectator to recognize the reciprocities of being. He never met the artist, but he went again and again, fascinated and deeply moved, to the exhibitions of the artist's work that were held in Paris in 1907, in the year following Cézanne's death. For a few weeks in October of that year, he let himself be obsessed by Cézanne's paintings, his technique and vision, his emergent modernism.

Objects in nature and from daily life, he realized, assumed the same significance in Cézanne's paintings as deeply held emotions, values, and beliefs. Rilke struggled to articulate this insight in his letters about the Cézanne exhibits: "To achieve the conviction and substantiality of things, a reality intensified and potentiated to the point of indestructibility by his experience of the object, seemed to him to be the purpose of his innermost work."[10] Here we see Rilke grappling with the resistance of language. He must speak of "things" and the "object" while trying to characterize Cézanne's understanding of "conviction" and "substantiality" in things he sensed and depicted. He summons "innermost" to help characterize the way in which the physical and objective world is simultaneously an inward one. All of this is more successfully enacted in the language of "The Bowl of Roses." In it, Rilke moves from writing about what painters do to doing it himself, using words while emulating a painter's subversive treatment of subject and object.

The idea of reciprocal gazing is easiest to sustain with a sculpted or painted portrait, since another gazer, a human being, is involved. We can all grasp the idea that the gazed-at figure in the portrait might be gazing back, and indeed there are jokes, horror stories, and legends built around just such a notion. Still, what about a landscape? That is more difficult, since a landscape, done for its own sake rather than as backdrop to a religious or historical subject, can sharply reduce the meaning and significance of the human. If we are to entertain the idea that the landscape is "perceiving" us as we perceive it, we must enlarge the idea of perception from the human to the nonhuman. The reciprocity of being must involve not simply humans and human perception, but also the whole of existence. In that sense, more is at stake in viewing a landscape than in viewing a portrait. If both are thought of as mirrors of a kind, then the second mirror is the stranger and more challenging.

The painter's choice of subject known as "still life" brings all this to a head. What is the point of looking at a bowl of fruit or a bouquet of flowers? In what sense could these inert objects (the French term for a still life is *nature morte*) possibly be said to reciprocate our attention, gazing back at us? Yet our regard for the still life as a legitimate genre implicitly argues that there is an answer to this question. It's easier to talk about "meaning" in a still life than to talk about "reciprocity of existence" and "mutuality of perception," but the two discourses are related, and Rilke sensed that fact. Thus it is that the first volume of the *New Poems* closes with a gorgeous and thrilling still life, "Die Rosenschale" (The Bowl of Roses).

Rilke was, so far as I know, the first poet to seriously undertake the creation of a still life in language, and he must have realized that with this poem he had gone further toward articulating his new sense of existence than ever before.[11]

No wonder he placed it in a key position. He had made a series of crucial deci-
sions about its structure that would enable him to bring it off successfully.

To begin with, the poem is by no means a "pure" still life. It has a frame,
and that frame takes the form of an implied narrative. The "you" whom the
speaker addresses seems to be a combination of that speaker's self and an
"anyone" who is in some sense the reader. This "you" has come to the bowl
of roses after seeing a disturbing fight between two boys. If we call this prior
experience a frame, we are borrowing from the language of the visual arts; if
we call it a prelude, we are borrowing from the language of music. In any
case, it is a past-tense event that ushers in the central present-tense event of
the poem, studying the roses.

In addition to this initial narrative gesture, the bowl of roses itself tends
to break down our normal sense of the border between art and life. How
many removes exist between the reader of the poem and the roses in the
garden? Are we looking at a painting of roses or, as seems more likely, at a
flower arrangement? If we are looking at a flower arrangement, we are
already witnessing something composed of and created from living things.
The roses, of course, are themselves a product of the gardener's art. If we are
looking at a painting of a bowl of roses, then additional creativity and artifice are involved. And then there is the translation of the entire experience
into language (and in this case an additional translation—from the original
language into the one I'm using). Whether it comes to us as a painting or a
poem, the initial creativity of the flower arrangement and, behind it, the
gardener's art are being studied, celebrated, and re-created.

These confusions about the degree and presence of artifice are ultimately
productive. Whether we are at two, three, or four removes from the garden
rose doesn't really matter in terms of what we understand and take away
from the poem. We might have attained our insights in the garden itself, and
the fact that art has aided us, three arts or four, is not crucial. This recognition helps destroy the dire gulf between life and art that the symbolists had
created. Art is simply an extension of nature or, more to the point, a series
of extensions, and visual art and language exist in a continuum with perception, sensation, thought, and emotion.

Rilke admits by his structure and his opening that with a poem, a language artifact, we will have sequence; we will move through the experience
in time. Thus, the narrative gesture represented by the frame is not an impu-
rity. It helps us move from the events of our own lives into the space created
for the roses. They are clearly an alternative, a way to get past human vio-

lence and to forget it.[12] The contrast is vibrant and unmistakable: The human tendency to aggression and conflict is juxtaposed with the serene existence of the flowers, cut, brought indoors, arranged, and waiting in a bowl. One reason to arrange some flowers or to compose a still life (a reason implicit in both activities) would be to provide an opportunity to contemplate, to admire and wonder, and to evoke a milder and less conflicted side of oneself. That would be a reason to view it, too. We do not, the poem implies, need a painter to show us how to do this. Paintings can exemplify contemplative insight into the nature of being, but they have no exclusive patent on the process, any more than poetry and philosophy do.

Nor is creativity a male realm; since the violence comes from boys and since the arts of flower arranging and rose growing are traditionally feminine practices, a subtle attack on male hegemony in the world, including the world of the arts, is implied. Rilke's protofeminism has not been much discussed, partly because of its subtlety, but readers can sense it in poems like this one, and it is part of his attraction to readers of both past and present.

The violence of the boys is disturbingly conveyed. The metaphors chosen to analogize their conflict—"like an animal attacked by bees; / actors, towering overstaters, / raging horses, crashing to collapse, / eyes rolling, baring their teeth / as if the skull was going to peel itself, / starting from the mouth"—are deliberately provocative and memorable. The peeling of the skull, as if the human face is merely a false mask of flesh, with the bone's truthfulness beneath, even evokes the memento mori tradition of still life paintings, where a skull or some other reminder of mortality directs the viewer toward a consciousness of death's presence in life, its ultimate meanings and domination.[13] The boys spell out death consciousness and death wish even as they roll and scramble in the dirt.

And yet they are boys. In their very youthfulness is some promise of possible change and maturity. Had the spectator been witnessing an adult conflict, the result might have been more disheartening. The boys may take their violence on into manhood, but they also have the opportunity to move past it, and in their own budding and flowering, their opening into existence, they still have an opportunity to commune with and even resemble the roses.

Metaphor has, of course, a different meaning in Rilke's new world, a world in which being is reciprocal and perception is mutual. Where figuration might once have been hierarchical, with an implied valuing of the human over the nonhuman (my love is like a red, red rose—but it is also of course more important than any flower), it is now equivalent. Everything is as valuable as everything else, and while metaphor may indeed serve human needs, that is not its sole function, nor does that function necessarily imply anthropocentrism. Moreover, if existence is now understood as fluid and metamorphic, with constantly shifting borders and transforming states of existence, then metaphor acts out that fact. Things change into other things and back again, and the shape shifting, the instability, is another way to remind language to stop reinforcing old categories and hierarchies and begin expressing new states of being. Metaphor is now a tool of thought and a potentially radical one.

Having used figurative language so vigorously in its opening stanza, the poem tends to be more abstract, even a bit hesitant, as it moves to contemplation of the roses:

> unforgettable, filled to the brim
> with the utmost expression of being, bending,
> yielding, unable to give, simply existing,
> that could ever be ours: utmost for us too.

> Silent life, opening and opening, no end in sight,
> a use of space that takes no space away
> from space that things around it need,
> an existence with almost no outlines, all background
> and pure inwardness

Only as the roses begin to assert their physical presence in the new space of our contemplative regard does analogy become possible, as if the ground had to be cleared and the figurative mode of thinking had to be reborn. In one phrase, "unable to give" ("Niemals-Gebenkönnen"), their frustration is evident, and their volitional limitations marked, while the surrounding phrases, "yielding" ("hinhalten") and "simply existing" ("dastehn," literally "standing there," but with an emphasis on the power of being), confirm their availability to our attention and delight, their rhyming with us by embodying "the utmost expression . . . that could ever be ours," the poet wrestling with the angel of syntax to pin down the complex truth of our relation to the roses. The conclusion, "utmost for us too," opens the possibilities expressed in the new stanza, which begins with the simple phrase "Silent life."

The third stanza now works to reconfigure our sense of space, which is usually based on our notions of our inward mental life and an outward physical world we move and perceive in, separate realms that may mirror each other but are forever differentiated. The roses seem to be denying this division. They are "a use of space that takes no space away," which is hard to visualize or understand. They have no outlines, somehow, and they are self-illuminated like lamps. Their strangeness, a "pure inwardness," is emphasized even as they begin to approach us analogically, since the question "do we know anything, anywhere, that's like this?" has two implied answers, first a "no" and then a recognition that we ourselves are potentially like this.

Emotion, we are told as the fourth stanza begins, is born "from the touch of petal to petal." This is a bold assertion that the inner world, familiar to our consciousness, is continuous with, even identical to, the material world we think of as exterior to our conscious selves. If we read this statement as simply saying that our emotions are awakened by the rose's petals, we miss the more radical point: emotion and petal (like love and peach in Cézanne) are the same, *in the same realm*, interacting and generative. Now we can go on into the rebirth of metaphor, in a world where it has an entirely different value.

The first figure of speech in this new world is the petal and eyelid association—"a petal comes open like an eyelid"—and through it the familiar Rilkean issue of gaze enters the poem. If petals are like eyelids, then eyes are implied, but the poem insists on exploring differences. Beneath these eyelids are just more eyelids, "closed, as though they had to be asleep / ten times deeper to shut down visionary power."[14] In other words, the special meaning that a human gaze can have in the world of poetry, where dreams and visionary power are released, is configured in the multiplication of petals around the core of the rose. The filtration of light through the darkness of the closed petals gives the rose both color and sexual energy ("the tangled group of stamens stirs and rears erect"). It is analogous to human processes but more emphatic, more moving, and more pronounced.

Now we find movement in the roses. We are ready for the paradox that the still life presents us—that just where movement was apparently absent, it reasserts its presence in a new and meaningful way: "look: / gestures from such small angles of eruption / they'd never be noticed if not for the way / their rays fan out to the cosmos." In this stretch of scale, this spectrum that runs from small angles to deep space, we have the overall paradox of the poem: Inwardness and outwardness are aspects of each other and of the same thing: being. Being registers both as intimacy and as grandeur. Microcosm and macrocosm are part of a constant exchange that affects roses as fully as it does the perceiving self.

Rilke has created a dynamic space in which metaphor translates human qualities out of the roses and back again, but in terms of reciprocity rather than hierarchy. If we had begun the poem with these comparisons, the old hierarchies would have asserted themselves. Here now, so deep in what we might describe as the roses' realm, the human metaphor is simply our own lifeline, our way of connecting our being with the being around us. The two stanzas in which we hear about Venus, embarrassment, coolness, self-absorption, and undressing before a lover are rich with human association, but they also contain reminders of paradox ("And *what* they shed: how it is light or heavy") and a transforming list that keeps the metamorphic nature of being before us ("a cloak, a load, a wing, / and then a mask"). That broader picture helps to check our anthropocentric temptation to simply read out of the roses those qualities that we can appropriate for ourselves.

That the roses' metamorphic capability is greater than merely that of reflecting the human is confirmed by the next stanza's opening rhetorical question: "Is there anything they can't become?" Rilke has now arrived at a plateau of confident and giddy invention. The exuberant handling of surfaces that follows no doubt has origins in his studies with Rodin and his hours contemplating Cézanne's canvases (not to mention his studies of baroque art and architecture), but his treatment here in no way feels derivative of any sculptor or painter. The voice of the poem rides on its own momentum, reveling in the matching of language to sensation, confident in its temporary mastery.

In this stanza Rilke particularly enjoys the extensions of implication that language can discover in color. We have the yellow rose, whose color evokes the rind of a fruit (the orange, presumably) and whose juice rhymes with it, both as a taste and a color, red-orange. We have the pink rose, which interacts with the air to invoke violet through taste association, picking up the idea of taste and aftertaste, sweet pink and bitter violet. And we have three white roses:

> And the one made of cambric, isn't it a dress
> to which the soft and breath-warm slip still clings,
> both of them tossed aside in morning shadows
> near an old pool in the forest?
> And this one, opalescent porcelain,
> easily shattered, a shallow china cup

filled with small, lit butterflies,—
and that one, which holds nothing but itself.

The riot of associations in this stanza, mixing textures, mythologies, feasting, and sexual desire, offers us a hugely satisfying set of interactions with the roses, and its conclusion, focusing on a rose that holds nothing but itself, sets up the powerful final stanza.

How can association so suddenly be cut off, leaving the rose holding nothing but itself? The essential paradox of being is that everything can interact without destroying uniqueness and that things can contain everything else and yet simply contain themselves. There is no limit to the associations and relationships of existence, which is no longer characterized by self and various kinds of otherness, and that means in turn that the self enjoys a kind of safety within the web of interactions that grants it its right to exist and be individuated. Everything is like that. The roses are like that, and we are like that.

My translation takes a small liberty with the opening of the penultimate stanza. The German reads "Und sind nicht alle so, nur sich enthaltend," which can be literally rendered as "And are not all so, only themselves containing." Thus, the German reader hesitates over the "all." It means, for a moment, "all the roses," then "everything," and then a subcategory of "everything," simply "everybody," that is, all of us. I have compressed this process by translating the phrase as "all of us."[15] That, to me, is the sense that emerges in the unfolding stanza, where readers are invited to make their life experience continuous with the list of things experienced. However, my choice of "us" is not limiting; the reader, by this point, need not and should not limit the category of perceivers and listeners to human beings. The category includes the roses, and "us" means all beings, all living things. So "aren't all of us like that" simply confirms the kinship with the roses that the poem has so fully and firmly established.

The masterful list that unfolds in this stanza combines concrete and abstract, inner and outer with an exhilarating freedom of reference. It argues that self-containment means a transformation of outer to inner, a distillation that resembles the roses' distillation of light beneath their eyelid-petals:

wind and rain and spring's great patience
and guilt and restlessness and masquerading fate
and the darkening of the earth at evening
and even the clouds that change and flow and vanish,

and even the vague command of the distant stars
all changed to a handful of inwardness.

That change, which characterizes human perceiving and experiencing and human living through time, is the same change that brings color, beauty, and blossoming to flowers. It is triumphantly natural, and it does not cut us off from nature, as we had once thought in our miserable isolation and self-consciousness; rather, it is the means by which we enact our kinship with the rest of existence. The resolution feels full and movingly affirmative, though it does not altogether banish reservations about the violence depicted at the opening or the "bitter aftertaste" that accompanies a world of change and inevitable loss. Nevertheless, its images stress sublimity, where awe and fear traditionally mingle and where the earth and the clouds and the starry heavens are taken in and successfully transformed. And it is given to us, in effect, on a platter or, in this case, in a bowl: *Nun liegt es sorglos in den offnen Rosen*. It now lies carefree in these open roses.

Most of the poems in *New Poems* (1907) are rhymed and metered. Many of them are sonnets. As the volume closes, however, a group of longer poems appears, using rhyme irregularly or not at all. These expansive, more free-wheeling poems engage the classical world, and the best known of them is the justly famous "Orpheus. Eurydice. Hermes." A reader coming through the volume will thus be somewhat prepared for the formal freedom of "The Bowl of Roses," but not for the subject and its treatment, which are notable after the group of classical, narrative-based studies. It stands among several ambitious poems that deal with mythic subjects, but it takes the idea of the still life to lengths and possibilities never before anticipated in poetry.

While the insights of this poem represent a culmination of Rilke's thought at this point in his life, they also forecast Rilkean ideas that are sometimes thought to be exclusive to the late and great *Duino Elegies*. The idea that being involves a dynamic interaction and reciprocity and that human interior life, consciousness, is a perfectly normal part of this process is famously articulated in the seventh and ninth elegies in particular. In the seventh, Rilke says:

even the most
visible joy
will reveal itself

only when we have
        transformed it within.

There's nowhere, my love,
        the world can exist
                except within.
Our lives are used up
        in transformations
                and what's outside us
always diminishing
        vanishes.

(Tr. David Young, *Duino Elegies*)

The ninth elegy is a kind of extended hymn to the world of things and the way that the human senses, along with human language, can celebrate their spiritual meanings and potentials. "Praise the world / to the angel / not the unsayable" argues Rilke, who goes on:

And these things
        that take their life
from impermanence
        they understand
                that you're praising them:
perishing, they trust
        to us—the most
                perishable of all—
for their preservation.
        They want us to change them
                completely
inside our invisible hearts
        into—oh endlessly—
                into ourselves!

(Tr. David Young, *Duino Elegies*)

Note the claim that objects and nonhuman parts of existence can exhibit understanding and longing and that they interdepend with human beings in an existential reciprocity of need and regard. If you praise a flower and can believe both that it understands you are praising it and that it trusts you to do so, your world is quite changed and your existence has a new meaning and function.

This is essentially the same insight that Rilke explained so beautifully in a letter to his Polish translator: "We are the bees of the invisible. We frantically plunder the visible of its honey, to accumulate it in the great golden hive of the invisible."[16] Making us bees is one more way of insisting on the natural and positive quality of this process. It is for one thing perfectly instinctual. It is has the same results—sweetness and light—that bees produce with their honey and wax. Again, the process makes art and life a contiguous and continuous process, and the artist, that lone priestly figure of the symbolist era, is returned to the social hive where common energies are joined for the greater good. The metaphor has implications that should remind us of the human/flower trope in the poem we have been examining. Moreover, it is poignant in relation to Rilke's own need for isolation and separation and to his somewhat crippled psyche; he can imagine himself as a rose in the garden of existence, but that tends to happen only in his poems and letters, a vision he can articulate for others but will tend to fall short of for himself.

In the spring of 1907, Rilke sent "The Bowl of Roses" to Hugo von Hofmannsthal, along with his new "Alcestis," in response to a flattering invitation to help inaugurate a new magazine, *Der Morgen*.[17] The response was gratifying. Hofmannsthal praised the language of the poem, sensing its newness and its innovative vision, and Rilke went on to place it, as I have mentioned, in its permanent home as the closing poem of the 1907 volume of the *Neue Gedichte*. That volume, then, ends with a revolutionary affirmation of human perception as a combination of self-possession and sharing, a gathering-in of being around a simple subject/object, a bowl of roses, that is also a giving out, a redefinition of the meaning of being and of our relation to the rest of existence.

The preceding discussion forms part of an attempt to address the larger question of the meanings and values of modernism. We like to presume that modern art arrives at a newness of perspective and awareness and that it somehow makes its break with conventions and tradition not simply as a repudiation of earlier art but also as a vehicle of new insight and understanding. Rilke's poem, it seems to me, passes that test unequivocally. Emulating the traditional and modernist practice of artists painting still lifes, it redefines the human consciousness and the human relation to space. It presents us with a rich experience in which we cannot quite say where art leaves off and nature begins. It questions materialist versions of reality that dominated eighteenth- and nineteenth-century thinking. In doing so, it returns us to preliterate modes in which the human self was understood as continuous with the rest of existence. Furthermore, it anticipates more recent discoveries in physics and quantum mechanics that confirm that same insight. In making "inner" and "outer" into a continuity, a sort of Möbius strip, it acts out the insights of phenomenology that constituted the first successful challenge in philosophy to Platonic and Cartesian versions of the world, systems that isolate the self and reinforce binary modes of understanding. It accomplishes all this by unorthodox (for poetry) choices of subject, procedure, and technique, offering us a poem unlike any that had been previously written. Modernism is well served here as the world around us is revivified and restored to us, making each of us artists and reconciling our consciousness to the world around us in those very moments when we are at our most natural and best.

2

William Butler Yeats writes

AMONG SCHOOL CHILDREN

I

I walk through the long schoolroom questioning;
A kind old nun in a white hood replies;
The children learn to cipher and to sing,
To study reading-books and history,
To cut and sew, be neat in everything
In the best modern way—the children's eyes
In momentary wonder stare upon
A sixty-year-old smiling public man.

II

I dream of a Ledaean body, bent
Above a sinking fire, a tale that she
Told of a harsh reproof, or trivial event
That changed some childish day to tragedy—
Told, and it seemed that our two natures blent
Into a sphere from youthful sympathy,
Or else, to alter Plato's parable,
Into the yolk and white of the one shell.

III

And thinking of that fit of grief or rage
I look upon one child or t'other there
And wonder if she stood so at that age—
For even daughters of the swan can share
Something of every paddler's heritage—
And had that colour upon cheek or hair,
And thereupon my heart is driven wild:
She stands before me as a living child.

IV

Her present image floats into the mind—
Did Quattrocento finger fashion it
Hollow of cheek as though it drank the wind
And took a mess of shadows for its meat?
And I, though never of Ledaean kind
Had pretty plumage once—enough of that,
Better to smile on all that smile, and show
There is a comfortable kind of old scarecrow.

V

What youthful mother, a shape upon her lap
Honey of generation had betrayed,
And that must sleep, shriek, struggle to escape
As recollection or the drug decide,
Would think her son, did she but see that shape
With sixty or more winters on its head,
A compensation for the pang of his birth
Or the uncertainty of his setting forth?

VI

Plato thought nature but a spume that plays
Upon a ghostly paradigm of things;
Solider Aristotle played the taws
Upon the bottom of a king of kings;
World-famous golden-thighed Pythagoras
Fingered upon a fiddle-stick or strings
What a star sang or careless muses heard:
Old clothes upon old sticks to scare a bird.

VII

Both nuns and mothers worship images,
But those the candles light are not as those
That animate a mother's reveries,
But keep a marble or a bronze repose.
And yet they too break hearts—O Presences
That passion, piety or affection knows,
And that all heavenly glory symbolise—
O self-born mockers of man's enterprise;

25

VIII

Labour is blossoming or dancing where
The body is not bruised to pleasure soul,
Nor beauty born out of its own despair,
Nor blear-eyed wisdom out of midnight oil.
O chestnut tree, great rooted blossomer,
Are you the leaf, the blossom or the bole?
O body swayed to music, O brightening glance,
How can we know the dancer from the dance?

THE SPEAKER walks through a long schoolroom, asking questions. The metaphoric charge of the first line is obvious enough—life is one long schoolroom, and questioning is the norm of our existence—but the base experience is drawn from the quotidian. Indeed, the self-portraiture in this poem is quite accurate as to time and place. Yeats was a senator in the newly instituted Irish Republic, and, as the recent (1923) recipient of the Nobel Prize for literature, something of a celebrity. He was a VIP, in other words, who made senatorial speeches about education reform and whose duties included this tour of a Montessori school in February 1926, a visit that helped shape a poem that eventually went well beyond it.

Sixty doesn't seem particularly old these days, but it did to Yeats, both personally and artistically. Poets are afraid of losing the edge that makes their youthful work interesting. Wordsworth's later years, for instance, constitute a grim object lesson. As he approached sixty, Yeats had begun to make old age a leading theme of his poems, and *The Tower* (1928), where this poem appears, is littered with complaints about aging and its frustrations. "That is no country for old men" is how it begins, for example, and the collection's title poem opens with "What shall I do with this absurdity . . . age that has been tied to me / As to a dog's tail?" and closes with the poet making his will.[1]

In the case of "Among School Children," sixty-year-old Senator Yeats, hearing about educational innovations, "the best modern way," begins to feel anachronistic and out of place. Age separates him from the children. Belief separates him from the elderly nun.[2] His mind wanders back to his long and unrequited love for Maud Gonne, the central theme of his early and middle poetry. Though married now and the father of two children very much like the ones in the classroom, he still returns to the subject of Maud and his humiliating obsession for her. He recalls her as a young woman, speculates on her appearance as a child, and considers her in her present state, a gaunt and aging beauty. For him she will always be a Helen of Troy, hence the epithet "Ledaean," a child of Leda—and Zeus.

As he meditates on the past and present Yeats may appear anything but modern. His sensibility links him to romantic love, a tradition at odds with modernism. His poem is rhymed and metered, tying him to traditional verse forms (ottava rima, in this case, the stanza we most associate with Byron). And he is candid about feeling out of place in the modern world of Montessori classrooms, indulging in memory and nostalgia. This "sixty-year-old smiling public man" is in fact deeply divided and confused, pitted against his own life in the way a symbolist poet might be. His interior life is dramatically at odds with his exterior setting and behavior. Instead of offering a radical subversion of the old subjective/objective gulf, as Rilke did, Yeats seems here to succumb to it completely.

In fact, however, these apparent contradictions to the poem's success as a modernist text constitute the essence of its modernism; they form part of a rhetorical strategy that Yeats had begun to employ as a way of moving from his symbolist phase to his embrace of modernism. The shift comes partly from a change of tone in his self-portraiture. The self-presentation of his earlier poems was sorrowful but dignified. Even as late as "The Wild Swans at Coole" (1917), he resembles romantic heroes like Childe Harold and the Keatsian protagonist of "Ode to a Nightingale."[3] As he responded to modernism, however, he began to experiment with comedy. Self-ridicule helped him to move away from his earlier persona and to repudiate and criticize his romantic stance, depicting himself and his poems as failing in various ways. Thus he represents himself in volumes like *Michael Robartes and the Dancer* and *The Tower* as variously helpless, speechless, frustrated, aged, and confused.[4]

From this tactic stems a new kind of success for the poem. The apparent disadvantage turns into an advantage. The "Yeats" inside the poem, in such cases, by looking bad, reveals the other "Yeats," the author, as more fully aware and in control. If the protagonist of "Among School Children" seems nostalgic, inattentive, and confused, then we must weigh that evidence against its ultimate source, the author. If we were dealing with a dramatic character, like Lady Macbeth, and an author, like Shakespeare, we would have no trouble distinguishing them. However, when an author such as Yeats makes a dramatic character of himself, using his own life, we must be able to distinguish them at some points and connect them at others. Ultimately, the two are one. It is not necessarily a triumphant unity; Yeats the lover and Yeats the maker often have trouble merging their perspectives and values. But old age gives both of them a sense of risk and frustration, and their common ground works to the artist's benefit. By letting us know that he knows the worst that can be said about him—that he is foolish about love, confused in his educational views, and eccentric in his personal thoughts—the poet gains a sly advantage, disarming criticism.

Self-deprecation has a long history in lyric poetry—one can cite Sappho and Petrarch as significant examples—and no one uses it more expertly than Yeats when transforming himself from a symbolist into a modernist. The divided self that was viewed as a lamentable weakness in romantic and symbolist poetry becomes a strength and emblem of his modernism. In a poem he wrote between 1917 and 1918 for example, "The Phases of the Moon," Yeats presents himself as working late in his tower, fruitlessly searching for the truth. Two of his creations, fictional characters named Owen Aherne and Michael Robartes, pause on the road outside and mock him for failing to understand certain mysteries of the cosmos about which they could have enlightened him. When the poem closes, the reader realizes that "Yeats" must have overheard and understood everything; otherwise, he could not be the author of the poem and could not report the conversation that makes fun of him. The tables are turned, and the joke is on Aherne and Robartes.[5]

The poetic self in these modernist texts is not presented as split in order to reinforce a symbolist aesthetic that laments the gulf between life and art, but rather to demonstrate continuity, a healthy connection with life. In "The Phases of the Moon," for instance, having his own fictional characters wandering by night through the neighborhood of his dwelling creates a confusion of Yeats's art and life that is ultimately much to his advantage. Deliberately confusing two things he had previously seen as drastically opposed might seem as though it risked compromising both, leaving him with no real life and no real art. The newly invigorated poems—I leave the issue of the life to the biographers—show otherwise.

When we reconnect the dramatized Yeats of the poems with the authorial Yeats who is their maker, we reconnect the parts of the divided self. Our act of reading solves his problem for him or shifts it to a new ground, where it is a problem in no way limited to the artist. Moreover, by constructing a failed or failing self inside the poem that is ultimately one with the more successful self outside, Yeats performs the same kind of Möbius strip effect that Rilke achieved, a subverting of the traditional split between self and world. The inner and outer worlds begin to seem interchangeable. His life and art become continuous with each other in a way that turns process into product and product back into process. We seem to see the poet composing as he goes, registering the thoughts that will shape themselves into poetry, and we find that the conclusion of the poem tends not to create a sense of rest and arrival so much as a nervous movement toward the next one.[6]

The total effect of this shift is not easy to grasp. For one thing, the formal elements of the poem—in this case eight eight-line stanzas of great technical elegance—may suggest a finished whole. But on closer inspection, many questions arise, some of them involving the poem's unusual syntax and punctuation. Moreover, the issues that precede it, fill it, and continue beyond it work to keep the poem unresolved and open-ended. The poet's life is always enacting itself, unfolding in time, and the art, by participating inextricably in that process, is also always in a state of becoming, never achieving full closure or completeness. Yeats begins the poem "questioning," poses new questions along the way, and ends with two famous questions that have sometimes been described as rhetorical. Nonetheless, rhetorical questions are intended to produce definite answers, and Yeats has none, either at the outset of the poem or at its close. He has only his emotional defiance of impossible ideals, aging, and temporal entrapments, his hope to be able to live in the present despite the fierce tug of the past and the terrors of the future. The poem loops back on itself, moving in and out of his life, part of an ongoing process of discovery and experiment.

Still, as I have suggested, the poem's inconclusiveness is by no means apparent in our early stages of contact with it. We are apt to be dazzled by its confident and capacious manner. The use of the demanding stanza, with the intricate rhyming (*abababcc*), all naturalized to the speaking voice and the wandering mind, bespeaks artistic confidence. And the poem's reach—to mythology, to various points in history, to large issues of human experience involving childhood, birth, motherhood, and old age—can also seem to argue for its mastery and control. It takes a thoughtful reader a good deal of time and energy to navigate the issues and references that fill the poem. Only at the end of that process can we stand back to survey the ways in which Yeats has left things unresolved. Let us begin, then, with the opening stanza.

The school inspection may look like a success, but the poem construes it as a failure. The problem is not that the school is bad or that Yeats has a patronizing attitude, as some critics have suggested, toward its methods and its personnel. Rather, the situation is one that constrains an absence of genuine human communication. Yeats questions and the nun replies, but what he learns from her is a list of activities that do not particularly differentiate this school from more traditional ones. If the result of Montessori education was that children learned to sew or that they were constrained to "be neat in everything," we would not find it innovative.[7] The idea that children's imaginations should be encouraged, that classrooms should be open, and that learning should be individualized is never specified.

The stanza's close—"the children's eyes / In momentary wonder stare upon / A sixty-year-old smiling public man"—leaves us with an impression of human interaction without real exchange of sympathy. The speaker sees the children seeing him, and he recognizes that all they see is an old man who is smiling, someone who is "public" and whose "private" self is therefore either uninteresting or inaccessible. Their wonder can be only momentary. The "stare" has no durable meaning and does not constitute an extension of their learning. It feels logical that Yeats is subsequently driven inward, hunting for sympathy in his past. We may wonder whether he understands Montessori education. There's a vague sense that it may be failing to achieve its stated goals.[8]

Seeing people see you and looking at yourself through their eyes, understanding what it is that they see, is an act of both sympathy and imagination. It overcomes the superficiality to which the gaze may be limited since it combines inner and outer worlds, a solution Rilke understood. The nun and the children may or may not have such imaginative capacities; it is the speaker who has them and uses them in this case. The poem must then focus on him, listening to and reporting his thoughts. The poem "overhears" the thoughts of the speaker in order that the poet may present and arrange them.

The second stanza, dipping into the speaker's memory, combines a visual stimulus with an aural one, a woman's tale of an incident in her childhood:

> I dream of a Ledaean body, bent
> Above a sinking fire, a tale that she
> Told of a harsh reproof, or trivial event
> That changed some childish day to tragedy—

The dying fire suggests her need for warmth and a lessening prospect of it. The speaker's memory is uncertain—was it a harsh reproof or a trivial event or something of both?—probably because he is focused on the pleasurable recollection of his empathic response:

> Told, and it seemed that our two natures blent
> Into a sphere from youthful sympathy,
> Or else, to alter Plato's parable,
> Into the yolk and white of the one shell.

Her recollection, perhaps of a teacher's or tutor's reproof, no longer matters to him. What's important is the way he feels that their "natures" merged, a oneness that reminds him first of the Platonic parable, recounted by Aristophanes in *The Symposium,* that gendered human selves are halves of a sphere that seeks to reunite itself. The sphere leads him to the thought of an egg.[9] Since Zeus raped Leda in the guise of a swan, she may have reproduced by laying eggs, from one of which Helen was hatched. That occasions a small joke, "altering" Plato, in which Yeats and Maud are not the two halves of a perfect sphere but the more natural, if less perfect, joining of a yolk and a white inside an eggshell. It's as if he returned with her to the equivalent of her mother's womb, to a sense of safety and completeness.[10]

Whichever analogy we choose, this introspective recollection of two people joined in "youthful sympathy" is a stark alternative to the classroom. It displaces the public with the private, and it may seem, by its vision of a moment of unity, to resolve a set of differences—man and nun, old and young—that limited the meaning of the first circumstance. However, because it is entirely interior and entirely lost in the past, the speaker's dilemma—a divided self and a tendency to nostalgia—is in no way resolved. His handling of the memory also suggests that he may be idealizing it. Furthermore, when he brings the memory back to the classroom in the next stanza and speculates on how much this or that little girl may resemble Maud as a child, he is in effect confronted again by the division between past and present, age and youth, public and private. Keeping the swan motif and remembering that swans are ungainly when they are cygnets, he suddenly finds it plausible that "a living child" he is looking at could be a replica of his love. The illusion of her presence and of time repeating itself is too much to bear; his heart is "driven wild."[11]

While the emotional surge that closes this stanza is quite moving, it is also inflected with a touch of the comic. For one thing, there is a deliberate tension between the rhyming couplet's tendency to completeness and closure and the emotional explosion it is reporting. For another, we realize that the speaker could be looking at an awkward or homely little girl, since "even daughters of the swan can share / Something of every paddler's heritage." If it walks like a duck, waddling, and quacks like a duck, it may still turn out to be a grown-up and graceful beauty, a swan, a Helen. But the distance between the myth of Helen and the mundane Irish classroom has ironic resonance even as it drives the old man's heart wild: with tenderness, with love, with the need to repress memory or even reject a brief upsurge of pedophilia.[12]

The fourth stanza's opening, "Her present image floats into the mind," summoned as if for comparison to the child, matches the "I dream" of the second stanza, signaling a return to reverie. It is a natural retreat from the violent emotion, and it brings the speaker forward into his own present, where Maud's old age and his own are the realities he needs to make himself face. "Better to smile on all that smile," and better to think of Maud's current image, gaunt and aged but still deeply attractive. The Quattrocento compliment, reflecting the speaker's ability to refer to history or mythology wherever he needs to, would seem to invoke a sculptor rather than a painter, since a finger is doing the fashioning of the face.[13] If I'm correct, the allusion qualifies the compliment sharply. Indeed, it puts the present-day Maud in the company of the scarecrow speaker, who, though he once had "pretty plumage," is now, in his own view, grotesque.

As the speaker moves decisively to put an end to his speculations about Maud—"enough of that, / Better to smile on all that smile, and show / There is a comfortable kind of old scarecrow"—he seems to have been reduced to involuntary actions and a deformity that makes him more an effigy than a human being. The reflexive smiling, connecting with the "sixty-year-old smiling public man" of the first stanza, is that of a doll or an automaton, and the simulacrum of the human in the tattered and weathered scarecrow is similarly reductive.[14] We have returned, apparently, to where we started, after some remembering and speculation, but there has been no real progress in resolving the problems of old age and the emotional preoccupations that saturate his memory. The poem is at its halfway point, and if it stopped here it would be a touching portrait of the various defeats that imagination tends to suffer in old age. Bodily decrepitude separates the elderly from the young and drives them inward to imaginative re-creation (and idealization) of moments in the past. They resign themselves to a widening gulf between their inner life, which is rich and vivid, and their outward appearance, which is increasingly ill-favored. The portrait is touching in its human truth, but it is also rather pathetic. Yeats, however, is not through with these issues; in fact, he is just getting under way.

Stanza five begins with another question, and it is the most complicated in the poem. Essentially, Yeats is asking whether a woman with an infant son would find childbirth and infant care worth facing if she could see the child at the age of sixty. Into that question, however, he inserts a clause about the baby that contains a complicated theory drawn from the mystical writings he was fond of. Basically, it is the idea that the soul is reincarnated by means of a temptation, "honey of generation," and that when it is trapped in life, in a body, it has three choices: to sleep, shriek, or struggle to escape.[15] Which it chooses will be decided by how much of its prior existence it can remember. If it recalls that existence, it will presumably shriek and struggle; if it is sufficiently drugged to forget, narcotized by its earthly life and its immersion in time and the senses, it will sleep, that is, accept its new imprisonment and "slumber" through the period of its incarnation, accepting life and ignoring its memory of heaven and of the larger existences and meanings that surround it.[16]

The inserted clause, once we have figured it out, shows a rather tragic mirroring between the mother and the fetus. If she had full knowledge of the future, she might not elect to give birth. Her perspective, limited by her immersion in time, protects her. If her fetus could recall the prior existence of its soul, it would not want to be born. In other words, any zest for life— sex, parturition, living in time, falling in love, growing old—is based more on illusion than on knowledge. The mother can narcotize herself with dreams of her son's glorious future—maybe he'll grow up to be president or pope someday—while the fetus will need to forget about its ties to eternity if it is to avoid having the miserable sensibility of a doomed prisoner. Both figures are linked to the old man who has just discovered that the present drives him back to a past where he is prone to idealize and to confuse reality and imagination. The mother lives upon an illusory sense of the future, the old man upon an illusory sense of the past, and the child-to-be upon an ignorance of both its prior and future forms of existence.

This is pessimistic enough to take the poem down to the bottom of possibility, an extreme response that most of us are unlikely to share. It's like the moment in Greek tragedy when the chorus tells us that it's better not to have been born at all. We recognize that the sentiment is appropriate to the circumstances, and we may even consider it to be true, but what are we to do? We're watching a play about suffering and, somewhat perversely, enjoying it. Later we'll have a nice dinner and maybe make love to someone and get a good night's sleep. We can contemplate the sentiment, in other words, but we can't live it; its extremity acts to reconcile us to our lives. Unable to agree or disagree totally, we hang suspended between possibilities, our awareness expanded and multiplied.

So the answer to the giant question that constitutes the entire fifth stanza must be both "no mother" and "any mother." No mother, the speaker suggests, would endure pregnancy and childbirth with full knowledge of her child grown old, but since no mother can (or should?) have full knowledge of time and perfect foresight, then any mother will in fact get on with it. She will go ahead and have the baby, future pope or president, just as the baby will probably let itself be drugged into an acceptance of life, and just as the miserable speaker is getting on with his tour, smiling and scarecrowlike, concealing a heart that's been driven wild with lust and nostalgia. We grant him the right to his implied answer to the rhetorical question ("no mother") partly because we see that he is just as involved in getting on with it as everybody else. He has no choice, really, despite knowing more, in his long schoolroom, than most people know. Nevertheless, if the question is rhetorical for Yeats the dramatic character, it is more open for us and for Yeats as the author of the poem. We probably know some mothers who don't mind the idea that their children will age and die. Mothers aren't as disgusted by old age or as benighted by dreams of glory as the speaker seems to think. Some children grow up to be presidents, after all. And Aristotles. And Yeatses. Maybe such accomplishments would indeed act to qualify "no mother" into "some mothers."

The next stanza appears to change the subject abruptly. We get Plato and Aristotle, two lines each, and then Pythagoras, for three lines.

> Plato thought nature but a spume that plays
> Upon a ghostly paradigm of things;
> Solider Aristotle played the taws
> Upon the bottom of a king of kings;
> World-famous golden-thighed Pythagoras
> Fingered upon a fiddle-stick or strings
> What a star sang or careless muses heard:

Only as the stanza closes do we learn its relevance to what has preceded it: "Old clothes upon old sticks to scare a bird." All these distinguished philosophers suffered old age and became scarecrows, "old clothes upon old sticks to scare a bird." In other words, the wisest men known to history have had the same human fate that the speaker shares with the mother and the infant: an involvement in time that makes old age a diminution and a curse, a burden that's difficult to bear.

Does this spread the pessimism further, or does it diminish it? If even wise and famous men finally become grotesque, is that disheartening, or, since misery loves company, is it comforting? One might be decrepit and scarecrowlike, but if one is also Aristotle, is that not some compensation? Is Yeats putting himself in their company? Again, the reader has a good deal of choice about how to interpret this move. Whatever our decision about its tone, we are unmistakably in the vicinity of a continuing and severe mind/body discrepancy.

The choices about tone are complicated by the way the wise old men are characterized. Plato comes off best—the image of what he thought nature was is quite beautiful, in my opinion—but he obviously lives in a climate of distrust and skepticism with respect to the material reality that surrounds us. Aristotle, the tutor of Alexander the Great, gets to spank a king of kings, but that doesn't do much to enhance his dignity. In the perspective of a Montessori understanding of how children learn he becomes an old-fashioned and rather unimaginative pedagogue. Pythagoras fascinates Yeats the most because of his own history of mystical studies. He gets to be "world-famous," but he also has the dubious distinction of possessing a golden thigh, which apparently makes him divine, though not immune to aging and death. His penetration into the mysteries of music and mathematics is thrilling—the reproduction of the music of the spheres, the very structure of reality—but it is also represented in terms of a fiddle-stick and some careless muses. It's a deliberate echo, as well, of the children learning "to cipher and to sing" in the first stanza. If the muses are careless or simply indifferent to divine secrets, a gulf is exposed between divine and human attitudes.

Aspects of these philosophers, in other words, foreshadow their reduction to scarecrows, making the stanza pleasing in the complex but unified tone it gradually adopts. It offers us ambiguous views of the achievements of human wisdom, but it also makes for an enjoyable and unpretentious characterization of the human condition. Our fellowship in temporality is, finally, one we can be rueful and wry about, developing a resignation that is humorous even as it is tragic and desolated. Insofar as geniuses, philosophers, and great artists share the ordinary mortal's discomforts and frustrations, the art/life gap is also silently bridged and imperceptibly dismissed.

Because this is a poem about men and women, it now turns back from the gallery of philosophers fiddling, spanking, and doubting to the mother from the previous stanza and the nun from the first. They are paired now in a kind of idolatry, the mother worshipping the idealized future image of her child, the nun kneeling before a statue of Mary or the crucified Christ. One might think the nun could have an advantage, attaching herself to something timeless and unlikely to weather into a scarecrow, but the speaker has bad news for her:

> But those the candles light are not as those
> That animate a mother's reveries,
> But keep a marble or a bronze repose.
> And yet they too break hearts—

Humans break their parents' hearts by not living up to their hopes and expectations. Figures of the ideal, on the other hand, break hearts by being eternal, removed, and unattainable. The candlelight recalls the firelight of stanza II. The animation of reveries echoes the speaker's dreaming and recollecting in II and IV and the mother's speculations in V. The marble or bronze repose of the iconic images recalls the fashioning Quattrocento finger in IV. In the classroom that Yeats visited, Raphael's "Madonna della Seggiola" was the reigning image, and Yeats knew enough about the nun's routine to understand that later that night and early the next morning she would be kneeling to pray by candlelight before images she worshipped wholeheartedly. To say that those images could be as heartbreaking as any that belonged more fully to time and human aging is to tell a hard truth and to dismiss the possibility of religion as a significant answer to the pessimism that the poem has proffered us. The recognition leads the speaker to lump together gods, myths, Christian icons, and the idealized images we create of our lovers and our children, addressing them under the general rubric of "presences":

> —O Presences,
> That passion, piety or affection knows,
> And that all heavenly glory symbolise—
> O self-born mockers of man's enterprise;

The final stanza, we begin to realize, will be an address to these assembled images. Calling them presences is an acknowledgment of their importance in our lives and their rootedness in our passions and our piety. Calling them mockers confirms that their difference from us, based in idealization, will sooner or later assert itself and break our hearts. The mother's hopes for her son will crumble. The inability of the nun to match her ideal will disappoint and discourage her. The icons are sirenlike, luring us to destruction. Because they resemble us, they inspire our trust and worship. Because they differ from us, they open a tragic contrast that disappoints and devastates us.

Calling them "self-born" is deliberately equivocal. It reminds us that they do not have to go through incarnation, pregnancy, aging, and death. Like Rilke's angels in *The Duino Elegies,* they are not betrayed by the honey of generation, drugged by the music of time. But "self-born" can also mean that they are generated out of our selves, born of our need for permanence and our resistance to our condition. In that sense, we own them and ought to be able to confront them as angrily as the speaker is doing. What they mock is "man's enterprise," which must include, in this context, our efforts in education, nation building, religion, and the arts. It must also include the Presences. We create them as part of human enterprise, this desire to make ourselves and the world better while we are a part of it, and they mock our efforts by simply being what they are, permanent and perfect, ultimately unlike our lives or us. Here is another chain of action and reaction, an endless strip that has but one surface.

It is wonderfully sweeping, this address that takes in so much of what it means to be human and of the dilemmas that time and mortality impose upon us. The speaker has forgotten his own problems. He now extends his sympathies to children, mothers, lovers, postulants, and pilgrims—to all who are both the makers and the victims of the heavenly glory they discover themselves drawn to and then separated from. The discourse hangs suspended as we move to the final stanza. Will the speaker's address be a prayer or a curse or both? What special form of language will be appropriate as an address to our idols and ideals, our self-born mockers?

The answer is a strange mixture of assertions and questions.[17] The poem's final stanza, which took Yeats a long time to work out, is the place where our interpretive capabilities are most severely tested, the rocks on which many a classroom discussion has foundered and many a critical vessel sunk almost without a trace. Here at the moment when the speaker sounds most assured and triumphant is where he also perhaps defeats himself. Here, when the poem seems set to arrive at a conclusion, come its most inconclusive images and its slipperiest language. Here, expecting closure, we are treated to a breathtaking open-endedness. All that, of course, is part and parcel of what makes Yeats a modernist, violating his own tradition and aesthetic to arrive at a new form of art and a new understanding of the creative process. We are in a space where a poem has never been before, hearing language used in a new way.

First the assertions:

> Labour is blossoming or dancing where
> The body is not bruised to pleasure soul,
> Nor beauty born out of its own despair,
> Nor blear-eyed wisdom out of midnight oil.

The poem has shown us that labor—childbirth, education, worship, love, soul making, philosophy, art—is very costly.[18] Now suddenly we are told that it is blossoming or dancing that isn't costly because body is not bruised to pleasure soul, blear-eyed wisdom doesn't require long and late study, and beauty isn't achieved at the cost of suffering and despair. What are we to make of this? Is the poem contradicting what it has painfully shown us earlier? Blossoming in plants and trees may not require "labor" in the human sense, but it certainly is not effortless. Nor is dancing, as any dancer can tell you.

Effort, yes—he says they are about "labour"—but perhaps only effort that feels appropriate, not so costly as to bruise and evoke despair or blear the eyes of the elderly wise: a balance, in other words, of cause and effect. That is one way we are apt to understand the assertions. They imply that the world might change, partly through more enlightened educational principles like those of Montessori, becoming an easier place in which to create and encounter beauty, wisdom, and spiritual affluence. Where the assertions say "is" we supply "should be," or we preface them with "Ideally" or "Preferably" or "In a better world."

Doing that, of course, puts us back in that human dilemma of imaginative projection that the poem has shown us as a universal characteristic: We move away from the present and toward the future and away from the real and toward an ideal that is probably impossible. So our "interpretation" of these lines involves us in being human, falling into time's trap and prison, joining ourselves to the nuns, philosophers, children, lovers, and artists who people its world. We can't be detached from that world, nor should we want to be. Reading is labor, too, after all. Interpretation is idealistic, a process that we think should have an end, a result that is satisfying and conclusive. It is hard to relinquish that possibility.

Now the questions:

> O chestnut tree, great rooted blossomer,
> Are you the leaf, the blossom or the bole?
> O body swayed to music, O brightening glance,
> How can we know the dancer from the dance?

The first is addressed to a tree, which means it can never be answered fully or literally, at least in the terms of human communication. If we are going to have a verbal answer from the chestnut tree, so magisterially evoked, we are going to have to supply it ourselves. The second is addressed to a body, and that poses problems as well. If I ask your body a question, will it answer, or will I get an answer from your mind, your spirit? You'll use your tongue and mouth, or you'll use your hand to write it, so your body will be involved, just as Maud's body, hunched over the fire, helped her tell her tale in stanza II. Still, in the old mind/body distinction, we expect answers from the former, not the latter.

However, what about "body language"? If I ask a dancer a question, that person may dance me an answer or even be content with a "brightening glance," deliberately limiting communication to the bodily as opposed to the linguistic or the mental. So getting a clear answer from a body may be as tricky, in the world of language, where this poem operates, as getting an answer from a tree.

I am not trying to raise unnecessary difficulties. I think there is always a good reason for specificity in poetry, so I want to ponder the particular word and image choices that Yeats makes. I think that careful readers of this poem will say that the questions look like the kinds of questions that have implicit answers, "rhetorical questions," but that, on closer inspection, turn out to lead to further questions and to uncertainties and difficulties. When they have said that, they have entered the territory of Yeats's modernism, where there is no place for easy answers and little help to be had from critical glibness and smokescreens of jargon.

Still, most readers will infer a kind of answer from each of the entities questioned. They will supply the voice of the tree, in effect, and have it say that it is, in its being and identity, the sum of its parts—leaf, blossom, bole, and its great roots as well. It is an answer that is at least partly suggested by the rest of the poem. It will lead on to a conjectured answer for the dancer's body, too: that dancer and dance must be inseparable during performance even though they may be distinguishable before and after.[19] The dance can be realized only through the dancer's body, acting in time, and their meanings come from the fact of performance and from their artistic fusion. A sense of exhilaration is evoked, surely, from the brightening glance and from the vigor and beauty we imagine is expressed bodily in choreographed movement.

Both of these conjectural answers acknowledge the necessity of time as an agency and matrix for being. Unlike the Presences, which seem to exist self-born and outside of time, the tree and the dancer can have their meaning only in time and through process. The root must grow, and the leaf must exfoliate, perish, and be replaced; the blossoming must occur in a natural cycle and a natural system. Similarly, the dance must have a duration; both its performing and its witnessing can occur only in temporal terms.

In that sense the final stanza has been held to "resolve" the poem because it contains an implicit affirmation of time. Coming after the assertions that seem to claim that being might be possible without excessive loss and suffering, they appear to argue for a vision in which being and becoming, process and product, are folded together into an artistic whole. It is a whole that appears to subsume other binaries—old and young, wise and ignorant, man and woman, loss and gain—as well. That might lead us further to say that Yeats is addressing the Presences insolently, dismissing them in favor of a more process-oriented and time-friendly view of human existence. In other words, like Rilke, he has come upon a phenomenological insight, a sense of the full meaning of being-in-the-world that acknowledges change and even ephemerality without sacrificing a sense of beauty.

Nevertheless, doubts are apt to linger and resurface. Isn't it odd that a poem that had earlier appeared to subscribe to belief in reincarnation and a consequent conviction about the immortality of the soul would now think it could repudiate or dismiss metaphysics in favor of embracing time, life-as-process, and human agency?[20] How can we be said to have gotten from the idea that souls are trapped in bodies, struggling to escape if they recall their divine origins, to the idea that bodies are absolutely necessary to the realization of beauty? And what about the aging bodies of W. B. Yeats and Maud Gonne? To address all of these questions it is useful first to survey briefly the history of this poem's interpretation, then turn to a consideration of how Yeats's dance with the new insights and meanings of phenomenology both accords with Rilke's and constitutes a sharp contrast.

Recent accounts of this poem and its ending have often been founded on the assumption that earlier views, characterized as formalist or New Critical, argued for the poem's completeness and for a triumphant unity achieved by its final line. Thus it was, for example, that Paul de Man took issue with such readings: "Although there are some revealing inconsistencies within the commentaries, the line is usually interpreted as stating, with the increased emphasis of a rhetorical device, the potential unity between form and experience, between creator and creation."[21] Anita Sokolsky followed this lead: "Most interpretations of the poem in effect fetishize its final lines, reading the whole poem as if its essence were condensed in them."[22] It isn't just the interpretations that are off, however. Yeats is at fault, too: "Yet the final stanza tries to recuperate these losses by asserting an image—the fusion of dancer and dance—meant to transcend the stubborn erotics of loss: an exorbitantly unearned image of sated yearning, born out of the exhaustion of thwarted desire."[23]

These commentators are distorting previous accounts to suit their own critical agendas. The critic they were most anxious to disagree with, Cleanth Brooks, actually anticipated their readings. He says, for example:

> Does Yeats choose idealism or materialism—the flowering chestnut or the golden bird whose metal plumage will not molt? Yeats chooses both and neither. One cannot know the world of being save through the world of becoming (though one must remember that the world of becoming is a meaningless flux apart from the world of being which it implies).[24]

This does not claim a unity of form and experience, and it does not fetishize the final lines. It is built on a recognition that, as Brooks puts it a moment later, "the human situation . . . is inevitably caught between the claims of both natural and supernatural."[25] *Both and neither. Caught between.* In other words, not unified, not resolved, and certainly not fetishized.

All three commentators are in fact saying very similar things. De Man is anxious to point out that the last line can be read literally as *wanting* to be able to tell dance and dancer apart.[26] This reversal, he suggests, undoes all the tidy packaging to which people subject the poem. Sokolsky is attacking "the impulse toward unity promoted by the New Criticism and its implicit retention of the ideal as a category," which is to her "inherently sentimental."[27] Yet Sokolsky also feels that "the thrill of modernism" constitutes "the ultimately inexpressible nature of experience, the strain to represent and to fail."[28] That is precisely the thrill Yeats is seeking and finding in this poem. It is also the thrill that Brooks is confirming when he says that "The poem is a dramatization, not a formula; a controlled experience which has to be *experienced*, not a logical process, the conclusion of which is reached by logical methods and the validity of which can be checked by logical tests."[29]

Brooks is not the first critic to be misconstrued, nor will he be the last. He is useful to bring back at this juncture because his emphasis on both the dramatic and the experiential provides a helpful line of inquiry for any account of how the poem's ending works in relation to what has preceded it. Yeatsian endings, especially in the later and modernist works, generally put us in places we didn't expect to be, leaving us to wonder how we arrived there. They are thrilling but also puzzling. I suspect they felt that way to the poet, too.

When I conjectured earlier that we need to distinguish between the dramatized Yeats inside the poem and the more competent version of Yeats who is its author, I did not mean to suggest that the latter has all the answers. He does not. But he is able to create an experience for us that will allow us both to participate in his persona's meditations and to detach ourselves from them. He is able to create a space in which we too are required to be creative and experiential. And we oblige him, even if we don't realize it.

The reader can, for example, decide that the final lines introduce a resounding unity or that they open up a gulf that reveals a crisis of meaning and signification. However, the articulation of such resolutions and chasms is a choice that a reader makes, not a conclusion so firmly built into the poem that no one can argue it or mistake its meaning. Just as the dancer must perform the dance, so must readers perform the poem, and that includes riding it to the conclusion of their choice, a conclusion dependent on mood, context, circumstances, values, and preferences.

We have seen that Rilke proposed and acted upon a new sense of being by ignoring old categories and hierarchies, giving animals, plants, and objects an equivalency of value and meaning in the totality of existence. The things he gazes at gaze back at him, and his inner life turns out to be continuous with the outer life around him. He demonstrates that meaning is born of relatedness, a web of existence, and that we do not create or control it or manage to exist separately from it merely by being subjective, perceiving selves. By making this move, as I suggested earlier, he found himself approximating the insights of phenomenology articulated in the work of Husserl and Heidegger. His insights also match up with discoveries that were occurring in the sciences, where an understanding of systems and relationships was displacing the older form of analysis that assumed intrinsic meaning in parts, adding up to wholes. Meaning, in this newer understanding of the world, is dynamic, the product of relations within ever-changing systems. That insight, emerging in science and the social sciences, was beginning to permeate the arts as well.

At first glance Yeats would seem to be rather far from such ideas. He is still obsessing about the mind and the body, the spiritual and the corporeal, and he seems to see the world in terms of the old split between his perceiving self and a reality of inert "matter" beyond it. But we know that Yeats was groping toward a new sense of systems and how they might work, using his wife's automatic writing to help build up a different picture of history and human behavior. We also know that after he finished writing up his mystical system, around 1925, his "instructors" recommended he embark on a course of reading philosophy. When he wrote "Among School Children" he was less taken up with mystical notions of gyres and historical cycles and more interested in epistemology, ontology, idealism (e.g., Berkeley), and the possible shortcomings of the Neoplatonic philosophies to which his associates in the Order of the Golden Dawn had subscribed. He was ready to repudiate some of those traditions or at least to question them. Becoming less of a spiritualist and more of a healthy, inquiring philosopher was thus a part of his current program as he strolled through that Montessori classroom. He could take some pride in the fact that his ideas were changing and that at the age of sixty he was still open to new possibilities, new questions, and new ways of seeing the world. That doesn't erase the bodily decrepitude that plagues him throughout *The Tower*, but it does offset it by a counterpoint of invigorated mind and imagination.

Yeats's particular form of modernism consists, I think, of taking the old divisions to such lengths that they begin to collapse of their own weight. Thus, in this poem, only after the protagonist has thoroughly aired his attachment to old beliefs about souls and bodies, ideal and real, eternal and temporal can he start to arrive at a glimpse of something else. The final stanza of the poem looks toward something different from all that has gone before. It does not try to "recuperate" loss so much as dismiss it, arriving at a redefinition. It uses its paradoxical assertions and broadening "rhetorical" questions to launch itself in a new direction, one that makes the ending a beginning. In that respect the different readings of the ending are a natural consequence of its ability to turn the world of the poem inside out, shedding it like a chrysalis.[30] What will follow cannot be known yet, but it will be different. It will be like Montessori education in trusting more to instinct, spontaneity, and the senses. It will free the protagonist from his litany of complaints and disappointed expectations. It will bring the scarecrow back to life and make him dance.

Yeats not only admired Maria Montessori's ideas about education; he had also followed up on them by reading the writings of the educational reformer and philosopher Giovanni Gentile, who helped put many of Montessori's ideas in practice in the Italian educational system during his time as minister of education. Gentile was a philosopher whose idealism (in the sense of repudiating materialism) was leading him along philosophical lines that could be said to ally him with phenomenology. He saw culture as an activity that involves a constant becoming. It is not an inert thing that can be studied and analyzed, taken apart and atomized, but a motion, a moving body, a dance and dancer. And Yeats, the school, the nun, and Maud are a part of it, indistinguishable from its totality of growth and motion. Their meaning inheres in their interrelatedness and extends beyond their immediate awareness of it. When Yeats entertains this insight, he can relinquish his desire to control and constrain that meaning, and insofar as he performs that relinquishment, he finds a way out of the poem at the end. It is not a way out that responds to analysis, which is still tied to the older model of knowledge and meaning, but it is a way out that can be danced and acted bodily, with the reader participating.[31]

We dance, then, without fully knowing that we dance. We dance with Yeats, Maud, Plato, and all the rest. The question of whether we need to know (distinguish, understand, know by means of and apart from) the dancer from the dance will formulate itself and then be left behind. It is a part of the dance, and it will pass us on to the next question and the next. We do not worry about part to whole or about definitive answers. We are subject to change in time, as is everything else in the system we belong to and participate in, and that is all right. It is acceptable in a way that was not the case before we reached this point.

Sometimes we need to remember the crucial role our bodies play in our very being, in our knowing, and in our delight. Aristotle spanks Alexander. Pythagoras has a remarkable thigh, and he fingers a fiddle-stick. The color on a child's cheek or hair can make our emotions explode inside us. The memory of a body bent over a fire can become as iconic as a crucifix. We blossom and we dance, part and parcel of our knowledge and part and parcel of our knowing. "Man can embody truth, but he cannot know it," Yeats wrote late in life.[32]

The final stanza has shown us that assertions are not very different from questions. They are relative to circumstance. However, there is definitely something celebratory and something affirmative in and around this relativity of meaning and expression. It is the recognition that beauty is a combination of labor and play—in the classroom, in love, in art, and in life.[33] It is the recognition that this is hard to achieve and sustain. Furthermore, it is the recognition that living emphatically in the present, with the realities that surround us, is preferable to living in the past or the future, fixated and seduced by impossible ideals. Life is not a sedation, a sleep that takes the soul away from its connection to the eternal. Yeats found that hard to admit, but when he came to it he came to some of his most thrilling insights and expressions. That, at any rate, is part of what I take away from the poem, and I believe that it is quite compatible with the insights that fill the conclusion of Rilke's poem. Both poems arrive at a conclusion that is also not so much a resolution as a blossoming or flowering, an opening out to the mystery of existence that is inexpressible and deeply affirmative.

3

Wallace Stevens writes

SUNDAY MORNING

I

Complacencies of the peignoir, and late
Coffee and oranges in a sunny chair
And the green freedom of a cockatoo
Upon a rug mingle to dissipate
The holy hush of ancient sacrifice.
She dreams a little and she feels the dark
Encroachment of the old catastrophe,
As a calm darkens among water lights.
The pungent oranges and bright, green wings
Seem things in some procession of the dead,
Winding across wide water, without sound.
The day is like wide water, without sound,
Stilled for the passing of her dreaming feet
Over the seas, to silent Palestine,
Dominion of the blood and sepulchre.

II

Why should she give her bounty to the dead?
What is divinity if it can come
Only in silent shadows and in dreams?
Shall she not find in comforts of the sun,
In pungent fruit and bright, green wings, or else
In any balm or beauty of the earth,
Things to be cherished like the thought of heaven?
Divinity must live within herself:
Passions of rain, or moods in falling snow;
Grievings in loneliness, or unsubdued
Elations when the forest blooms; gusty
Emotions on wet roads on autumn nights;

All pleasures and all pains, remembering
The bough of summer and the winter branch.
These are the measures destined for her soul.

III

Jove in the clouds had his inhuman birth.
No mother suckled him, no sweet land gave
Large-mannered motions to his mythy mind.
He moved among us, as a muttering king,
Magnificent, would move among his hinds,
Until our blood, commingling, virginal,
With heaven, brought such requital to desire
The very hinds discerned it, in a star.
Shall our blood fail? Or shall it come to be
The blood of paradise? And shall the earth
Seem all of paradise that we shall know?
The sky will be much friendlier then than now,
A part of labor and a part of pain,
And next in glory to enduring love,
Not this dividing and indifferent blue.

IV

She says, "I am content when wakened birds,
Before they fly, test the reality
Of misty fields, by their sweet questionings;
But when the birds are gone, and their warm fields
Return no more, where, then, is paradise?"
There is not any haunt of prophecy,
Nor any old chimera of the grave,
Neither the golden underground, nor isle
Melodious, where spirits gat them home,
Nor visionary south, nor cloudy palm
Remote on heaven's hill, that has endured
As April's green endures; or will endure
Like her remembrance of awakened birds,
Or her desire for June and evening, tipped
By the consummation of the swallow's wings.

V

She says, "But in contentment I still feel
The need of some imperishable bliss."
Death is the mother of beauty; hence from her,
Alone, shall come fulfillment to our dreams
And our desires. Although she strews the leaves
Of sure obliteration on our paths,
The path sick sorrow took, the many paths
Where triumph rang its brassy phrase, or love
Whispered a little out of tenderness,
She makes the willow shiver in the sun
For maidens who were wont to sit and gaze
Upon the grass, relinquished to their feet.
She causes boys to pile new plums and pears
On disregarded plate. The maidens taste
And stray impassioned in the littering leaves.

VI

Is there no change of death in paradise?
Does ripe fruit never fall? Or do the boughs
Hang always heavy in that perfect sky,
Unchanging, yet so like our perishing earth,
With rivers like our own that seek for seas
They never find, the same receding shores
That never touch with inarticulate pang?
Why set the pear upon those river-banks
Or spice the shores with odors of the plum?
Alas, that they should wear our colors there,
The silken weavings of our afternoons,
And pick the strings of our insipid lutes!
Death is the mother of beauty, mystical,
Within whose burning bosom we devise
Our earthly mothers waiting, sleeplessly.

VII

Supple and turbulent, a ring of men
Shall chant in orgy on a summer morn
Their boisterous devotion to the sun,

Not as a god, but as a god might be,
Naked among them, like a savage source.
Their chant shall be a chant of paradise,
Out of their blood, returning to the sky;
And in their chant shall enter, voice by voice,
The windy lake wherein their lord delights,
The trees, like serafin, and echoing hills,
That choir among themselves long afterward.
They shall know well the heavenly fellowship
Of men that perish and of summer morn.
And whence they came and whither they shall go
The dew upon their feet shall manifest.

VIII

She hears, upon that water without sound,
A voice that cries, "The tomb in Palestine
Is not the porch of spirits lingering.
It is the grave of Jesus, where he lay."
We live in an old chaos of the sun,
Or old dependency of day and night,
Or island solitude, unsponsored, free,
Of that wide water, inescapable.
Deer walk upon our mountains, and the quail
Whistle about us their spontaneous cries;
Sweet berries ripen in the wilderness;
And, in the isolation of the sky,
At evening, casual flocks of pigeons make
Ambiguous undulations as they sink,
Downward to darkness, on extended wings.

(Collected Poems)

THE RICH AND SENSUOUS language of this poem lays immediate claims upon us. The diction is a curious mix of plain and fancy. The rhythms feel confident, and, along with the sonorities, they draw us forward, fascinated. Yet the poem's progression, which is never quite narrative, never quite drama, never quite an oration or measured argument, is difficult to grasp. Does "Sunday Morning" possess an overall unity, or is it a group of poems around a common subject, somewhat arbitrarily associated? And if its unity consists of its repeated challenges to the authority of Christianity, exactly why is religion such a dominant concern?

Reading "Sunday Morning" has been likened to entering a picture gallery and coming upon one colorful canvas after another.[1] The first "painting" we see is informal and domestic, touched with exotic hues and details. The final one is a great panoramic landscape. In between, we discover a considerable variety of picturesque styles and tonalities. At the time Stevens wrote the poem, he was experiencing enthusiasm for new developments in the visual arts. The people he knew in New York, who included collectors of modern art like Walter Arensberg and modern artists like Marcel Duchamp, had given him "permission," we might say, to break out of a certain decadent preciousness in his own poetic style and to experiment with language and form in startling and exciting ways. The New York Armory Show of 1913 had jump-started American modernism in all the arts. One task of a poet was to figure out how the innovations in sculpture and painting could be translated into language to help lay the foundation of a new poetics.

Becoming a modernist while remaining American was the task that confronted the next three poets in this study. Stevens, Williams, and Moore can all be differentiated from poets like Pound, Stein, H.D., and Eliot, who threw in their lot with modernism while living in Europe. This is not to say that those writers weren't profoundly American, too, in various ways; it is simply to acknowledge that those who stayed at home were pressed to think about how to formulate their modernism in distinctly local terms. Place and landscape play a significant role in their experiments, and direct responses to certain facts of American culture characterize their poetry.[2] In Stevens's case that response was to the limitations, as he saw them, of traditional Protestant Christianity. For him, it formed an obstacle to art and to modernism, one that he felt he must address directly. Thus his first great modern poem is, among other things, a concerted attack on organized religion. The criticism of religion, in his understanding, opens the door to innovation and achievement in the realm of art.

While tradition in the form of religion may be rejected in "Sunday Morning," traditional poetry is by no means unwelcome there. As we respond to the poem's images, we are also responding to Stevens's command of traditional verse-paragraphs, a use of blank verse that draws on Shakespeare, Milton, Wordsworth, and Browning, shaping a steady but highly flexible iambic pentameter. The regular fifteen-line stanzas feel rather like unrhymed sonnets.

Given this use of blank verse and picturesque images, might not the poem be called romantic? In its concern for the human relation to the natural world and to questions of the supernatural, it certainly displays something of a romantic sensibility. Moreoever, its kinship with the great romantic odes of Keats, Coleridge, and Wordsworth has been much noticed. At the same time, we sense how American this poem is. Whatever it owes to the English romantics, it would never be confused with their poetry.

How about transcendentalist, then, that American version of the romantic? That is closer, but it will not suffice as an identifying tag either, because there is something distinctly modern about this poem's approach and atmosphere. The attitude toward Christianity is harsher and more explicit. The poem's tones are elusive and complicated, from line to line and stanza to stanza. Ironic reflections abound. The sonorities often slide sideways, reaching a parodic pitch, as in the passage about Jove in stanza III. And romantic sensibility is clearly being mocked in the passage about the boys, the maidens, and the fruit that closes stanza V, just as a tone of burlesque tends to dominate stanza VI.

Something about this poem's way of looking at the world, its manner of posing issues, its spirited voice, and its notions of beauty locates it in the early part of the twentieth century.[3] Separating its European elements from its American ones and its transcendentalist elements from its modern ones is part of our challenge here as readers. Having experimented with modernism in several shorter poems, Stevens apparently felt ready to formulate a kind of artistic Declaration of Independence. "Sunday Morning" stakes a claim to a new aesthetic, distinctly modern and distinctly American, and it is both the articulation of a thesis and the most impressive demonstration of that thesis.

The poem emerged rather suddenly. Stevens had written very promising poetry while an undergraduate at Harvard, but he had then given it up while he explored careers, first in journalism and then in the law. All the while living in New York City, he was reading widely and keeping a journal, as well as writing love letters to his future wife, Elsie. He wrote some poems for her as a part of this courtship in 1906 and 1907 but made no attempt to publish or show them to other readers at that time. His own Sunday mornings during this period tended to be given over to long walks in the country. His adventures in exploring the natural world had culminated, in a way, during a hunting trip to British Columbia with his employer. There, at the age of twenty-two, he seems to have had a full realization of what the natural world meant to him, especially in its character as wilderness, and some commentators have seen this vacation as a kind of spiritual and intellectual turning point for the young Stevens.[4]

Ten years later, established as a lawyer and settled in his marriage, still living in New York, Stevens found himself responding enthusiastically to new developments in the arts. He experienced the 1913 Armory Show and the growing collection of modern art that belonged to the collector and connoisseur Walter Arensberg. Gatherings at Arensberg's apartment included like-minded people who were founding little magazines and writing experimental poems. Stevens now began writing again and showing poems to friends in the Arensberg circle like Carl Van Vechten and William Carlos Williams.[5] The next ten years were quite productive, producing most of the poems in his first collection, *Harmonium* (1923).

Most of what he wrote in these beginning years was quite different from "Sunday Morning." The poems tended to be sketchy and imagist, playful and experimental, clearly responding to the developments in cubism and the dada movement. The poem that opens *Harmonium* is typical of this period:

EARTHY ANECDOTE

Every time the bucks went clattering
Over Oklahoma
A firecat bristled in the way.

Wherever they went,
They went clattering,
Until they swerved
In a swift, circular line
To the right,
Because of the firecat.

Or until they swerved
In a swift, circular line
To the left,
Because of the firecat.

The bucks clattered.
The firecat went leaping,
To the right, to the left,

And
Bristled in the way.

Later, the firecat closed his bright eyes
And slept.

(Collected Poems)

The celebration of energy here, along with the severe and precise use of geometrical representation and the free verse, eschewing rhyme and meter, evokes the paintings of the futurists and cubists. The addition of Oklahoma, bucks, and firecat introduces American details to a manner that would otherwise be associated with European modernism. The deliberately flat ending, along with the resistance to obvious beauty and ready metaphorical decoding would have shocked and outraged traditionalists, while delighting those who were taken by the newness and the confrontational manner of modernist painting, music, and poetry. Knowing that Stevens was associating with Marcel Duchamp at the time, one can imagine that artist's appreciation for the poem, reciprocating the poet's fascination with Duchamp's experiments in sculpture and painting. Stevens's desire to create an American version of modernism is easy to identify and understand in such a case.

Nevertheless, "Sunday Morning" is trickier. Written in 1915, in the midst of a series of more obviously modernist experiments, it seems to stand out as an articulation of an American and modernist aesthetic. It looms up above the smaller experiments like a mountain among foothills. We need to ask how this grand set of statements helped both to define and to extend the more obvious modernist experiments that surround them.

One clear answer lies in the issue of religion and the sacrilegious. A redefinition of the sacred, in terms of the human and natural realms, lies at the heart of the poem. For Stevens, no true modern art could be created, especially in America, before the issue of religion was settled. There was a significant tension around the subject in his own mind, given his religious upbringing and his wife's steadfast piety. Resolving the question of the quarrel between religion and art as comparable manifestations of human spiritual need was therefore paramount to him.

To address it, he turned back to the writings of George Santayana, his teacher at Harvard, using them to help inform this extended consideration of the role of religion and art in human life.[6] Santayana had argued that poetry and religion were essentially the same thing, with the advantage going to poetry because it does not require or perpetuate dogma. Subscribing to this, Stevens wanted, as part of his artistic declaration, to announce the ways in which he felt that poetry could replace organized religion. He wished to resolve, both in and for himself, an issue he saw manifesting itself everywhere in his culture. When Sunday morning came around, you were supposed to be in church or in Sunday school. If you were raised that way and chose not to be in church, you then had to deal with a sense of guilt, an uneasiness, and a depression that could make the free and open time of Sunday oppressive. The week seemed to organize itself around the question of your obedience or apostasy.[7]

Rightly or wrongly, Stevens felt that Americans could not create their own vigorous and original artistic culture until they freed themselves from their puritanical Protestant heritage. The tomb in Palestine needed to be acknowledged as a foreign place where a historical figure named Jesus had died—just that and nothing more. It was in exploring and trying to resolve such issues that Stevens suddenly found he could write in a particularly eloquent and extended style, turning away from the playful and opaque experimentation of his concurrent poems and drawing on the romantic and Miltonic tradition that seemed to be reserved for larger issues. His explicitness about the drawbacks of organized religion shocked Harriet Monroe, the editor of *Poetry*, to whom he sent "Sunday Morning."[8]

Stressing both the foreignness and the historical remoteness of Christianity thus becomes one strategy by which Stevens reinforces his views. The here and now is an America, sunny, capacious, and newly modern, where one might enjoy oneself on a Sunday morning. The encroachment upon this pleasure comes from a far-away time and place, a distant oppressiveness that stifles the spirit, darkening and silencing the world. Stevens fought that oppression in himself, and of course he wished his wife and neighbors could fight it, too. Whether or not they could and whatever their sentiments and pieties, he meant to stake out his antitheological and proaesthetic position. He needed to clear his own artistic ground for a new start in a new world, a place where Sunday and morning could acquire an entirely new meaning.

So we begin with a domestic interior. The emphasis is on sensuous pleasure: a bathrobe elegant enough to be called a peignoir and some imported tropical pleasures, including bright fruit, stimulating coffee, and a pet bird from the rainforest, being given what is perhaps its weekly moment of freedom from its cage. Even the rug will feel exotic in this context since the bird takes its leisure there.[9] Even though it is simply called "rug," more than one commentator has decided it must be oriental, evidence of the lively imaginative response we bring to this scene.

While we may be disposed to think of this domestic scene as a painting, we are not able to identify it in terms of any one painter, school, or period. Domestic interiors had been a subject for paintings ever since the seventeenth-century Dutch began to cultivate them. Women at leisure, in what was known as deshabille,[10] a subgenre falling between the formal portrait and the nude study, had been a frequent subject for French painters in the nineteenth century. More recently, artists such as Whistler, Sargent, and Manet had shown elegant women in exotic robes and dressing gowns, sometimes with pets nearby. Meanwhile, the emphatic use of colors, orange and green, naturally evokes postimpressionist and Fauvist painters like Matisse, Bonnard, Van Gogh, and Gauguin. The painterly associations, in other words, are rich and complex, and they aid the reader's imagination without specifying a particular period or style.[11]

For a moment the sensuous and exotic pleasures seem to dominate; they "mingle to dissipate"—the verb is probably chosen for its innate ambiguity—the Protestant Sunday morning preoccupation with biblical matters. But their dominion, attractive though it may be, is not enough to overcome the woman's upbringing and psychology. We move inward to discover that as she "dreams a little," a natural extension of her relaxed "complacencies," there comes a "dark encroachment" of an "old catastrophe," presumably the Crucifixion. The domestic interior is displaced by a rather spooky seascape, calm and silent, with water lights and a procession of ghosts heading for Palestine. It is as though the living and dead alike are compelled to join this ghastly Easter parade. The progression of the entire stanza is from sunny "complacencies" to gloomy "sepulchre," and the pungent fruit and cockatoo wings are swept along, as is the woman's sunnier mood, by the tremendous force of religious preoccupation.

The drama, combining inner and outer, may recall the drama in Yeats, but the differences are instructive. It is not an "I" but a "she." The meditative space is subjective but not personal. It does not express the situation of the speaker and, through that, connect to the author. And the resort to darker imaginative landscapes is involuntary and unwelcome, not a refuge from contemporary reality but rather a sinister invasion by tradition. The stanza's repeated words and phrases, especially "wide water, without sound," in successive lines, underline its portrayal of obsession and a sort of spiritual kidnapping.

We should not be surprised, then, that the woman's experience provokes the speaker/narrator's direct protest: "Why should she give her bounty to the dead? / What is divinity if it can come / Only in silent shadows and in dreams?" Having presented her and delighted in her, just as a painter might in his model, he now wants to protect her from the "dark encroachment" that disrupts her sensuous enjoyment and spoils her Sunday. He wants to assume that her sensibility matches his, but the reader senses his urge rather than his success. He may or may not understand her mind and emotions. This problematizing of their situation opens a creative space in which the reader faces choices and entertains speculations that may undermine the speaker's authority.

In any case, the speaker is sure of his ground: He wants to counterbalance "the thought of heaven" with the beauty of the earth:

> Shall she not find in comforts of the sun,
> In pungent fruit and bright, green wings, or else
> In any balm or beauty of the earth,
> Things to be cherished like the thought of heaven?

The speaker is stacking his argument by making religion a "thought," located in a mental realm of silent shadows and dreams, a "dominion" of something long gone—bloody, lugubrious, and preferably forgotten—while the humanist side gets the real and material things that can be touched, smelled, tasted, and listened to. The world of the senses is firmly associated with pleasure, both physical and aesthetic, while the world of dogma is presented as a threat that turns sense experience vague and dark, silencing and obscuring it.[12] For the woman in deshabille, it is a matter of her reconciling her inner world with the outer one:

> Divinity must live within herself:
> Passions of rain, or moods in falling snow;
> Grievings in loneliness, or unsubdued
> Elations when the forest blooms; gusty
> Emotions on wet roads on autumn nights;
> All pleasures and all pains

Sadness is more acceptable on these terms, a cool companion to pleasure. The mix of weathers and seasons with interior events, both painful and pleasurable, feels quite persuasive. It is also recognizable—we may invoke Rilke and Yeats by now, as colleagues—in terms of the modernist attack on the discontinuities of inner and outer, spirit and matter. One thing that is crucial to the argument is the imagination's ability, aided by the senses and sense-memory, to mix and match experiences, acting not only in the present but also retrospectively. The ability to remember "the bough of summer and the winter branch" gives one the ability to balance and compare, relishing sense experience and offsetting the painful with the pleasurable. That is the kind of spiritual activity the poem endorses, as against religious activities involving guilt, fear, and the anticipation of heavenly reward. By the time the speaker closes this section with "These are the measures destined for her soul," the main issues of the poem have been fully set out. The rest will be variations on this theme.[13]

The first variation, in stanza III, is a sort of potted history of religion. Its tongue-in-cheek tone is signaled in part by the excessive alliterations:

> Jove in the clouds had his inhuman birth.
> No mother suckled him, no sweet land gave
> Large-mannered motions to his mythy mind.
> He moved among us, as a muttering king,
> Magnificent, would move among his hinds.

This is the first phase of human religion, in which the deity's otherness is stressed. It will do for Zeus, for Jupiter, and for the Jehovah of the Old Testament. The stories of these deities' relations with their human subjects emphasize their inequality and the sense of subjection to their arbitrary behavior (Zeus and Europa, etc.). The absence of any interdependence between the human and the divine is next replaced by the idea of the Incarnation: "Until our blood, commingling, virginal, / With heaven, brought such requital to desire / The very hinds discerned it, in a star." This brings us to the Christian Nativity and to a mingling of the divine and the human. Now it is not a matter of arbitrary exercise of power, but rather, as in Rilke, human desire ascending and aspiring to the condition of godhead. The next step, Stevens's speaker is happy to suggest, might be to let the human take over the divine altogether: "Shall our blood fail? Or shall it come to be / The blood of paradise? And shall the earth / Seem all of paradise that we shall know?" It's clear how the speaker, from the attitudes expressed in stanza II, thinks these questions should be answered: no, yes, and yes. He sees a natural evolution of spiritual belief from the positing of gods as others, through the incarnation of divinity in human form, to a final human acknowledgment of independence from supernatural beliefs. The prospect is welcomed:

> The sky will be much friendlier then than now,
> A part of labor and a part of pain,
> And next in glory to enduring love,
> Not this dividing and indifferent blue.

The tone has moved from burlesque treatment of religious mythology to humanist declaration of kinship with nature. Divinity is humanized now as part of the activity of the imagination.[14]

As stanza IV opens, the woman speaks. The situation becomes more fully dramatized, a dialogue or debate in which we realize that she has perhaps been listening to the speaker's arguments and wishes to respond:

> She says, "I am content when wakened birds,
> Before they fly, test the reality
> Of misty fields, by their sweet questionings;
> But when the birds are gone, and their warm fields
> Return no more, where, then, is paradise?"

This question, which echoes Keats's great odes, is a lyrical expression of two contrary things: the human response to nature and the human resistance to natural change. It is cast in terms of morning, a summer dawn with birdcalls beginning and a preliminary mist. It also provokes an emphatic response from the speaker, who once again rehearses the history of religion, this time in terms of versions of the supposedly perfect world from which humanity fell and/or the perfect world to which it aspires to return. He lists a string of phony oracles and paradises, sometimes using archaic terminology ("chimera," "golden underground," "isle / Melodious, where spirits gat them home"), in order to dismiss them. None of them

> has endured
> As April's green endures; or will endure
> Like her remembrance of awakened birds,
> Or her desire for June and evening, tipped
> By the consummation of the swallow's wings.

His response takes her language and imagery into account, matching her misty morning with a protracted summer evening and birds that are active at dusk and adding a kind of superword, "consummation," to clinch his argument. Green endures, we learn, and so do sensations of memory and desire; ideal constructs, meanwhile, come to seem ephemeral.

We should note in passing that their "dialogue" is not very direct. He does not say "your remembrance." He still discusses her as though she occupied a different space or time, such as a picture, and he stood commenting on her. Yet her responses, as stanzas IV and V both demonstrate, suggest that she can listen to him as well as object. The implications of this point again to the complications of modernist art, where the destabilizing of the speaker's authority and singularity opens the text and furnishes a more creative role for the reader.

When stanza V opens as IV did, we realize that his mockery of various human inventions of paradise has not settled her objections: "She says, 'But in contentment I still feel / The need of some imperishable bliss.'" Fair enough, we might say, taking her point. If he talks of "desire" for June and evening, why not also acknowledge her desire, "feel[ing] the need," for lasting bliss? Why must pleasure be ephemeral? Who says we can't have a paradise where beauty and happiness are prolonged indefinitely? Her contention turns out to be precisely the provocation the speaker needs to spring his most direct and powerful argument, couched as an aphorism that echoes Plato's "Necessity is the mother of invention": "Death is the mother of beauty; hence from her, / Alone, shall come fulfillment to our dreams / And our desires." The sentiment matches those that Rilke and Yeats have expressed less directly. It can also be traced back to the romantics, particularly to Keats and especially to his "Ode on Melancholy."[15]

The logic of this is tricky: If our dreams and desires include paradise, how can death bring any kind of fulfillment for them? The implied answer is that desire for false beauty (i.e., permanent beauty) is illegitimate. If the beauty is genuine, it will be bound up with change and death. That insight is further addressed in stanza VI.

The dramatized confrontation has somehow made the unusual directness possible. Moreover, Stevens now borrows from religion the habit of positing deities; his is admittedly constructed for the occasion, but a goddess of death is an especially convenient personification to summon at this point.[16] We learn that she "strews the leaves / Of sure obliteration in our paths," paths associated variously with sorrow, triumph, and tender love, and that she "makes the willow shiver in the sun" and "causes boys" to proffer fruit. As the maidens taste the fruit "and stray impassioned in the littering leaves," the poem slides into a burlesque manner again. These boys and maidens sound rather like the silly lovers in *A Midsummer Night's Dream*. However, the central phrase and concept, "Death is the mother of beauty," continues to resonate, spreading out from the poem's center to dominate its aesthetic and outlook.

We do not know whether the woman is convinced or simply silenced. Whichever is the case, the speaker takes over for the final three stanzas. He presents her as hearing a voice in stanza VIII, but she utters no further objections to his viewpoint. She has served her purpose, provoking his eloquent outbursts and opening new space in which readers may speculate on the complications of the questions the speaker is trying to settle authoritatively. Her implied presence continues to trouble both the surface and the depths of the poem, allowing us to see the speaker as a version of Stevens who, like the "Yeats" who wanders through "Among School Children," is less capable or comprehending than the author. His emphatic declarations are deliberately undermined by a whisper of objection that suggests, for example, that he has not managed to persuade his target audience. We may admire his sentiments, framing them in terms of his rejection of religion and celebration of a humanist aesthetic, but we do so with an awareness that they can isolate him—from the woman, from his neighbors, and from the potential audience for his art. He is not a ludicrous comic hero like Crispin, whom Stevens made the protagonist of his uneven long poem, "The Comedian as the Letter C," but he has in common with Crispin a mixture of success and failure that complicates our perspective.

Stanza VI is a series of rhetorical questions, over nine lines, followed by an exclamation and then a reiteration of the key phrase from stanza V, "Death is the mother of beauty." In the questions, paradise is mocked for being made up of natural beauties that in their essence necessarily imply change and loss: ripe fruit, unchanging sky, rivers that never make it to the ocean or even touch their own banks. The absurdity is summarized: "Why set the pear upon those river-banks / Or spice the shores with odors of the plum?" And the absurdity provokes a kind of crocodile tear, feigning sympathy: "Alas, that they should wear our colors there, / The silken weavings of our afternoons, / And pick the strings of our insipid lutes!" Alas, indeed. The denizens of paradise (which means for Stevens, I think, both the Eden from which Adam and Eve presumably fell and the heaven to which humankind is supposed to aspire in the afterlife) sound like pallid imitators of life, emulating its sensations but unable to make them effective because of their prolongation. To "spice the shores with odors of the plum" is necessarily to admit that fruit ripens and falls and that sensations like smell are ephemeral. The mockery of heavenly phoniness is swept aside in favor of a ringing and mysterious close: "Death is the mother of beauty, mystical, / Within whose burning bosom we devise / Our earthly mothers waiting, sleeplessly." The final image captures the human paradox triumphantly. We see Death and acknowledge her creation of beauty, but we also resist, positing mothers who are waiting up for us, as if we were tardy children. This "devising" disrupts the truth of Death and the vision of her "burning bosom." It is an understandable nostalgia—who does not want his or her mother back, want a reunion and a life after death?—but, in the speaker's view, it needs to be looked at skeptically. Of course we do this, he suggests, but we also need to step back from it. No mothers wait sleeplessly for us, in Stevens's view of the matter; we need to let them rest and accept the fact of their sleep, their death.

If we trace the presence of the feminine through the poem, we can say it has been both troublesome and enriching to the arguments the speaker is pursuing. The woman raises objections to his dismissal of the supernatural and the eternal. Motherhood is problematic to the gods and to humans; no mother suckled Jove, but Jesus attained his incarnation through Mary, whose traditional color blue has become "dividing and indifferent," as the sky in stanza III. Maidens and mothers are displaced somehow by the mother who turns out to be Death, the mother in whom we devise our mothers waiting sleeplessly for us.[17] But through her mothering authority, Death brings labor and generation and the consequent desire for more permanence back into the poem's foreground.[18] Small wonder, then, that the pagan celebration envisioned in stanza VII turns out to be male, a religious ritual of nature worship performed exclusively by men:

> Supple and turbulent, a ring of men
> Shall chant in orgy on a summer morn
> Their boisterous devotion to the sun,
> Not as a god, but as a god might be,
> Naked among them, like a savage source.

They may or may not be clothed. The speaker doesn't specify, although the nakedness of the sun, the sunlight "as a god," along with their dew-covered feet (instead of shoes or sandals) has led many commentators to reasonably infer nakedness in the men. As for summer and morning and sunlight, it begins to be clear how their recurrence in the poem establishes an emerging foundation for a natural religion.

Again, we are apt to think of paintings. Matisse's famous ring of naked dancers was not all male, but it certainly comes to mind.[19] So do the naked male bathers of painters like Eakins and Cézanne. For Stevens's readers, moreover, in 1915, the image might well have summoned up not a painting but a recent and famous modernist performance, Stravinsky's *Rite of Spring* as produced by Diaghilev and choreographed and danced by Nijinsky.[20] The orgiastic music and the frankness of the dancing constituted a landmark of modernist primitivism that achieved a rapid notoriety. A ring of dancing men could also be said to call up Native American practices that were beginning to be discussed by Stevens's generation in their search for alternatives to mainstream European culture. In many tribes it was primarily the men's business to dance, while the women served as spectators and commentators.

These men, however, do not literally take the sun to be a god. They are post-Christian, representing a reborn paganism, and their praise does not mistake the sun for something else. Rather, it acknowledges how divinity can be personified metaphorically, "as a god might be." There's no question about the human origin of their practice: "Their chant shall be a chant of paradise, / Out of their blood, returning to the sky." There's also no question but that it replaces traditional religion in its eloquence and praise:

> And in their chant shall enter, voice by voice,
> The windy lake wherein their lord delights,
> The trees, like serafin, and echoing hills,
> That choir among themselves long afterward.

This is not a muttering king moving among his hinds, but a celebration of the holiness and beauty of the natural world, reinforced by biblical language and traditional associations of worship. The result is a "heavenly fellowship":

> They shall know well the heavenly fellowship
> Of men that perish and of summer morn.
> And whence they came and whither they shall go
> The dew upon their feet shall manifest.

In other words, their bond is partly in the recognition of their common mortality.[21] The dew speaks of it eloquently by standing, as is usual in Stevens, for the ephemeral nature of all life in this world. Words like "perish," "whence," "whither," and "manifest" continue the heavy borrowing from traditional religious discourse, and they make the tone of this stanza almost impossible to capture. It can seem profoundly serious in its vision of an earth-oriented and humanist religion of the future, and it can simultaneously register as slightly parodic and tongue-in-cheek, a send-up of the whole idea of communal worship and religious ritual. This simultaneity, which characterizes so much of the poem, has always intrigued readers and, insofar as they could stand to leave matters unresolved, made them acknowledge its elusiveness.

Does this all-male ritual signal a final gulf between men and women, especially on the subject of worship? Hardly. But it certainly continues the poem's framing of questions about belief in terms of gender. Stevens brings his female opposite back one more time in the next stanza, to hear what he considers a truth, but then he turns his face to the American wilderness. The implication seems to be that men are in advance of women—as represented primarily by the poet's mother and by Elsie, although Harriet Monroe can be included, given her insistence on censoring the poem—in questioning traditional religion's relevance to modern American life. The men forge on ahead in this area, and the women are free to follow if they choose. That it should be cast in terms of gender may seem unfair to later readers, but it is scarcely surprising in its reflection of Stevens's own life and circumstances.[22] And the ways in which it enhances the interest and drama of the poem are not altogether a disadvantage.

The final section of the poem has two distinct parts, a report of the woman's hearing a voice, followed by a summary of humanity's position with relation to the natural world. The implicit relation between the two parts seems to reflect the kind of interaction found elsewhere in the poem: hearing about the death of the historical Jesus and dismissing the idea of resurrection and paradise seems to release the poem into some of its most eloquent speech and imagery. In that sense we can say that the engagement of Christian and pagan viewpoints, with the pagan displacing the Christian, happens one final time, achieving an emphasis that is particularly memorable.

Bringing the woman back at least raises the possibility that the entire poem has been a drama in her mind. It also undermines, once again, the full authority of the speaker, which in turn, as I have suggested, opens new speculative (modernist) space for the reader. She "hears" a "voice that cries": "The tomb in Palestine / Is not the porch of spirits lingering. / It is the grave of Jesus, where he lay." The voice is "upon that water without sound," where her dreaming feet were passing in stanza I. It sounds disembodied and authoritative, as if it were a supernatural utterance. Who is speaking? History? Common sense? Reason? We are left to speculate.

We are also left to speculate on her response. One critic assumes that the lines that follow represent her insight.[23] In that reading all of the different positions of belief expressed in the poem become her territory, part of her mental theater, with this the final one. It's an intriguing suggestion. However, since we have been acutely aware of a difference between her viewpoint, drawn away from her pleasures toward her sense of duty to Christian belief and ritual, and that of a speaker who comments on her and argues against her distraction, I think most readers will feel that she is more or less dismissed here, left to ponder what she has heard. One can liken her to a passive Mary, hearing a kind of anti-Annunciation. Turning away from her, in effect, the speaker moves stage front to chant the final lines, representative once more of the position of atheism and paganism he has been championing. She may hear his voice, and she may or may not assent. The question is left open.

The final unit can be broken into two subsections. The first is extremely generalized:

> We live in an old chaos of the sun,
> Or old dependency of day and night,
> Or island solitude, unsponsored, free,
> Of that wide water, inescapable.

"We" is all humanity. The "old chaos," which replaces the "old catastrophe" of stanza I, is both the literal origin of the solar system and the sentiment that we cannot look to the disorder of nature for signs of a purposeful creator. The sun is the sun, not a god and not a mirror of a deity practicing "intelligent design." It confers a "dependency" on us because, no matter how ingenious our technology and civilization, the basic facts of day and night continue to rule our lives. This dependence upon the fact of the earth circling the sun and rotating as it goes can also be expressed as an "island solitude," like Robinson Crusoe's. There is no deity to share our island/planet with us, no "sponsor" of our activities. This leaves us "free," but it also maroons us. The reappearance of the "wide water," which invokes the size and majesty of the oceans as well as the vastness of outer space, reinforces the sense of being marooned in an immensity. Some readers will find this negative and forbidding, though I do not think that Stevens found it so. For him, "unsponsored" and "free" outweigh "dependency," "inescapable," and "chaos."

The reason I do not think Stevens found the insight depressing is contained in the lovely description and invocation of the natural that follows.[24] Generalizations are now replaced by images of considerable beauty and power:

> Deer walk upon our mountains, and the quail
> Whistle about us their spontaneous cries;
> Sweet berries ripen in the wilderness;
> And, in the isolation of the sky,
> At evening, casual flocks of pigeons make
> Ambiguous undulations as they sink,
> Downward to darkness, on extended wings.

It turns out that our "island solitude" is shared, in fact, by creatures and plants whose existence is relatively independent of ours. We may think of mountains as "our mountains," and we may hear the whistling and spontaneous cries of the quail "about us," locating them in relation to where we are. Nonetheless, the deer walk whether we see them or not—they usually make sure that we don't—and the quail are well hidden, while the berries ripen whether or not we eat them. Since they ripen "in the wilderness," it's much more likely that the bears and birds get them.

The flocks of pigeons, too, come home to roost whether we witness or ignore them.[25] Their undulations are ambiguous partly because it is hard to tell whether they intend to fly more or cease flying. In addition, undulations, as the whole poem has taught us, are always likely to be ambiguous, to mean flux and chaos on the one hand and to mean beauty on the other, in this case the beauty of birds: cockatoos, swallows, and pigeons. They are birds of paradise—of the real paradise, that is, this earth we share with them.

The American wilderness, the great biosphere that the American settlers found waiting to explore, to fear, to conquer, and to conjure, is a fact that finally outweighs the tomb of Jesus and any of the old mythologies of death and resurrection. Voros quotes from a journal that Stevens was keeping shortly after his trip to British Columbia:

> I thought, on the train, how utterly we have forsaken the Earth, in the
> sense of excluding it from our thoughts. There are but few who
> consider its physical hugeness, its rough enormity. It is still a

disparate monstrosity, full of solitudes + barrens + wilds. It still dwarfs + terrifies + crushes. The rivers still roar, the mountains still crash, the winds still shatter. Man is an affair of cities. His gardens + orchards + fields are mere scrapings. Somehow, however, he has managed to shut out the face of the giant from his windows. But the giant is there, nevertheless.[26]

This sounds more like the romantic version of the sublime than the quiet wilderness depicted in the final stanza. However, its more general sentiment, that we separate ourselves from nature at great risk to our psychic health, is a particularly American sentiment, framed in terms of a direct response to the size and majesty of the continent. Having had it, Stevens had been waiting to put it in a poem; it bursts forth in "Sunday Morning" as a long-delayed and deeply cherished insight, and it helps identify the poem as both modern and American—modern because it rejects an important part of tradition and asks for new insights and a new beginning, sponsored by a new aesthetic, and American because it finally frames the issues of newness in relation to the landscapes and wildlife of the New World.

The poem ends with evening and darkness, as it began with morning and sun, acknowledging in this arc the "dependency of day and night." But the image of enveloping darkness, which is also a rest and homing for the pigeons, is reassuring and different from the "dark encroachment" of catastrophe. This time it is not a disruption of the sunny Sunday but a natural complement to it. It is evening. There's likely to be a vivid sunset of the kind that Hudson River and American Luminist painters loved to depict. The birds are casual, performing a familiar and daily act. The darkness is night, but it is also some of the other things darkness has come to mean. The darkness is death, and, in Stevens's understanding of the matter, that involves a frank acceptance of human mortality and its interpenetration with beauty, the central insight of the poem.

This is not to say that the ending does not also carry an elegiac edge; earth's presences become absences all too readily, always, as the woman has clearly felt; her consciousness of loss qualifies and shadows the narrator's more optimistic affirmations, enriching and deepening the poem enormously.

This splendid and memorable ending makes it hard to understand Harriet Monroe's pressuring Stevens in a way that made him both cut the poem and scramble the order, putting this closing stanza second. She certainly does not seem to have grasped the poem in its entirety. Furthermore, Stevens's cooperation with her, presumably a compromise bred of the temptation to appear in her magazine, was purely temporary. When he put *Harmonium* together, he "rehung" his exhibition in its original order, fully understanding that, while the stanzas/sections can be viewed, read, and studied separately, there is a crucial order of arrangement that takes us from the woman in the peignoir, among her coffee and oranges and cockatoo, to the vast American landscape at the end.

The reader will perhaps think of some points of comparison between this poem's close and the memorable closures of "The Bowl of Roses" and "Among School Children." All three arrive at a new definition of the human condition, one that tries to reconcile us with a world of change and flux, arguing for an interaction between humanity and nature that traditional beliefs and practices had managed to obscure. A common purpose among the modernist poets seems to have been emerging in the years in which these poems were written. Rilke, Yeats, and Stevens, on very different terms, can be said to mount a double attack: on transcendentalist philosophies on the one hand and materialist philosophies on the other. They feel their way forward to a third alternative, in which body and spirit are interdependent aspects of each other, inseparable in their activities and meanings.[27] This is nothing less than an attempt to redefine the human, for it locates the understanding of what it means to be human in this world, in this life, and it does so in order that readers may participate in it and feel their humanity more fully and more truly in the music and candor of the poems.

4

William Carlos Williams writes

JANUARY MORNING

SUITE:

I
I have discovered that most of
the beauties of travel are due to
the strange hours we keep to see them:

the domes of the Church of
the Paulist Fathers in Weehawken
against a smoky dawn—the heart stirred—
are beautiful as Saint Peters
approached after years of anticipation.

II
Though the operation was postponed
I saw the tall probationers
in their tan uniforms
                    hurrying to breakfast!

III
—and from basement entries
neatly coiffed, middle aged gentlemen
with orderly mustaches and
well-brushed coats

IV
—and the sun, dipping into the avenues
streaking the tops of
the irregular red houselets,
                         and
the gay shadows dropping and dropping.

V

—and a young horse with a green bed-quilt
on his withers shaking his head
bared teeth and nozzle high in the air!

VI

—and a semicircle of dirt-colored men
about a fire bursting from an old
ash can.

VII

            —and the worn,
blue car rails (like the sky!)
gleaming among the cobbles!

VIII

—and the rickety ferry-boat "Arden"!
What an object to be called "Arden"
among the great piers,—on the
ever new river!
            "Put me a Touchstone
at the wheel, white gulls, and we'll
follow the ghost of the *Half Moon*
to the North West Passage—and through!
(at Albany!) for all that."

IX

Exquisite brown waves—long
circlets of silver moving over you!
enough with crumbling ice crusts among you!
The sky has come down to you,
lighter than tiny bubbles, face to
face with you!
            His spirit is
a white gull with delicate pink feet
and a snowy breast for you to
hold to your lips delicately!

X

The young doctor is dancing with happiness
in the sparkling wind, alone
at the prow of the ferry! He notices
the curdy barnacles and broken ice crusts
left at the slip's base by the low tide
and thinks of summer and green
shell-crusted ledges among
                    the emerald eel-grass!

XI

Who knows the Palisades as I do
knows the river breaks east from them
above the city—but they continue south
—under the sky—to bear a crest of
little peering houses that brighten
with dawn behind the moody
water-loving giants of Manhattan.

XII

Long yellow rushes bending
above the white snow patches;
purple and gold ribbon
of the distant wood:
                    what an angle
you make with each other as
you lie there in contemplation.

XIII

Work hard all your young days
and they'll find you too, some morning
staring up under
your chiffonier at its warped
bass-wood bottom and your soul—
out!
—among the little sparrows
behind the shutter.

XIV
—and the flapping flags are at
half mast for the dead admiral.

XV
All this—
            was for you, old woman.
I wanted to write a poem
that you could understand.
For what good is it to me
if you can't understand it?

            But you got to try hard—
But—
      Well, you know how
the young girls run giggling
on Park Avenue after dark
when they ought to be home in bed?
Well,
that's the way it is with me somehow.

(Collected Poems)

LESS MEDITATIVE and more interested in immediacy and detail than the poems we have examined so far, this "suite" that Williams composed as he was finishing up a volume to be published later the same year—*Al que quiere!* (1917)—is exhilarating. It is a poem that both declares and enacts its aesthetic directly and with an elation that is infectious. That Williams chose to put it first in the *Selected Poems* he put together many years later is indicative of the importance he attached to it.[1] He saw it as a fitting entrance to his distinctive achievement as a poet.

The reader grasps immediately that while this poem is in sections, like the Yeats and Stevens poems, those sections have a different character and meaning. Unlike the ottava rima stanza Yeats was using or the measured fifteen-line verse paragraphs of "Sunday Morning," these sections are irregular. They vary in length and are jagged in appearance, with indentations, dashes, and exclamation marks. Especially in sections III through VIII, all of which begin with "and," they carry the sense of being items in a list. Although the roman numerals suggest a formal order, the varying lengths and tones of the stanzas counteract that sense of order. As it moves forward, the poem exploits a simultaneous sense of unity and dispersal, threatening its own coherence with an openness that adds drama and a certain measure of suspense: Will Williams be able to persuade us finally that this hodgepodge of impressions and sensations can function as a successful artistic whole?

The author's subtitle, calling the poem a "suite," invokes a musical analogy: a set of dances in the same key (the older meaning) or a composition with a number of movements and no particular requirements as to the number and character of those movements (the more recent meaning). However, the poem's visual emphasis, by which I mean both its look on the page and its obvious propensity for sharply rendered visual details, is pronounced enough to divert us from a musical analogue to the visual arts. "January Morning" resembles a series of quick sketches, an album of snapshots, or a cinematic montage. Whether we imagine turning the pages of a sketchbook, inspecting a display of photographs, or watching a film, the sense is of quick glimpses and shifting attention. All the analogies involve a sense of movement, one that feels rapid and energetic.

The constant distraction from one impression to the next, with meanings created by the juxtaposition of moments and images, is thus a leading characteristic of the poem. In that sense, it might be described as a demonstration of Williams's revision of imagism. Like the imagists, he found that concentrating on detail and rendering it precisely, with a minimum of interpretation or commentary, helped release in him a sense of new possibilities for poetry. But the "pure" imagist poem had a tendency to seize the moment and then come to rest, as in Pound's famous example from 1913:

IN A STATION OF THE METRO

The apparition of these faces in the crowd;
Petals on a wet, black bough.

This haikulike moment of recognition, combining the urban with the rural, the personal with the impersonal, is complete in itself. Nonetheless, what if you sense that its true energy lies not so much in the individual images as in the meaning released by their juxtaposition?[2] Then you will want a poetics that allows you to continue the juxtaposing, a procedure for launching yourself from image to image to image, implicitly celebrating the energy of movement. Imagism up on its feet and dancing, we might say, becomes futurism and vorticism.[3] The movement and energy are not for their own sake; instead, they function in response to the implicit recognition that meaning is created in the space *between* the images, through relation and what it does to alter and enliven them, just as musical harmony arises in the relations between notes.

One way to emphasize the particular value of movement and juxtaposition is to speed them up a little. The Yeats and Stevens poems move at a fairly stately pace, while Williams hurries, darting and glancing, eager for the next sensation and then the one that will follow it, coming to rest only after he has fully demonstrated the value of the journey. If his poems are machines made out of words, they tend to be built for speed. His line, his diction, his handling of form, and even his punctuation all contribute to our sense that his poems reflect the restless, rapid pace of modern American life, a world of business, hurry, and constant change.

I say "the value of the journey" because this poem is mainly a record of an excursion. We sense that almost immediately and can readily summarize the sequence: A young doctor gets up before dawn on a winter morning for an errand that takes him to the Hudson River, where he crosses on the ferry from New Jersey to Manhattan.[4] He notices many objects and people along the way, communing with himself as he goes, and at the end he offers his solitary experience to someone else as a necessary implication of his aesthetic.

Along the way some questions arise that cannot, I think, be answered definitively. Is the doctor going to visit a patient in the city? Is the death he contemplates in section XIII the outcome of his visit, as though he arrived too late to help his patient? Does he also ride the streetcar at some point? Where exactly is he when he contemplates the rushes and the "distant wood" in section XII? Are all of the first seven sections set in and around Weehawken? Are the "probationers" male medical students or female nurses in training or both? The fact that the poem doesn't settle all of these matters definitively is testimony to the interpretive space that Williams has left open for the reader. Our freedom of conjecture and our sense that the poem is a kind of kit for assembly are additional essential aspects of its emerging aesthetic.[5] It is not made by an artist who wants our overriding sense of him to be that of his mastery and control. We are to join him, rather, in his discovering and his experimenting.[6] The vulnerability that results from this shift was especially costly to Williams: Readers, critics, and other poets second-guessed him all his life, mistaking his openness of design and method for sloppy craftsmanship. Yet he never sacrificed his poetics in response to these doubts. His consistency is persuasive, even heroic.

The well-known literary forebear to this poem is Walt Whitman's "Crossing Brooklyn Ferry." Both poems use their ferry crossings to contemplate the meaning of the river, the achievement that the city represents, and of course the symbolic nature of any such crossing, a journey from one existence to another, even perhaps from life to death. The differences between the two poems, however, feel even more instructive than the similarities. Whitman, for example, is anxious to connect: with other passengers who are currently sharing or have previously had his experience, as well as with the generations to come. His cataloging of his sensations, meanwhile, is both ample and leisurely. Williams, on the other hand, tends to quickness and economy, and he emphasizes the solitary character of his pleasure— "alone / at the prow" in section X, he might as well be the only passenger on the ferry—until the very end.

Probably the most significant tension in Williams's aesthetic during this time lay in the problem of the artist's relation to his audience. Modernists made much of not caring what the public thought and whether it approved or understood. The cubists and dadaists with whom Williams had been associating had taken this stance to an extreme, delighting in the resistance and anger they stirred up.[7] *Al que quiere!* translates as "To whoever wants it," and its use of a foreign phrase in the title compounds its air of austere mystery. Anticipating the resistance of readers and reviewers, the original edition's dustjacket was deliberately impudent:

> You, gentle reader, will probably not like it, because it is brutally powerful and scornfully crude. Fortunately, neither the author nor the publisher care much whether you like it or not. The author has done his work and if you *do* read the book you will agree that he doesn't give a damn for your opinion.[8]

This bravura transfigures itself, finally, into the moving gesture of communication in the final section of "January Morning," but until and because of that moment, we realize that all of Whitman's emphasis on camaraderie and democratic sentiments has been quietly resisted or ignored.

Williams was caught in a bind; as an American poet he was clearly continuing in the democratic tradition of his great predecessor, whereas as a modernist he knew he was emphasizing newness, courting unpopularity and dislike. His split views are even reflected in his uncertainty about his volume's title. He wrote to Marianne Moore:

I like the Spanish just as I like a Chinese image cut out of stone: it is decorative and it has a certain integral charm. But such a title is not democratic—does not truly represent the contents of the book, so I have added: AL QUE QUIERE! or THE PLEASURES OF DEMOCRACY. Now I like this conglomerate title.[9]

The publisher, who was more interested in the modernist spirit than in the Whitmanian continuity, talked Williams out of this idea, but it perfectly illustrates the rift in his current aesthetic. "The Pleasures of Democracy" may be inflected with some irony, but the thrust of the volume is, again and again, emphatically populist. It celebrates America and argues for its local beauties. It insists on exposing social problems and challenging hierarchies. Above all, it holds out for a society in which poetry matters and is widely read and discussed.

The poem's opening section helps define a number of important features in Williams's new aesthetic. It is emphatic as to place—"the domes of the Church of / the Paulist Fathers in Weehawken"—but it is also casual about the uniqueness of place. The speaker is not embarrassed to discover beauty in what must have seemed an unlikely locale. He is not claiming to have discovered great overlooked architecture that we should plan to visit or that Weehawken is somehow the equivalent of Rome. Rather he is celebrating contingency and openness, suggesting that beauty will manifest itself in unlikely ways and places if we allow ourselves to abandon preconceptions. On the one hand, few people would be likely to journey to Weehawken to admire the Paulist Church; on the other hand, they might have their heart stirred by seeing that church's domes in the right circumstances. A relativity of place, coupled with a recognition of the value of spontaneity, makes space and time less opposed and less significant than they had seemed. All roads need not lead to Rome, and history can be misleading, as can strict categories that rank aesthetic pleasures, thus restricting the experience of beauty.

There's something deliberately liberating and democratic about this recognition. For a long time Americans tended to feel they must travel to Europe to see great architecture and to experience major cultural achievements. Williams's own generation of poets included Pound, Eliot, and Stein, who felt they needed to exile themselves in Europe to develop properly as artists. Williams contradicts these views by arguing that an early January morning—being up and observant as the sunrise crosses Manhattan and then spreads across New Jersey—is sufficient circumstance for transformative recognitions, a stirring of the heart:

I

I have discovered that most of
the beauties of travel are due to
the strange hours we keep to see them:

the domes of the Church of
the Paulist Fathers in Weehawken
against a smoky dawn—the heart stirred—
are beautiful as Saint Peters
approached after years of anticipation.

Change your routine a little, and you can renew your sense of the beautiful without having to travel a great distance or spend years anticipating your visit to major monuments.[10]

That the comparison is cast in religious terms, involving two churches, raises the issue of pilgrimage and, as in Stevens, the question of religion's relation to art. From this beginning a reader could expect religious art to be the subject of the poem, an expectation quickly dissipated by the list of beauties that follows. It is not a Sunday morning, but a weekday and a workday. People are not making pilgrimages (religious or aesthetic) or attending Mass but going about their business in the bustling American economy. It soon becomes clear that the domes are beautiful not because of their spiritual associations but because their shapes in the smoky dawn provide a momentary and exciting visual stimulus. Williams invokes and then displaces the religious element of American life with a casualness that Stevens might have envied. The pilgrim/tourist who hopes to see Saint Peter's is replaced by a busy young doctor who can have his heart stirred nearer to home and without having to affiliate himself with a faith.

In aesthetic terms, the New World is given an independence from the Old World, while spontaneity—an unplanned glimpse—takes precedence over a reverence for tradition and the careful design of aesthetic experiences that may involve "years of anticipation." What seems like a casual choice, then, becomes an important beginning, one in which issues of freedom, tradition, aesthetic experiences, and spiritual affiliations all become a sly pronouncement of Williams's new way of going about the discovery and celebration of beauty.

This decoupling of the religious and the spiritual is reinforced by the probationers who people the second section:

II
Though the operation was postponed
I saw the tall probationers
in their tan uniforms
    hurrying to breakfast!

"Probationers" was used originally to identify religious postulants. By the time Williams wrote the poem, it had become a term for newly admitted student nurses. Perhaps it referred to medical students as well, since the adjective "tall" suggests a group of men rather than a group of women (male nurses were fairly uncommon at the time). Since an operation has been postponed, we realize that the context is medical rather than religious. These young people are hungry, so they naturally hurry to breakfast as the first manifestations of quickness and energy that rise up to counter the cold and darkness of winter. Having seen the domes and had his heart stirred, the poem's protagonist, eventually identified as a young doctor, is now open to a set of delighted discoveries, all of them revealing a kind of secular but mystical life-force at large in the world.

Thus "neatly coiffed" middle-aged men emerge from "basement entries" in section III. Their grooming bespeaks their sense of self-respect and order, and their emergence into the newly lit world makes them resemble moles or bears coming out of hibernation. They brush their coats every morning, presumably, but on this particular morning that activity seems to bespeak their affiliation with the world's regeneration. January may be the dead of winter, but it is also the year's beginning. A sunny day in January naturally makes us think ahead to spring.

As light bathes the world, its illumination brings renewal, as in section IV:

—and the sun, dipping into the avenues
streaking the tops of
the irregular red houselets,
        and
the gay shadows dropping and dropping.

Again, the diction and detail exhibit an aesthetic that is not based on orthodox notions of symmetry and order. It is part of the visual and spiritual delight that the sun is "dipping" and "streaking" and that the working-class brick houses, while they tend to have a uniform shade of red, are otherwise "irregular" and less than impressive ("houselets" would seem to be a coinage suggesting their cramped and miniature character). Even the "shadows," which might traditionally be associated with gloom, are "gay," a willing group of unruly participants in the morning's onset.

The exuberant horse in section V is readily associated with the probationers, the emerging gentlemen, the streaking sun, and the gay shadows. It may be an accident that his bed-quilt, an acknowledgment of the cold, is also green, but the color contributes to the excited sense that, despite the dark and cold, the world's hidden energy is once more on the loose. The close-up—"bared teeth and nozzle high in the air"—transforms an animal that would normally have been old or tired into another youthful spirit.

In the same paradoxical fashion, the semicircle of "dirt-colored men" huddled around an "old / ash can" in section VI seems at first glance to testify to the cold and misery of January. They are pathetic figures. However, they have made a fire, and its movement, a "bursting," links it to all the other movements: hurrying probationers, emerging gentlemen, streaking sun, dropping shadows, and, most of all, the shaking and whinnying horse.[11] It is as though light itself is a divine presence in the world, and, while it manifests itself most of all in the dawn, it also comes down to earth and bursts out in unlikely places. That it can be found bursting from "an old / ash can" makes it positively phoenixlike.

The marriage of earth and sky, which could remind Christian readers of the Incarnation and pagan readers of similar mythic moments, is next made evident in the streetcar tracks of section VII: "—and the worn, / blue car rails (like the sky!) / gleaming among the cobbles!" The metal of the tracks, polished by the passage of countless streetcars, reflects the light and the intense color of the sky. The reflection is a kind of mystical moment of recognition. That the blue car rails gleam delights him. That their color links them to the heavens is his simultaneous flash of recognition. We have gone from humans and houses to a horse and an ash can. Now, the lowest and humblest things testify to the miracle of light as well; among the cobbles the worn rails shine.

A more openly religious poet such as Gerard Manley Hopkins would make the spiritual ramifications of this more explicit. He can notice the shine on earth left by a plough and watch for fire exposing itself from inside "blue-bleak embers" in "The Windhover," details that he links to Christ's

Incarnation and sacrifice. His claim in another poem that "The world is charged with the grandeur of God" and that "It will flame out" is cast in openly theological terms, since he is testifying as a Jesuit, secure in his faith. Williams is proffering similar claims, but on manifestly nontheological terms. Any reader who might wish to can connect a specific theology to this catalogue of flarings and shinings, but the poem, while it does nothing to prevent that, does not require theology to pursue its vision of light as a manifestation of an energy that we respond to spiritually. He has brought sentiments that might find theological expression entirely over into the aesthetic realm, where they are more readily associated with visual art and its delights than with any sort of doctrine.

Now, as we board the ferry, the poem's pace slows and its tones shift, growing more loquacious and more reflective. The visual manifestations of light are temporarily interrupted as the protagonist is bemused and distracted by an unusual use of language: The boat's name turns out to be "Arden." We move onto the water, and we also encounter Shakespeare. Is this a distraction from the poem's ecstatic progress, or is it a confirmation of what Williams is celebrating?

While calling a ferry "Arden" involves a certain grotesqueness, it also represents an implicit acknowledgment of the power of literature. The source of the ferry's name, the pastoral forest in Shakespeare's *As You Like It*, strikes Williams as both absurd and touching:

> VIII
> —and the rickety ferry-boat "Arden"!
> What an object to be called "Arden"
> among the great piers,—on the
> ever new river!

A forest should not be confused with an urban ferry, perhaps, but the fact of the "ever new river" helps reconcile the name and the object through its implicit recognition that nature's powers of renewal are also reflected in our best literature. Three hundred years after its composition, Shakespeare's play continues to make its presence and meaning felt here in the New World, where a new poet is redefining pastoral, the old habit of praising the simple and the rural.[12] This insight allows the protagonist to link exploration and imagination in an amused fashion:

> "Put me a Touchstone
> at the wheel, white gulls, and we'll
> follow the ghost of the *Half Moon*
> to the North West Passage—and through!
> (at Albany!) for all that!"

Touchstone, the realist clown who debunks the idealism of pastoral, is now imagined as the pilot who will commandeer the boat for the purpose of continuing Henry Hudson's attempt to find a nonexistent passage to the Pacific.

Journeying up the river evokes a good deal of American history and culture. The *Half Moon*'s is not the only ghost here. Some readers will think of Mark Twain; others may remember the Hudson River School of painters. The amount of river travel, both exploratory and commercial, that makes up the earlier years of American history, comes briefly to bear on the poem's casual river crossing.

As for Hudson's unsuccessful quest, which gave the river its name, if it is ever to happen, it will have to happen in the imagination, especially from Albany (where an imaginative breakthrough is at least as surprising as the discovery of beauty in Weehawken) on. Underneath the joking, Williams is serious about his notion that art, experimental and daring, can pick up the responsibility for America's destiny in ways that other enterprises have had to abandon. Allied with Shakespeare's jester, a cynic who nevertheless acts from loyalty and love, he feels that his explorations of the continent can yield a success scarcely envisioned until now. He teases himself and guards his heady excitement with ironic apostrophe and exclamation, but his sense of kinship with both Shakespeare and Hudson is one more way of signaling the excitement he feels about his art and its emerging possibilities.[13]

The ferry journey occupies sections VIII through XII. Exhilaration continues to buoy up the protagonist. In section IX, continuing his use of apostrophe, he addresses the river:

> Exquisite brown waves—long
> circlets of silver moving over you!
> enough with crumbling ice crusts among you!
> The sky has come down to you,
> lighter than tiny bubbles, face to
> face with you!
>   His spirit is

a white gull with delicate pink feet
and a snowy breast for you to
hold to your lips delicately!

Here we have another marriage of heaven and earth. The first three lines are ambiguous: We are not sure whether the circlets of silver are made by light, manifesting life and renewal, or by ice crusts, bespeaking winter. But the next set of details resolves the matter, partly through personification and anthropomorphic treatment: The sky is a white gull (already evoked as a force of nature in the apostrophe of section VIII), and its landing on the river is a kind of ritual kiss.

This consummation leads the protagonist into a dance of happiness, disregarding both decorum and weather.[14] As he presents this moment to us in section X, Williams metaphorically divides himself: He is the third-person narrator, and he is, we assume, also the dancer. This is precisely the kind of move that signals his emergent modernism. He is challenging the convention that requires the poem's speaker to be a stable and predictable entity, securely related to the authorial self. Similar moves are evident in the Rilke, Yeats, and Stevens examples:

The young doctor is dancing with happiness
in the sparkling wind, alone
at the prow of the ferry! He notices
the curdy barnacles and broken ice crusts
left at the slip's base by the low tide
and thinks of summer and green
shell-crusted ledges among
                    the emerald eel-grass!

That sparkling wind is full of dazzling inspiration. No wonder the doctor/ poet is happy. And no wonder he continues to find that the details of reality, closely observed, have a way of revealing their hidden beauty. His imaginative summoning of the opposite season has a specificity of detail—shell-crusted ledges and emerald eel-grass—that matches the material present, diminishing the traditional opposition of reality and imagination.

Does a ferry have a prow? It has two, in fact, which also serve as sterns. The doctor seems to be on the New Jersey end of the boat, looking back toward the ferry slip it has just left, noticing the barnacles and crusted ice that the tide has exposed. Whether at prow or stern, he is a kind of pagan celebrant, able to summon the summer in his imagination even as he concentrates on the actualities of winter. The dancing, an event both primitive and modern, as it also was in Stevens, recalls another fine Williams poem of this period, inspired by the 1916 visit of the Ballet Russe to New York:

DANSE RUSSE

If I when my wife is sleeping
and the baby and Kathleen
are sleeping
and the sun is a flame-white disc
in silken mists
above shining trees,—
if I in my north room
dance naked, grotesquely
before my mirror
waving my shirt round my head
and singing softly to myself:
"I am lonely, lonely.
I was born to be lonely,
I am best so!"
If I admire my arms, my face,
my shoulders, flanks, buttocks
against the yellow drawn shades,—

Who shall say I am not
the happy genius of my household?

(*Collected Poems*)

Here again the difference between Williams and Stevens is instructive. The latter envisions a future moment when naked men will dance together in worship of the sun. It will resemble a pagan past, but it will be modern in its hypothetical understanding that the worship involves the sun "not as a god but as a god might be." Williams, lacking companions, simply undertakes the dance himself, underlining its inherent comedy by emphasizing the privacy it requires. It may acknowledge the rising sun as "a flame-white disc / in silken mists / among shining trees," but it has to be performed behind "yellow drawn shades." He appropriates a ritual that other modern artists have created, one that is freed from theological obligations and that, by allowing him to be pagan and primitive while he is also suburban and familial, liberates him into a secure identity as "the happy genius" of his own household. The dance on the ferry boat's prow/stern bespeaks the same kind of breakthrough, a solving of the need to be both modern and pagan while also going about one's business in New Jersey and New York. The successful invocation of summer in the midst of winter links his imagination with the phoenixlike fire in the ash can and makes him the happy genius of the changing seasons, at home in any of them.

The dance on the prow also evokes a similar moment in a long poem Williams had begun several years earlier, called "The Wanderer," and included, in its latest version, in the 1917 collection. The first section of that poem, "Advent," records the poet's early sense of his vocation and his encounters with a goddess figure who represents his exuberant and rather untidy muse. She takes the form of a crow the first time he sees her, and then, on a ferry ride similar to the one in "January Morning," she is identified with a seagull:

> But one day, crossing the ferry
> With the great towers of Manhattan before me,
> Out at the prow with the sea wind blowing,
> I had been wearying many questions
> Which she had put on to try me:
> How shall I be a mirror to this modernity?
> When lo! in a rush, dragging
> A blunt boat on the yielding river—
> Suddenly I saw her! And she waved me
> From the white wet in midst of her playing!
> She cried me, "Haia! Here I am, son!
> See how strong my little finger is!
> Can I not swim well?
> I can fly too!" And with that a great sea-gull
> Went to the left, vanishing with a wild cry—
> But in my mind all the persons of godhead
> Followed after.

> (*Collected Poems*)

At first she is a tugboat, hauling a barge and boasting of her strength. When she announces that she can fly, however, she reverts to the form of a bird, this time a white one. This mystical moment is presumably being invoked and re-created in sections IX and X of "January Morning" several years later.[15] Crossing the river to Manhattan naturally reminds Williams of his encounter with the muse three years earlier. The two sections thus mark a moment of confirmation in the poet's struggle with his developing aesthetic. Out on the river, between the city and his suburban home, he affirms his artistic freedom and vision once again, aligning himself on the ever-new river with Hudson, Whitman, Shakespeare, and the modernist artists whose work he keeps encountering in his Manhattan visits. No wonder he feels exhilarated!

The next two sections develop a quieter and more reflective mood, a coming down from the excitement of the dance in sparkling wind. The poem shifts back from third person to first person, adding a claim of special knowledge as the protagonist's gaze now travels further, to take in the geological features of the vista that can be observed from the ferry, a vista that includes the man-made towers of Manhattan and, contrasting with them, the rocky cliffs on the river's western side. He claims an intimate knowledge of the region:

> XI
> Who knows the Palisades as I do
> knows the river breaks east from them
> above the city—but they continue south
> —under the sky—to bear a crest of
> little peering houses that brighten
> with dawn behind the moody
> water-loving giants of Manhattan.

It is an amused contrasting of city and suburb, moody giants close to the water and little peering houses up on the cliffs, but it is mainly notable for its scope. As the most panoramic moment in the poem, it is another affirmation of the artist's confidence in his art. He can journey between two venues with confidence. In Manhattan he will find modernists such as Duchamp, Man Ray, Picabia, and Stieglitz, urging him by their theory and practice to create a new art. In New Jersey he will find his family, his medical practice, and his working-class patients. These two worlds will be gradually reconciled in his poetry. Crossing and recrossing, he will remind himself of the strength he takes from each.

To absorb this large vista and its full meaning requires both positioning and experience, a capaciousness of vision that contrasts nicely with the close detail in the section that follows:

XII

Long yellow rushes bending
above the white snow patches;
purple and gold ribbon
of the distant wood:
           what an angle
you make with each other as
you lie there in contemplation.

The composition here is extremely painterly, based on contrasting colors, the careful observation of foreground and background, and the attractiveness of the contrasting lines. The angle created by the bending rushes and the bicolored ribbon of the woods would presumably form an effective composition for a canvas, harmonizing oppositions through tension and balance. Here it is simply re-created in words, confirming the artistic powers of observation that the protagonist employs on his journey and his consistent openness and alertness to his environment. The "contemplation" is surely his, but it is attributed to the rushes to suggest how complete his identification with the world around him has become.

The moment in which the reeds and the protagonist are at one, in "contemplation," now gives birth to its opposite reaction, the human sense of mortality that sooner or later separates us from the renewable and impersonal energies of nature. The reeds, the woods, the river, and the season all belong to a giant harmony of change, renewal, and constancy. For the individual self, it is a different matter. We work, we die, perhaps grotesquely, and then *maybe* we join the natural order, in a sort of liberation:

Work hard all your young days
and they'll find you too, some morning
staring up under
your chiffonier at its warped
bass-wood bottom and your soul—
out!

> —among the little sparrows
> behind the shutter.

The doctor may have been called to pronounce someone dead, or he may have arrived to find his patient in this state. In quick succession we have the passing of a life, the moment of death from the point of view of the corpse, eyes fixed open upon a surface of furniture that is normally hidden from view. Then an imagined liberation, the soul joining the sparrows outside the shuttered room and, without going to heaven or joining an orthodox after-life, finding a freedom among the most common of birds. The young doctor, who is working hard all his young days, and the reader are left with a number of questions, none of them fully answerable. Is the soul's escape pleasurable? Will it lead to some kind of personal immortality, or is it just a dissipation into the environment?

The poem leaves these issues to us, even as it marks, in section XIV, one more observation from the ferry trip: "—and the flapping flags are at / half mast for the dead admiral." Admiral Dewey, who died on January 16, 1917, was the hero of Manila, a much-admired man who had briefly considered running for the presidency around 1900. His career spanned much of the nineteenth century, including the Civil War, where he fought in the battle of New Orleans. His presence in the poem, which is also of course an absence, brings history back to bear on the poem, connecting him with Hudson, another "admiral," and raising the issue of America's destiny. America was getting ready to go to war again in 1917, as it had with Spain in 1898. The country was divided on this matter, although it would soon assent in a wave of patriotism, just as it had to the Spanish-American War.

For Williams, however, issues of national destiny and foreign policy are displaced by the commonplace matters he faced in his own life as a doctor. The flapping flags at half mast are a momentary distraction. The deaths of public figures, we note, are commemorated solemnly. For most of us, however, it's the more common fate involving the chiffonier and the sparrows. And death is still something final, however it is marked or commemorated. Its grotesqueness may be inescapable, but its involvement with the ongoing life that the flapping sparrows and waving flags represent seems inescapable, too. The "divine" energy that drives the poem and inspires its maker is still present in the wind that flutters the flags and the noise the sparrows make beyond the shutters, unseen but boisterous. We die, all of us, as individuals. Yet something persists, something lives on, connecting us to the light and movement that exist around us in the seasons and cities we inhabit.

The last section startles and pleases us with its direct address: "All this—/ was for you, old woman." It is not the first direct address in the poem, but the others were apostrophes of one sort or another—to the waves, to the rushes, to anyone who might "work hard all your young days" and then die. They did not feel so conversational, so intimate, such an unmasking or such a deliberate giving of a gift. The gesture is partly retrospective, a look back at the suite of images and dances, "All this," and it is partly confessional: The solitary pleasures of the observant doctor, re-created in words, had an ulterior purpose of pleasing someone else. We do not know exactly who the old woman is, so we are free to conjecture: a patient (the one who died?), a muse, or someone who does not really care for poetry or for the new kind of poetry Williams has been shaping? We know now it was his mother he especially had in mind.[16] But we also feel, whenever we read the poem, that the poet is nakedly confessing his need for an audience:

> I wanted to write a poem
> that you would understand.
> For what good is it to me
> if you can't understand it?

We realize suddenly that the poem's plain language, its loving attention to local details, and its straightforward presentation of season, persona, mood, and pleasure all have one emphatic motive. Communicability has been the driving force behind its organization, its form, and its energy. It has quietly dismissed that part of modernism that cultivated obscurity and shock and that thrived on difficulty and confrontation.

Now that Williams has become a kind of classic, that clarity of purpose and successful directness of voice have come to seem unequivocal and uncontroversial. However, we need to remember what most people thought poetry was and should be in 1917. They expected rhyme and meter and "poetic" diction, a sort of warmed-over romanticism. They expected moralizing and a safe reading experience, the reader spoon-fed comforting truths and insights, an atmosphere in which the poem's meanings and sentiments were fully disclosed. No doubt Williams's mother was prouder of her son's efforts to be a doctor than of his poems, and no doubt she, like most readers, found his work shocking in its form and content (there's a good deal of frankness about sexual desire in *Al que quiere!* that doesn't happen to manifest itself in this particular piece). So her "understanding" is crucial to the poet and also representative of his problems with his audience; he wants to communicate with them, but not safely and not on traditional terms. He would like them to join him in the risks he is taking:

> But you got to try hard—
>
> But—
>
> Well, you know how
> the young girls run giggling
> on Park Avenue after dark
> when they ought to be home in bed?
> Well,
> that's the way it is with me somehow.

The girls are irresponsible, but their youthful energy is understandable, pardonable, even necessary to their maturing. They can't help exceeding the boundaries the older generation has set for them, and an "old woman," sharing their gender and having long years of experience in seeing people grow up, can surely overlook their naughtiness, shake her head at it perhaps, and indulge it at the same time. If she can do that for those girls, then she can do it for the poet, whose "apology" is really an affirmation of his connection to the rest of humanity and his youthful high spirits. He leaves it to her to nod her head and allow him his excesses.

As for Park Avenue, that is one more illustration of the poem's deliberate confusing of locations. Most readers will think of Manhattan's Park Avenue, a dignified location resistant to youthful high spirits. The poem's choice of a well-known street in its apparent destination seems perfectly appropriate. But Williams was also thinking of Rutherford's Park Avenue and knew, of course, that his mother would, too. So the place of departure and the place of arrival are deliberately confused once again, like the prow and the stern of the ferry boat. Whitman would have understood the geographical wordplay, and so would many of Williams's New York modernist friends, people like Maxwell Bodenheim and Alfred Kreymborg. Both Park Avenues work equally well for the poem's purposes, and both are necessary to its full success. Taken together, they sum up much of its playfulness, both of construction and of reference.

The tonal curve of the final section, I believe, is from serious to playful as well. The opening stanza is quite moving, a gesture of vulnerability and deep affection. Once it has been made, the poet can relax from it, choosing an analogy that seems to dismiss the seriousness of his artistic enterprise by comparing it to harmless hijinks. Nevertheless, the opening still resonates as he admits to a certain loss of control in his two uses of "Well" and his final "somehow." The open-endedness of "somehow" leaves it to the reader to decide how seriously to take the poem and how much unity to attribute to it. Its variety has concealed a remarkable consistency, but Williams is not insisting on that in his closure; he signs off with a "somehow" and leaves the completion of the design to the old woman—and to us. If we "try hard" we can "understand" what he has done, and that will have made it all worthwhile.

Looking back at what the poem has included and the ground it has covered, we can see how much Williams has accomplished in an apparently casual and informal fashion. His poem is spiritual and even mystical in character, but its mode is emphatically secular. It celebrates life, especially in the various manifestations of light and energy it delightedly discovers, but it also faces the fact and finality of death. The poet has brought European history and culture, Saint Peter's, Shakespeare, and Henry Hudson into a successful relation with his attempts to shape an aesthetic that is both modern and American. We could say that he displaces them, but we can also recognize that they inhabit the poem without dominating it. These moments and personages of history and "high" culture have been made to coexist with ordinary things such as reeds, ice crusts, barnacles, a seagull, sparrows, a horse with a green quilt on his withers, streetcar rails, and a fire in a trash can. Moreover, the poem has managed to suggest through its cataloging of impressions that all of these things are equally interesting and have an equivalent value and meaning. As in the Rilke poem, hierarchic notions of being have been turned sideways and made to occupy a poem in which human things and nonhuman things have an equivalency of being and therefore of value. I find this phenomenological shift to be far more radical than any of the impudent gestures of the Dadaists. It challenges tradition more thoroughly and offers a more sweeping redefinition of meaning. It is, in short, modernism at its best.

Williams has taken a ferry ride that might once have symbolized a crossing between two worlds, life and death. He has demythologized it, transforming it into an emblem for the inclusiveness of his art. Manhattan is where he goes to get "permission" to abandon traditional notions of how to write poetry and what to value in art. He is liberated there from the past and from conventions, social and artistic. Rutherford is where he must return to his family, his medical practice, and the blue-collar realities of his patients. There he can root the new poetry in the gritty soil of twentieth-century American life. If swallowing the filthy water of the Passaic is what it takes, he will do that. If equating himself with an adolescent girl giggling on Park Avenue is what it takes, he will do that, too. And he will wait for his mother and others to see the wonderful newness and rightness of what he is doing.

Most moving of all, perhaps, is the candid way in which he has addressed the conflicting urges of his art: the desire for independence on the one hand and the need for connection on the other. His poem acts out a drama whereby he first has an essentially solitary and ecstatic experience on a winter morning, at sunrise, a visionary sense of connection to something more or less divine. He then finds a way to transform the experience into language, into a musical "suite," hoping at last to communicate it to a representative listener/reader. A high-spirited piece of newfangled poetry becomes a solemn gift, a gesture of human connection that holds out the hope that we can "understand."

To whoever wants it. It took a long time for Williams's message to reach some of his readers, and it took a long time to understand how it fit into the larger story of modernism. But he was patient. He could put it there in the poems and wait for us to find it. And eventually we would.

5

Marianne Moore writes

AN OCTOPUS

of ice. Deceptively reserved and flat,
it lies "in grandeur and in mass"
beneath a sea of shifting snow-dunes;
dots of cyclamen-red and maroon on its clearly defined pseudo-podia
5   made of glass that will bend—a much needed invention—
comprising twenty-eight ice fields from fifty to five hundred feet thick,
of unimagined delicacy.
"Picking periwinkles from the cracks"
or killing prey with the concentric crushing rigor of the python,
10   it hovers forward "spider fashion
on its arms" misleadingly like lace;
its "ghostly pallor changing
to the green metallic tinge of an anemone-starred pool."
The fir-trees, in "the magnitude of their root systems,"
15   rise aloof from these maneuvers "creepy to behold,"
austere specimens of our American royal families,
"each like the shadow of the one beside it.
The rock seems frail compared with their dark energy of life,"
its vermilion and onyx and manganese-blue interior expansiveness
20   left at the mercy of the weather;
"stained transversely by iron where the water drips down,"
recognized by its plants and its animals.
Completing a circle,
you have been deceived into thinking that you have progressed,
25   under the polite needles of the larches
"hung to filter, not to intercept the sunlight"—
met by tightly wattled spruce-twigs
"conformed to an edge like clipped cypress
as if no branch could penetrate the cold beyond its company";
30   and dumps of gold and silver ore enclosing The Goat's Mirror—

that lady-fingerlike depression in the shape of the left human foot,
which prejudices you in favor of itself
before you have had time to see the others;
its indigo, pea-green, blue-green, and turquoise,
35   from a hundred to two hundred feet deep,
"merging in irregular patches in the middle lake
where, like gusts of a storm
obliterating the shadows of the fir-trees, the wind makes lanes of ripples."
What spot could have merits of equal importance
40   for bears, elk, deer, wolves, goats, and ducks?
Pre-empted by their ancestors,
this is the property of the exacting porcupine,
and of the rat "slipping along to its burrow in the swamp
or pausing on high ground to smell the heather";
45   of "thoughtful beavers
making drains which seem the work of careful men with shovels,"
and of the bears inspecting unexpectedly
ant-hills and berry-bushes.
Composed of calcium gems and alabaster pillars,
50   topaz, tourmaline crystals and amethyst quartz,
their den is somewhere else, concealed in the confusion
of "blue forests thrown together with marble and jasper and agate
as if whole quarries had been dynamited."
And farther up, in stag-at-bay position
55   as a scintillating fragment of these terrible stalagmites,
stands the goat,
its eye fixed on the waterfall which never seems to fall—
an endless skein swayed by the wind,
immune to force of gravity in the perspective of the peaks.
60   A special antelope
acclimated to "grottoes from which issue penetrating draughts
which make you wonder why you came,"
it stands its ground
on cliffs the color of the clouds, of petrified white vapor—
65   black feet, eyes, nose, and horns, engraved on dazzling ice-fields,
the ermine body on the crystal peak;
the sun kindling its shoulders to maximum heat like acetylene, dyeing them white—
upon this antique pedestal,

92

"a mountain with those graceful lines which prove it a volcano,"
70 its top a complete cone like Fujiyama's
till an explosion blew it off.
Distinguished by a beauty
of which "the visitor dare never fully speak at home
for fear of being stoned as an imposter,"
75 Big Snow Mountain is the home of a diversity of creatures:
those who "have lived in hotels
but who now live in camps—who prefer to";
the mountain guide evolving from the trapper,
"in two pairs of trousers, the outer one older,
80 wearing slowly away from the feet to the knees";
"the nine-striped chipmunk
running with unmammal-like agility along a log";
the water ouzel
with "its passion for rapids and high-pressured falls,"
85 building under the arch of some tiny Niagara;
the white-tailed ptarmigan "in winter solid white,
feeding on heather-bells and alpine buckwheat";
and the eleven eagles of the west,
"fond of the spring fragrance and the winter colors,"
90 used to the unegoistic action of the glaciers
and "several hours of frost every midsummer night."
"They make a nice appearance, don't they,"
happy seeing nothing?
Perched on treacherous lava and pumice—
95 those unadjusted chimney-pots and cleavers
which stipulate "names and addresses of persons to notify
in case of disaster"—
they hear the roar of ice and supervise the water
winding slowly through the cliffs,
100 the road "climbing like the thread
which forms the groove around a snail-shell,
doubling back and forth until where snow begins, it ends."
No "deliberate wide-eyed wistfulness" is here
among the boulders sunk in ripples and white water
105 where "when you hear the best wild music of the forest
it is sure to be a marmot,"

the victim on some slight observatory,
of "a struggle between curiosity and caution,"
inquiring what has scared it:
110   a stone from the moraine descending in leaps,
another marmot, or the spotted ponies with glass eyes,
brought up on frosty grass and flowers
and rapid draughts of ice-water.
Instructed, none knows how, to climb the mountain,
115   by businessmen who as totemic scenery of Canada,
require for recreation
three hundred and sixty-five holidays in the year,
these conspicuously spotted little horses are peculiar;
hard to discern among the birch-trees, ferns, and lily-pads,
120   avalanche lilies, Indian paint-brushes,
bear's ears and kittentails,
and miniature cavalcades of chlorophylless fungi
magnified in profile on the moss-beds like moonstones in the water;
the cavalcade of calico competing
125   with the original American menagerie of styles
among the white flowers of the rhododendron surmounting rigid leaves
upon which moisture works its alchemy,
transmuting verdure into onyx.
Larkspur, blue pincushions, blue peas, and lupin;
130   white flowers with white, and red with red;
the blue ones "growing closer together
so that patches of them look like blue water in the distance";
this arrangement of colors
as in Persian designs of hard stones with enamel,
135   forms a pleasing equation—
a diamond outside, and inside, a white dot;
on the outside, a ruby; inside, a white dot;
black spots balanced with black
in the woodlands where fires have run over the ground—
140   separated by aspens, cat's paws, and woolly sunflowers,
fireweed, asters, and Goliath thistles
"flowering at all altitudes as multiplicitous as barley,"
like pink sapphires in the pavement of the glistening plateau.
Inimical to "bristling, puny, swearing men

145 equipped with saws and axes,"
this treacherous glass mountain
admires gentians, lady-slippers, harebells, mountain dryads,
and "Calypso, the goat flower—
that greenish orchid fond of snow"—
150 anomalously nourished on shelving glacial ledges
where climbers have not gone or have gone timidly,
"the one resting his nerves while the other advanced,"
on this volcano with the blue jay, her principal companion.
"Hopping stiffly on sharp feet" like miniature ice-hacks—
155 "secretive, but with a look of wisdom and distinction, but a villain,
fond of human society or the crumbs that go with it,"
he knows no Greek,
"that pride-producing language,"
160 in which "rashness is rendered innocuous, and error exposed
by the collision of knowledge with knowledge."

"Like happy souls in Hell," enjoying mental difficulties,
the grasshoppers of Greece
amused themselves with delicate behavior
165 because it was "so noble and so fair";
not practiced in adapting their intelligence
to eagle-traps and snow-shoes,
to alpenstocks and other toys contrived by those
"alive to the advantage of invigorating pleasures."
170 Bows, arrows, oars, and paddles, for which trees provide the wood,
in new countries more eloquent than elsewhere—
augmenting the assertion that, essentially humane,
"the forest affords wood for dwellings and by its beauty stimulates
the moral vigor of its citizens."
175 The Greeks liked smoothness, distrusting what was back
of what could not be clearly seen,
resolving with benevolent conclusiveness,
"complexities which still will be complexities
as long as the world lasts";
180 ascribing what we clumsily call happiness,
to "an accident or a quality,
a spiritual substance or the soul itself,

an act, a disposition, or a habit,
or a habit infused, to which the soul has been persuaded,
185 or something distinct from a habit, a power"—
such power as Adam had and we are still devoid of.
"Emotionally sensitive, their hearts were hard";
their wisdom was remote
from that of these odd oracles of cool official sarcasm,
190 upon this game preserve
where "guns, nets, seines, traps and explosives,
hired vehicles, gambling and intoxicants are prohibited;
disobedient persons being summarily removed
and not allowed to return without permission in writing."
195 It is self-evident
that it is frightful to have everything afraid of one;
that one must do as one is told
and eat rice, prunes, dates, raisins, hardtack, and tomatoes
if one would "conquer the main peak of Mount Tacoma,"
200 this fossil flower concise without a shiver,
intact when it is cut,
damned for its sacrosanct remoteness—
like Henry James "damned by the public for decorum";
not decorum, but restraint;
205 it is the love of doing hard things
that rebuffed and wore them out—a public out of sympathy with neatness.
Neatness of finish! Neatness of finish!
Relentless accuracy is the nature of this octopus
with its capacity for fact.
210 "Creeping slowly as with meditated stealth,
its arms seeming to approach from all directions,"
it receives one under winds that "tear the snow to bits
and hurl it like a sandblast
shearing off twigs and loose bark from the trees."
215 Is "tree" the word for these things
"flat on the ground like vines"?
some "bent in a half circle with branches on one side
suggesting dust-brushes, not trees;
some finding strength in union, forming little stunted groves,
220 their flattened mats of branches shrunk in trying to escape"

from the hard mountain "planed by ice and polished by the wind"—
the white volcano with no weather side;
the lightning flashing at its base,
rain falling in the valleys, and snow falling on the peak—
225 the glassy octopus symmetrically pointed,
its claw cut by the avalanche
"with a sound like the crack of a rifle,
in a curtain of powdered snow launched like a waterfall."

(*Selected Poems*)

THIS LONG AND DIFFICULT poem, which closes with an avalanche, is itself something of an avalanche—of information, quotation, scientific detail, and playful language.[1] It's an eccentric map, a wild collage, a grand fugue, and a meditation on the North American wilderness. It is also a highly self-conscious moment in modernist practice and an elusive reconfiguring of aesthetic principles and cultural truths. Readers are entitled to wonder why it should be called poetry at all since its use of the line does not seem to establish or sustain strong or regular rhythms, its voice is "prosy," and the many quoted passages are obviously from prose sources, untransformed. Moore is clearly willing to risk a good deal of what was traditionally associated with poetry in order to arrive at something new. Her daring and her degree of experimentation are more evident than in any of the poets discussed in the previous chapters.

As the subject gradually emerges readers may long for a narrative or an unfolding logical sequence, some traditional form of ordering to help orient us.[2] But we do not have those things, nor do we even have a single authoritative voice, as in most poems. A patchwork babble of quotations inhabits the poem, supervised, to be sure, by a presiding artistic sensibility but bewildering nevertheless in its multiplicity. Like the octopus of its title, the poem seems to be able to reach out in several directions at once. And like the rugged and challenging peak it describes, a mountain whose size and height discourage most climbers, it has probably defeated many readers over the years. One of a group that Moore wrote in the early 1920s when she was at her most experimental, it requires considerable patience and attention. However, it also rewards close reading and rereading. It is a masterpiece of modernism, not to mention a unique example of what we might call the American sublime.

To survive in this poem we need to suspend many of our normal expectations and assumptions about poetry. There is, for one thing, the strongly prosaic quality of its language and movement. I used to feel that Moore had no ear for the music of language, a response that others have also had to Williams. The truth of the matter, however, is that while she is capable of highly musical moments—the eagles, for instance, "hear the roar of ice and supervise the water / winding slowly through the cliffs"—she is much more interested in starting again, grounding her poem in an artistic humility, building music slowly out of her rediscovery of it in prose, finding poetry among the many prosaic explanations and facts of the world around her.

Just as Williams came to feel that he could not ride on the shoulders of Keats, whose poetry he had adored and emulated, but must instead begin to find his own music and lyricism in the world around him, the world of New Jersey, so Moore begins with pamphlets, articles, and scientific information. They constitute *her* New Jersey, we might say, resisting transformation. We watch her struggling to transmute these materials into something approaching genuine poetry, and we begin to realize that she is perfectly willing to let the reader be witness to her struggle and all of its attendant difficulties. A poem that might have been refined into lyrical smoothness and consistency is deliberately left rough and multiplicitous, involving us in its own gestation and growth, its necessary imperfections.

Here in "An Octopus" the poetic line becomes a tentative and extremely elastic unit. Since there is only one stanza break in the whole text, we can say that the stanza is jettisoned as a significant means of ordering the text. So we are left, really, with an "organization" based on a very difficult handling of syntax: large, sometimes gigantic sentences, twenty-nine of them.[3] Moreover, many of these "units" require patient negotiation. The first is a sentence fragment, broken between the title and first line. It is followed by a sentence that runs for seven lines, then another of six, then four, then five, then sixteen. The longest sentence in the poem runs twenty lines. These trailing sentences tend to be packed with diverse information. We need them in order to follow the discourse and voice of the text, but they often shift subject and tone without warning. Getting from sentence to sentence is actually rather like a mountain climb, finding your handholds and footholds, hoisting yourself carefully and patiently upward.

Most notably, perhaps, "An Octopus" is a poem that is especially difficult to take in because it tends to undermine its own forms of organization—an elaborated metaphor, a mountain climb, a series of catalogues, and a meditation on the beauty of nature—even as it makes use of them. I would, of course, like to make the process of reading the poem simpler and easier for the reader, but in doing so I am in danger of undermining the very subversiveness of Moore's unique modernism. I must proceed with caution.

Moore herself was a bit daunted, later in life, by the wildness and inclusiveness of some of her own experiments, particularly by the elastic definition of relevance she had allowed herself. Her later "revision" of her own earlier poems, which was not so much revision as simple subtraction, savage pruning, did not, in my view, serve them well. The poems she wrote in her midthirties are both her best and her most purely modern, and they deserve our careful attention in their fullest form.[4]

By calling the poem an example of the American Sublime, I have also taken a step toward identifying its subject, Mount Rainier in Washington. Nevertheless, that identification is by no means a simple matter for the reader of the poem. Rainier is never named, though "Big Snow Mountain," a Native American name, comes up at line 75, and "the main peak of Mount Tacoma," also the Native American name, is mentioned in line 199.

And then, of course, there is the matter of the title. Even after we have seen the completion of that title in the first two words of line 1, "of ice," we remain uncertain about the actual subject for the first fifteen to twenty lines of the poem. The focus seems to shift abruptly and without warning between the undersea creature, an octopus, and the metaphoric comparison of that creature to a large glacial mountain that, in an aerial view, has an octopus-like shape from the radial extension of its many glaciers. Lines 2 and 3, for example, extend the mountain subject initiated by "of ice,"—"it lies 'in grandeur and in mass' / beneath a sea of shifting snow-dunes"—but line 4 describes an actual octopus—"dots of cyclamen-red and maroon on its clearly defined pseudo-podia"—and line 5 seems to be examining an artifact: "made of glass that will bend—a much-needed invention." Then come two more glacier-mountain lines—"comprising twenty-eight ice fields from fifty to five hundred feet thick, / of unimagined delicacy"—followed by six that take us back under the sea:

> "Picking periwinkles from the cracks"
> or killing prey with the concentric crushing rigor of the python,
> it hovers forward "spider fashion
> on its arms" misleadingly like lace;
> its "ghostly pallor changing
> to the green metallic tinge of an anemone-starred pool."

Eventually we may be able to attribute all of these details and this behavior to the glacier, but at the outset they function mainly to distract us with the actualities of the creature known as an octopus. The notes, which refer us to articles on octopuses in popular magazines, reinforce the literal application as against the metaphoric.

Only at line 14 does the poem clearly settle into what turns out to be its main subject. There are detours along the way (e.g., we'll hear about an octopus again at line 207), but the closing lines, which once more characterize it briefly as a "glassy octopus," offer an impressive panorama of the mountain, with "lightning flashing at its base, rain falling in the valleys and snow falling on the peak," a vista that helps us incorporate and summarize the myriad details of its existence that have been offered to us along the way.

This initial playing with a subject—it's a mountain! no, it's an octopus! no, it's a mountain!—before settling into it will strike many readers as irresponsible. It involves, for one thing, a destabilizing of the way metaphor normally works. Saying "an octopus of ice" and then hovering between the octopus on the one hand and the mountain and its glaciers on the other, as if trying to decide which is figurative and which is literal, makes us feel as though we are being teased about our confidence in decoding figurative language.

That destabilization, as it turns out, affects the entire poem. Long after we have abandoned the undersea creature, we continue to inhabit the poem partly at the surface of language. We realize that we cannot proceed without resorting to analogy and figuration, but we've become aware that a recognition of likeness is also a forgetting of difference and that our casual habits of comparison can provide a distorted approximation of reality.

This challenging of language habits, especially those long associated with the practice of poetry, shifts our sense of our environment. We have moved into unfamiliar territory. On the glaciers or underwater, we are out of our element.[5] We proceed with caution, and the interface between human and nonhuman, which we normally visit with greater confidence and assurance, becomes a place where we feel both fear and wonder, the two characteristic emotions of the aesthetic experience called "the sublime."

Romantic writers of the nineteenth century revived and cultivated the classical notion of the sublime, an aesthetic category of the beautiful, and they duly stress fear and wonder, often in connection with mountains, as Shelley does in "Mont Blanc" and Wordsworth in his accounts of crossing the Alps and of climbing Mount Snowdon in *The Prelude*. The particular modification that modernists added to this recipe was amusement. Emily

Dickinson and Walt Whitman begin it in the American tradition; their moments of sublimity often tend to be flecked with humor. Although I would not describe her treatment of Mount Rainier as satirical, Moore is certainly richly amused, particularly by the differences between the human and nonhuman realms.

Mountains and wildernesses tend to dwarf and intimidate us, and we have various strategies, many of them linguistic, for coping with their implicit devaluation of the human. Moore finds our efforts touching and sometimes hilarious, and she is able to include that response without destroying either the awe or the sense of danger that the aesthetic experience of the sublime is traditionally said to include.

What happens at the outset, I think, is that she is bemused by the strangeness of calling the mountain an octopus of ice. Moore's keen interest in zoology and natural history would not let her be casual about bringing together two complicated and unlike things on the basis of one simplified likeness. She was fascinated by the uniqueness of animals and knew, for example, that "the term 'octopus' embraces a large number of species, all of repulsive appearance, and all of a very characteristic shape and mode of life."[6] Yes, the glacial "arms" of Rainier, from an aerial view, resemble the tentacles of an octopus. But what about the fact of the sea? Well, perhaps the mountain can be said to lie beneath "a sea of shifting snow-dunes" (line 3), one weak analogy thus propping up another. Still, what about the paleness of the snow and ice? Well, octopuses do have times when they develop "a ghostly pallor" (line 12), one aspect of their tendency to change color frequently.[7] An even stranger conjunction arises from the fact that an octopus may have "dots of cyclamen red and maroon on its . . . pseudo-podia" while the glaciers have occasional redness from the worms and plants that live in them.[8] For a moment the glaciers and the cephalopod match up, and then they fall away from each other again.

By teasing the "octopus of ice" metaphor that she found in the guidebook, playing with it to see both its possibilities and its limitations, Moore introduces us to the characteristic rigor of her world, a rigor that extends to language and information about the nonhuman. If the Imagists had objected to the fuzziness and "emotional slither" of the symbolists and the Georgian poets, an extension of their doctrine might argue for a more precise and even scientific handling of both language and subject. Moving confidently in this climate of newness, Moore takes the issue of how well or how badly language renders experience and fact as far as she possibly can. Metaphor, that poetic staple, will not be taken for granted. It will be used of necessity, but it will also be questioned and tested.

In addition, the poet wants to be straightforward about her marshalling of sources. She reads widely and keeps track of her information. Since she had recently encountered, for example, a list of "needed inventions" that includes "glass that will bend," she connects it to the idea of "an octopus of ice," indicating that nature has, in effect, gotten there ahead of us.[9] Moreover, since she had carefully read articles about octopuses, she will import not only information from those sources but actual phrases as well. In addition, in courteous notes she will refer curious readers to the location of her sources in case they want to be better informed.

So the bewildered reader is subjected, as the poem opens, to a metaphor that is explored and questioned and to a flurry of quotation marks that seem to multiply the voices of the poem, mixing the authorial voice with a chorus of commentators and experts.[10] Moore does not quote other poets, but she mines the writings of naturalists and essayists, philosophers and theologians, articles in newspapers and magazines and guidebooks for poetic phrases and striking ideas.[11] The quotations are summoned to aid her in her project of re-examining certain issues: the human relation to the natural world, the strengths and weaknesses of poetic discourse, and the limits and peculiarities of human knowledge.

An octopus, as Gertrude Stein might put it, is an octopus is an octopus. A mountain is a mountain is a mountain. If the two meet, the meeting will be temporary and amusing, and the possibilities and limits may prove memorable. As we leave the first metaphor behind, we advance with a sense of greater caution and heightened spookiness, uncertain about comparisons and wondering whether an inert feature of landscape may have the weirdness and "crushing rigor" of the octopus and python. Fear and wonder. And some amusement.

If readers have come this far into the poem, some thirteen lines, they have probably also by this time visited Moore's notes and discovered that Moore's most frequent source for this poem is a guidebook published by the Department of the Interior called "Rules and Regulations," part of a series in *The National Parks Portfolio*. When Moore visited Washington in 1922, this pamphlet had been newly republished, and as she and her brother Warner undertook to climb Rainier, they must have consulted it often. The pamphlet is far from being a simple list of rules and regulations, although they

visit the poem, for example, from line 191 through line 199. It also contains a good deal of information about the geology, flora, fauna, and weather of the area, and some of the writing approaches eloquence.

Rather than make her poem her own meditation on the meaning and majesty of the mountain, Moore makes it instead a kind of conversation with the writers of the Department of the Interior guidebook, as well as with other sources in her wide reading.[12] She is partly delighted that her own government is capable of creating national parks—they were a fairly recent phenomenon in the 1920s—and publishing a rich account of one of the country's natural wonders. However, she is also interested in how a poet may contribute to such an account, going beyond what the official publication manages. Her enterprise is conducted with a sense both of collaborating and of teasing.

In a way, the pamphlet can be equated with her brother, Warner, with whom she had a close and lively relationship.[13] The two of them had spent two days on the mountain in July 1922, climbing as high as some ice caves on the glacier with a party of tourists and a guide. Marianne and her mother were visiting the area because Warner's ship, the USS *Mississippi*, was in dry dock and he was stationed at Bremerton, Washington.[14] Marianne and her mother returned to the area the following summer, traveling through the Canadian Rockies by train, a trip that allowed her to acquire further material for the poem. By late summer of 1923, she was working on the poem and would do so off and on for another year.[15]

An ordained minister, Warner was in the navy and was already the father of a growing family. He took a keen interest in his sister's poetry and presumed sometimes to tell her how to improve it. In his maleness and his occupation of several socially sanctioned roles, he was connected to the official and the conventional in ways that Marianne was keeping clear of. Associating with modernists in New York (Dadaists, Cubists, Precisionists, etc.), reviewing writers such as Williams and Cummings for *The Dial*, befriending unorthodox couples like H. D. and Bryher, and closely following other new writers like Pound and Eliot with evident admiration, she necessarily saw herself as outside the establishment, challenging its orthodoxies and extending its borders.[16] Still, her relation to things both official and traditional could be friendly and fruitful, just as it was with Warner, with a tolerance on both sides. Thus the "official" version of Rainier is never really satirized or repudiated. Neither, however, is it entirely sanctioned. The guidebook's confidence about its ability to express, control, and sum up the mountain, not to mention its being centered on rules and regulations, is seen as misplaced and sometimes quite foolish. What the mountain means will always lie beyond the official account or any set of rules, ensconced in a territory that the poet can inhabit because she is not contained or constrained by the discourse or the understanding of officialdom.[17]

As we begin our tour of the mountain, we meet the fir trees, seeing them more clearly with some help from John Muir ("the magnitude of their root systems") and John Ruskin ("each like the shadow of the one beside it"), two poetic naturalists. Seeing them clearly frees us from the arms of the octopus ("these maneuvers 'creepy to behold'") and allows us to appreciate "austere specimens of our American royal families." If a democracy is to have royal families, they must be trees, natural aristocrats that have no association with a class system. Furthermore, if the rock "seems frail next to their dark energy," it also attracts us with its colors and weathering patterns, which are "recognized by its plants and its animals." This recognition, which affirms the circulation of energy and meaning in the mountain's ecosystem, is contrasted in lines 23–25 with the behavior of the tourist: "Completing a circle, / you have been deceived into thinking that you have progressed, / under the polite needles of the larches." If lost in the woods, we would travel in circles, thinking we were getting somewhere. Our cultural notions about progress may be similarly delusional; we think we go forward when in fact we repeat our mistakes. Moore was looking for ways of expressing her deep distrust of social progress and male overconfidence, a concept that the First World War had badly shaken; she does not resort to gyres and cones and seances, like Yeats, but to sly truths about what we are like when our tendency to disorientation is exposed. Other Moore poems, like "The Fish" (1918) and "A Grave" (1921), use the sea to establish the same insight. Away from our cultural markers, we wander in circles, lost.

Language distracts us, too. Because a mountain lake is called "The Goat's Mirror," we are "prejudiced in favor" of it even before we can compare it with others: "that lady-fingerlike depression in the shape of the left human foot, / which prejudices you in favor of itself / before you have had time to see the others." Anthropocentric, we would like to believe that goats share our love of self-regard. We also tend to use our own bodies—fingers and feet—to establish connections with the nonhuman. When the names of things and their descriptions establish such connections, however falsely, it prejudices us in their favor.

Moreover, the description that follows, partly Moore's own precise riot of colors and partly the guidebook's observations about patterning and weather changes, does make the lake an enchanting presence.[18] Precision of observation and exactness of expression are beginning to have their intended effect on us. Having been given a list as explicit as "indigo, pea-green, blue-green, and turquoise" and having noticed that the colors merge "in irregular patterns . . . where the wind makes lanes of ripples," we are not likely to want to settle for subsequent observations that are any less exact.

Mention of the goat may be what triggers the catalog of animals that basically organizes the next eighty-nine lines of the poem. We have a quick list—"bears, elk, deer, wolves, goats, and ducks"—and then a more leisurely catalog, starting with the "exacting porcupine" and the well-traveled rat (a kind of signature for Moore), followed by "the thoughtful beavers" and the bears.[19] That the source, a popular guidebook called *What to See in America*, can characterize the beavers only by comparing them to humans—"careful men with shovels"—is another example of our anthropocentric tendencies, held up for our amusement.[20] The bears, meanwhile, are given Moore's own poetic validation by "inspecting unexpectedly / ant-hills and berry-bushes." Omnivorous, they show up anywhere and anytime, foraging, driven by appetite.

I said that the catalog of animals is an organizing device, but the sentence that begins at line 49 illustrates Moore's somewhat subversive and chaotic way of handling both syntax and information in this poem. Syntactically, it is a characterization of the bears' dens and therefore relevant to the animal catalogue. Experientially, it is an explosion of mineral names and attributes:

> Composed of calcium gems and alabaster pillars,
> topaz, tourmaline crystals, and amethyst quartz,
> their den is somewhere else, concealed in the confusion
> of "blue forests thrown together with marble and jaspar and agate
> as if whole quarries had been dynamited."

The distracting details trump the syntax, making it more a pretext than an ordering device, and it becomes evident that the presiding voice is more committed to accumulating interesting details than pursuing "responsible discourse."[21] Just as the bears' den is "concealed in the confusion," so is the fact that the sentence is "about" the den; we are meant to stay bewildered and somewhat overwhelmed by the wealth and confusion of the natural world.

The next two sentences illustrate the same technique. They deal with the mountain goat, but the first manages to distract itself with the paradoxical waterfall "which never seems to fall," while the second, even as it details the goat's features, manages to introduce us to "cliffs the color of the clouds," "dazzling ice fields," and a "crystal peak," culminating in a view of the mountain that recognizes its kinship, aesthetically and geologically, with Fujiyama, of which it turns out to be an exploded version. Even this summary of that sentence, which runs from line 60 to line 71, has not had room for the draughts that "issue" from the "grottoes" in its opening, partly because I am not sure whether they are "penetrating" for their temperature or their smell![22]

To have come this far in the poem, then, is to have learned to suspect metaphor, to accept syntax as a pretext for other kinds of expression, to appreciate precision in terminology, and to welcome sharp detail. We are being retrained both in terms of how we might want to read a poem and also, more fundamentally, in how we might see ourselves in relation to the nonhuman world that surrounds us, often beyond the reach of both language and understanding. We can contemplate the word "waterfall" for its beauty and oddness, just as we can contemplate the thing it refers to, "an endless skein swayed by the wind," as something marvelous and mysterious, more poetic, finally, than the name, which captures its fundamental function but misses its paradoxical quality. Even an apparently casual use of adjectives, as in "exacting porcupine," may drive us to the dictionary to consider etymology and usage, emerging with a clearer sense of the word's history and meanings—stemming from Latin, which means "to drive out," and associated with severity and extraction—and a richer sense of how porcupines operate, leaving their quills in would-be predators. There is no hurrying this process; it is a reeducation that requires time and a willingness to rethink suppositions that many of us have never examined closely.

The catalogue of fauna continues—"Big Snow Mountain is the home of a diversity of creatures" (line 75)—and turns out to include humans, specifically those most at home in the wilderness, "the mountain guide evolving from the trapper" (line 78), but who have no more privileged a place in the list than the nine-striped chipmunk, the water ouzel, or the white-tailed ptarmigan who follow them. The eagles, however, since there are eleven varieties, are allowed to be a bit more dominant. Their passage runs from line 88 to line 102, and it stresses their powerful eyesight (though they are "happy seeing nothing") and the panoramas they witness:

> they hear the roar of ice and supervise the water
> winding slowly through the cliffs,
> the road "climbing like a thread
> which forms the groove around a snail-shell,
> doubling back and forth until where snow begins, it ends."
> (lines 98–102)

The eagles are followed by the marmot, musical and comical, and the marmot gives place to the spotted ponies, which have been introduced to the park to carry visitors and supplies up the mountain. The ponies appear at line 110, in a bravura passage that integrates them with the local flora, preparing the poem for a shift of attention from fauna to flora:

> these conspicuously spotted little horses are peculiar;
> hard to discern among the birch-trees, ferns, and lily-pads,
> avalanche lilies, Indian paint-brushes,
> bear's ears and kittentails,
> and miniature cavalcades of chlorophylless fungi
> magnified in profile on the moss-beds like moonstones in the water;
> the cavalcade of calico competing
> with the original American menagerie of styles
> among the white flowers of the rhododendron surmounting rigid
>   leaves
> upon which moisture works its alchemy
> transmuting verdure into onyx. (lines 118–28)

Glory be to God, as Hopkins says, for dappled things! The riot of detail integrates the ponies and tourists with the rest of the environment, camouflaging them in order to press the point that America has "a menagerie of styles" that preceded the human presence, which introduced the horses. If our own motley additions should try "competing" with this world, they will simply be overwhelmed by its abundance—wildflowers, fungi, lakes, and streams, the alchemy of moisture—and its sheer power.

We must learn to assent to this "cavalcade of calico" and to the larger "menageries of styles" if we want to inhabit the world of this poem comfortably. We may want to pause over a particularly delightful name that gives evidence of close appreciation—"avalanche lily" is my own favorite here—or stop to contemplate the vivid picture of mushrooms dotting moss beds like moonstones under water. Or we may simply want to feel, as Moore puts it in another poem, that "it is a privilege to see so / much confusion."[23] The writing is rich and abundant because the natural world is that way, especially in places where human presence has had relatively little impact.[24]

Lines 129–44 extend the catalog of wildflowers that began in the ponies' passage. It begins and ends with listing, while in between we visit the world of human art, given to decorating with patterns, a realm that emulates nature and, by imposing patterns, orders and distorts it:

> Larkspur, blue pincushions, blue peas, and lupin;
> white flowers with white, and red with red,
> the blue ones "growing closer together
> so that patches of them look like blue water in the distance";
> this arrangement of colors
> as in Persian designs of hard stones with enamel
> forms a pleasing equation—
> a diamond outside, and inside, a white dot;
> on the outside, a ruby; inside, a white dot;
> black spots balanced with black
> in the woodlands where fires have run over the ground—
> separated by aspens, cat's paws, and wooly sunflowers,
> fireweed, asters, and Goliath thistles
> "flowering at all altitudes as multiplicitous as barley,"
> like pink sapphires in the pavement of the glistening plateau.

This is a passage that Moore decided to cut from the poem when she "revised" so much of her work for a compendium titled *Complete Poems* in 1951. The poem can certainly survive without it, but its removal feels arbitrary, born of a desire to curb the abundance and wildness that rightly luxuriate there. As poetry, it is no less purposive or germane than any other part of the poem. Its juxtaposition of human artifice and natural abundance mixes irony with delight, as elsewhere in "An Octopus." Indeed, characterizing the overall tone of the poem as *affectionate irony* helps us see how the poet positions herself with relation to the subject and how she helps the reader handle the profusion of knowledge and detail.

What follows was cut as well. It continues the catalogue of wildflowers, but it also touches on the human tradition in ways that are crucial to our understanding of Moore's purpose. It begins by contrasting the human attitude toward "this treacherous glass mountain," seen as "Inimical to 'bristling, puny, swearing men / equipped with saws and axes,'" with the hospitable quality of its relations to plant life: "this treacherous glass mountain / admires gentians, lady-slippers, harebells, mountain dryads, / and 'Calypso, the goat flower—/ that greenish orchid fond of snow'—." That's how it ends as well, admiring the blue jay and then admitting that

> he knows no Greek,
> that "pride-producing language,"
> in which "rashness is rendered innocuous, and error exposed
> by the collision of knowledge with knowledge."

This characterization of the Greeks and their language turns out to be crucial to what follows, a consideration of Greek civilization that finds it inadequate to any full understanding of the American wilderness and the phenomenon that is Mount Rainier. A careful reader can still figure out the meaning of the contrast, but the absence of this transition in the cut version has led at least one commentator to suppose that Moore is praising the Greeks in this poem. In fact, although her attitude is quite complicated, in the main she is contrasting civilization, as developed and practiced by the Greeks, with the North American wilderness she has been celebrating. The stanza break—the only one in the poem—indicates an important transition, and the original text, with its comments about pride, rashness, and knowledge, provides a firmer progression than does the cut version.

The final section of the poem, in my reading, is a small crisis in aesthetics and faith. Moore does not, I think, have any real solution, Christian or pagan, to the problems that arise on the interface between wilderness and civilization. What she does affirm, I believe, is that the art that lives on that interface, in other words this poem, cannot complacently rely on Greek values like "smoothness" or aesthetic principles that, before modernism, called for "neatness of finish." So ambiguous is her tone and so varied are her observations that commentators have differed widely about what is being stressed in this section. I think the first question we must try to answer is this: Why, in a poem about Mount Rainier, should we bring up the Greeks at all?

Admiration for classical civilization was pervasive in the culture Moore grew up in. American democracy saw itself as extending an important principle of social order discovered by the Greeks. Greek art was an ideal that artists were urged to emulate, and Greek architecture had been the model for the Greek Revival buildings that spread across the land. In all of this, it was the Apollonian side of Greek culture—the setting of boundaries, the imposition of order, the delight in harmony and symmetry—that was being celebrated.[25] Yet what would the skillful and mentally agile Greeks do with something like Mount Rainier? Its size and ruggedness would surely have been inimical to their values:

> "Like happy souls in Hell," enjoying mental difficulties,
> the grasshoppers of Greece
> amused themselves with delicate behavior
> because it was "so noble and so fair";
> not practiced in adapting their intelligence
> to eagle-traps and snow-shoes,
> to alpenstocks and other toys contrived by those
> "alive to the advantage of invigorating pleasures."

In her later version Moore removed the characterization represented by "grasshoppers," a metaphor that stresses smallness and delicacy, along with the hedonism and thoughtlessness allegorized in the fable of the grasshopper and the ant.[26] Still, the metaphor is useful since the contrast builds itself around the love of delicacy and pleasure on the one hand as opposed to the hearty and demanding world of alpenstocks, snow-shoes, and eagle traps on the other. Nature, as represented by North American mountains, is not so much something to conquer as to cope with. The Greeks eventually logged off all the timber in their own mountains, destroying their fertile environment in the process of building ships and elaborating their technology:

> Bows, arrows, oars, and paddles, for which trees provide the wood,
> in new countries more eloquent than elsewhere—
> augmenting the assertion that, essentially humane,
> "the forest affords wood for dwellings and by its beauty stimulates
> the moral vigor of its citizens."

In old countries the forests will mostly have been tamed and converted to the needs of technology. In new countries, partly through their abundance and scope, they will be more eloquent. They may seem to support the "essentially humane" idea that they serve our needs, giving us timber for housing, but their beauty will be more intact and less clearly within our control, and the guidebook thinks that that kind of beauty stimulates moral vigor.

Moore is difficult to detect behind these quotations, but I believe she is focusing on the newness and rawness of nature in her own country, as opposed to those parts of Europe that have seen the longest and fullest human habitation. She is not so much interested in praising or criticizing the Greeks as she is in saying how different the stages of civilization are and how, in the raw, new American West, nature is not something we can view complacently as falling within our control or existing simply for our use. Its beauty is more its own, and if we are to derive "moral vigor" from it, that vigor must be based on our clear recognition that the human view of things is not always and everywhere the only one or the central one. To tell Greeks that they are disabled by anthropocentric attitudes would simply bewilder them; to tell Americans that, in the Cascades and during the 1920s, might well get their attention and make them thoughtful:

> The Greeks liked smoothness, distrusting what was back
> of what could not clearly be seen,
> resolving with benevolent conclusiveness,
> "complexities which still will be complexities
> as long as the world lasts";
> ascribing what we clumsily call happiness,
> to "an accident or a quality,
> a spiritual substance or the soul itself,
> an act, a disposition, or a habit,
> or a habit infused, to which the soul has been persuaded,
> or something distinct from a habit, a power"—
> such power as Adam had and we are still devoid of.

Greek resolutions and "conclusiveness" are clearly illusory, if the contradicting quote is to be believed. It comes from an odd text that the Moore family had had around all of Marianne's life, an eighteenth-century evangelical tract that was enormously popular in America, going through many printings. Baxter's *The Saints Everlasting Rest* becomes a stick to beat the Greeks with here, but it is not used to displace Greek paganism with Christian faith. After its acknowledgment of complexities, it is shown floundering toward a definition of happiness, which it seems unable to arrive at. Its certitude about complexities is replaced by a tentative syntax. After it has been shown dithering through a series of terminological choices, the author's voice cuts in, like Alexander chopping the Gordian knot, to clarify its Christian view of a fallen world, citing Adam's happiness and human-kind's subsequent loss of that happiness. But seeing the natural world as what we fell away from does not lead Moore into any direct expression of Christian sentiments about salvation and resurrection. It simply displaces the Greek "solutions" with the recognition that the human/nature interface is and will continue to be a problematic site for us—and for art.

One more round with the Greeks:

> "Emotionally sensitive, their hearts were hard";
> their wisdom was remote
> from that of these odd oracles of cool official sarcasm,
> upon this game preserve
> where "guns, nets, seines, traps and explosives,
> hired vehicles, gambling and intoxicants are prohibited;
> disobedient persons being summarily removed
> and not allowed to return without permission in writing."

It is indeed difficult to imagine Greek civilization deliberately protecting an environment, especially a wilderness. Toward untamed nature their hearts were indeed hard, and the intentional limits placed on human use for the protection of the wildlife and plants in "this game preserve" are a relatively new feature of human civilization, one that Moore wants to celebrate even as she finds the list of rules somewhat amusing. What amuses her, of course, is the reminder of Eden and the human fall, when the "disobedient persons" were sent packing.

The rules remind us that we are, in a sense, intruders when we set out to climb the mountain:

> It is self-evident
> that it is frightful to have everything afraid of one;
> that one must do as one is told
> and eat rice, prunes, dates, raisins, hardtack, and tomatoes
> if one would "conquer the main peak of Mount Tacoma . . ."

What follows is surely not from the same source: "this fossil flower concise without a shiver, / intact when it is cut, / damned for its sacrosanct remoteness—." These characterizations of the "main peak" are thoughtful recognitions of the human difficulty of trying to embrace it in thought, much less climb it. A "fossil flower" is itself a kind of paradox, something past and present, dead and living, beyond our understanding in being "concise without a shiver" and remaining "intact when it is cut." That Rainier might also be cursed for the sheer difficulty of getting to the area and then getting up the mountain must also be acknowledged. Most people won't take the trouble, just as most won't bother to figure out a poem this complex and inclusive.

Moore is now getting ready to align the mountain not only with the octopus but also with this very poem-portrait of it. To that end, she surprises us by comparing it with Henry James: "like Henry James 'damned by the public for decorum'; / not decorum, but restraint; / it is the love of doing hard things / that rebuffed and wore them out—a public out of sympathy with neatness." Late James novels like *The Golden Bowl* and *The Wings of the Dove* do indeed loom like unclimbable mountains for most readers. James's love of doing hard things looked only like decorum or neatness to a public that misunderstood his modernism. His elegant sentences and nuanced psychological observations were in fact more like rugged mountaineering than like an excess of decorum or neatness. The widespread misunderstanding of his art triggers an outburst: "Neatness of finish! Neatness of finish!" Both neatness and finish are beside the point. Because the Greeks liked smoothness, we tend to look for that in our own art and to mistake James's stylistic experiments and elegantly shaped sentences for decorous and neat effects that are not, for Moore, at issue in his relentless exploration of human psychology. The wilderness within matches the wilderness without, and Moore, treating the sublime and unmanageable aspects of nature, is in a different, but comparable, artistic dilemma. The difficulty of James's novels and of Moore's poem is the difficulty represented by full and powerful representation, a pairing of searching observation and too much detail: "Relentless accuracy is the nature of this octopus / with its capacity for fact." Bringing the octopus back reminds us of the way that metaphor, closely examined, could not do justice to the mountain, which needed fact, close detail, and a passion for accuracy.

At this juncture "this octopus" means, most of all, the very poem we are reading.[27] Moore recognizes, and hopes we recognize, that her failure to achieve "neatness of finish" here is in fact a triumph of adaptation, a poem better fitted to its rugged subject. In the lines that follow, then, we must, as we encounter the pronoun "it," understand that it refers simultaneously to the mountain, the octopus, and the poem:

> "Creeping slowly as with meditated stealth,
> its arms seeming to approach from all directions,"

it receives one under winds that "tear the snow to bits
and hurl it like a sandblast
shearing off twigs and loose bark from the trees."

If a poem can match the strangeness of an octopus and the violence of the mountain's weather, it will be an unnerving experience. And language will become problematic since simple nouns like "tree" will not suffice for the relentlessness of its representation:

Is "tree" the word for these things
"flat on the ground like vines"?
some "bent in a half circle with branches on one side
suggesting dust-brushes, not trees;
some finding strength in union, forming little stunted groves,
their flattened mats of branches shrunk in trying to escape"
from the hard mountain "planed by ice and polished by the wind"—

One of the most admired poems of the time was Joyce Kilmer's "Trees," which begins with the famous line: "I think that I shall never see / A poem lovely as a tree." We are a far cry from that kind of complacency in language and art. Kilmer can remain at a level of generality in which it is safe for him to use the noun as though it actually had clarity and accuracy. However, he can never take us up the mountain to the tree line in violent weather to really see and study the stunted pines that exist on that margin between tree life and no tree life. Having thus come closer to the reality behind and beyond the noun, we can be released from the grasp of the octopus/poem, which can now close with a vivid panorama:

the white volcano with no weather side;
the lightning flashing at its base,
rain falling in the valleys, and snow falling on the peak—
the glassy octopus symmetrically pointed,
its claw cut by the avalanche
"with a sound like the crack of a rifle,
in a curtain of powdered snow launched like a waterfall."

So attentive have we become to word choice and metaphor that we are even likely to ponder the shortcomings here: a "claw" rather than a tentacle and a "curtain" launched like a "waterfall." Moore must continue to manage her subject with inadequate means, quoting directly from other writers' only partially adequate similes and acknowledging that she often falls short of the potential of her subject. Still, this closing vista is extremely powerful, with its reminders of fire—volcano and lightning—and its multiple states of water—rain and snow, a curtain, and a waterfall. We have come a long way from our first tentative consideration of whether we were examining an octopus or a group of glaciers radiating from a huge volcanic peak in the Cascades. As the poem closes, the mountain and the octopus reunite, made similar this time not by a casual use of metaphor but by the effort that has brought them together in this mindful and passionately accurate poem.

Moore's huge and complicated collage, a formidable experience for any reader, is certainly not very much like a Henry James novel.[28] What it does resemble in many ways is its near-contemporary modernist classic, T. S. Eliot's *The Waste Land*. Eliot's poem, newly published and widely praised in 1922, would undoubtedly have been in Moore's mind as she worked on her own long collage poems, "Marriage" and "An Octopus," in 1923. The use of quotations to build up a layered and polyphonic texture, giving a lyric poem some of the elements of a drama, would clearly appeal greatly to such an omnivorous reader, who was already making scrapbooks and journals to record her reading and her sightseeing and to compare her own impressions of the world with those of other writers. Indeed, she might have felt that women, who had been creating composite objects like quilts and scrapbooks for a long time, had a better hold on the possibilities of collage than any man might.[29] Eliot had struggled mightily with his material—"On Margate Sands / I can connect / Nothing with nothing"—and it had required Pound's editorial intervention to bring his poem to completion. Moore labored alone, "happy seeing nothing" like her eagle, feeling her way and feeling less anxious, perhaps, about completeness and closure.[30]

She approached her task, in any case, with confidence and enjoyment. She did not seek to replicate Eliot's peculiar lyricism; her quotations do not so much evoke speaking as reading, and the flatness and ordinariness of prose interest her more than the scraps of song, overhead conversation, and mythic allusion that interest Eliot. Moreover, Eliot's pessimism, his focus on the decline of civilization and culture, and his tendency to dwell on the unpleasant and the unsettling would naturally invite reworking to someone with a more positive outlook.[31] Ezra Pound, about this time, had embarked on the *Cantos*. His, too, would be a backward-looking search through European cultures (and later through Asian ones) for values that would counterbalance the tragedy of World War I. But an American poet who elected to stay at home could perhaps counter all of this Eurocentrism, as Stevens and Williams were doing as well, by a healthier prospect, faced in a nation with a future, in this case by an encounter with the great American wilderness that remained half explored and half understood. Stephen T. Mather, the assistant to the secretary of the interior in charge of national parks, had put the matter unequivocally in his "Presentation" in the *National Parks Portfolio*:

> This nation is richer in natural scenery of the first order than any other nation; but it does not know it. It possesses an empire of grandeur and beauty which it has scarcely heard of. It owns the most inspiring playgrounds and the best equipped nature schools in the world and is serenely ignorant of the fact. In its national parks it has neglected, because it has quite overlooked, an economic asset of incalculable value.[32]

Moore is not interested in the economic assets, but she does take up the aesthetic ones. Embracing the modernism that produced works like Picasso's *Still Life with Chair Caning* and Eliot's *Waste Land* and would soon produce *Ulysses* and the *Cantos,* Moore could bring her own distinctive vision to these practices. It might include, as James's had, a subtle affirmation of American experience that the other artists lacked.[33] Her very first note for the poem contrasted Rainier with the historical circumstances that had produced the recent world war: "An octopus of ice / so cool in this age of violence."[34]

One could turn from the disasters of history and civilization to the unspoiled vistas of the Cascades with something like relief. Here was something that even Greek philosophy fell short of understanding or accounting for. Here was a refuge, even a shrine. Here was a "Paradise" where an American Adam and Eve, Marianne and Warner, might absorb and recognize the holiness of the natural world.[35]

Marianne and Warner could not stay in the park or the paradise. He was her brother, for one thing, and he was already married, a "fallen" state that the companion poem, "Marriage," would take up. Nevertheless, they could look back on their visit with wonder and affection, and the great mountain could become an aesthetic touchstone for things they valued and shared. Marianne's mother, with her emphatic Christian piety, could be included, too, though Marianne takes care that the Christian sentiments of her sources, like Baxter and Newman, do not enter the poem. Shelley's mountain confirmed his atheism. Wordsworth's reinforced his incipient faith.

Keeping clear of the deliberate paganism of Stevens and the more casual paganism of Williams, Moore nevertheless aligns herself with them aesthetically as an exponent of the new, thus freeing art from tradition and making it an instrument of both private and public discovery.

Perhaps she made her poem too hard. Perhaps she made it too rough and unruly, like the great natural site it commemorates. When it was done, Moore lapsed into a seven-year silence as a poet, and when she resumed composition she exercised a tighter control on both subject and structure, doubting her earlier prolixity. But her accomplishment in "An Octopus" remains an example of her early modernism at its most original and visionary.[36]

6

Eugenio Montale writes

MEDITERRANEAN

A whirlwind's vortex
showers some nasty jeers
upon my resting head.
The earth scorches, crosshatched
by twisted pinetree shadows,
and the sea's below me, veiled,
partly by branches, also by haze
that the ground itself, in gasps,
gives off from time to time.
Louder, then softer, the sound of boiling water
strangling itself
next to a stretch of shoals, comes up to me—
or sometimes a bomb of spume
explodes against the rocks.
I raise my eyes, the braying stops
above my head; and flung
out and down toward the water's uproar
arrowing blue-white, there go two jays.

Ancient One, I'm drunk on the voice
that comes from your mouths when they gape
like green bells, throw themselves back
and then dissolve.
The house of my far-off summers
was near you, you know,
in that country where the sun
scorches and mosquitoes cloud the air.
Now as then you turn me to stone,
sea, but I no longer
hold myself worthy of the solemn

admonition of your breath. You taught me first
that the tiny commotion of my heart
was merely a moment of yours;
that deep within me was
your perilous law: to be vast, diverse,
and yet fixed—
and to empty myself of all filth
like you, who fling to your beaches
among seaweed   corks   starfish
the rubbish of your depths.

Sometimes clambering down
these dry ravines, swollen just now
with autumn moisture,
I couldn't quite feel at heart the wheel
of seasons and the relentless
drip of time;
yet the inkling of your presence
panting in that air, so still before,
surprised me,
filling my spirit,
among the rocks that lined the path.
Now, I told myself, the very stone
wants to break free, stretch
toward an invisible embrace;
hard matter sensed
the abyss approaching, and it flinched;
and the tufts of the eager reeds
spoke to the secret waters,
shaking, saying *Yes*.
You vastness, you rescued
even the stones from their suffering—
all your carousing offset
those immovable finite things.
I climbed on down through heaps of rocks,
with salty gusts arriving
in my heart; the tense ocean
was like a game of ringtoss.

With this same joy
the lost plover
swoops through the narrow gorge
down to the shore.

I've loitered, sometimes, in the grottoes
that you favor, huge
or narrow, shadowy and sad.
Seen from inside, their openings
outlined a robust architecture
against a field of sky.
Out of your booming heart
ethereal temples rose
with spires flashing lights—
in the lucent blue a city of glass
rose slowly from the mist
and its roar was more like a whisper.
The dreamed country surfaced from the swell.
Out of the hubbub came the evidence.
The exile was back in his uncorrupted home.
So, father, to one who watches,
your unleashing teaches a heavy law.
And there is no escaping it;
if I were to try, even pebbles on the path
would contradict and judge me,
petrified suffering without a name,
or the shapeless wreckage
tossed aside by the torrent of life
in a tangle of branches and straw.
In the destiny that's shaping
I may experience respite;
an end to fear, that's all.
This, says the surf in its mess and its rage,
and *this*, the calm swell says as well.

I arrive at unexpected moments
when your inhuman heart, as now
divided from mine, strikes terror.

Then your music is all dissonance,
your every move unfriendly.
I fold back into myself, drained
of strength, your voice seems lost.
I gaze at the rockslide
that stretches down toward you,
at the cliff that juts above you,
crumbling, yellowish, furrowed
by rainwater channels.
My life is this dry slope,
a middle, not an end, road open to
widening rivulets, slow-motion landslide.
And it's this as well, this plant
born out of devastation
facing the blows of the ocean
and the unpredictable gusts of wind.
This patch of soil where nothing grows
has cracked itself to sprout a daisy.
In it I hesitate, facing the sea that assails me,
still missing its silence in my life.
I look at the glittering earth,
at air so serene it grows dark.
What's welling up in me, sea,
could easily be the rancor
each son feels toward his father.

Nobody knows what's coming
tomorrow, dark or joyful;
maybe the road we take
will bring us to untouched glades
where youthful waters murmur endlessly;
or maybe a last descent
into a fatal valley,
down into darkness, no more morning light.
Maybe foreign shores
will welcome us again, we'll lose
our memory of the sun, our minds
will drop the jingling rhymes we knew.

The fable that, yes,
contained our very lives
will turn to the dark tale
no one wants to tell!
One thing will still be passed along,
father: a little bit of your gift
will always survive in these syllables
we bring along with us, these buzzing bees.
We'll journey far and still we'll keep
an echo of your voice, the way dull grass
in shaded courtyards between houses
never quite forgets the sunlight.
And a day will come when these soundless words
that you engendered in us, nourished
on lassitude and silence,
will seem to some brother heart
to savor of Greek salt.

I'd like to be pocked and essential
as one of the salt-eaten pebbles
you toss around;
a timeless splinter, evidence
of a cold, unyielding will.
Instead, I've been one who watches intently
in himself and others the boiling away
of a fleeting life—a man who defers
the act that no one then destroys.
I wanted to find the evil
which eats away at the world, the tiny flaw
of a lever that throws the cosmic machine
out of gear; and I saw all
the events of the moment
ready to separate and collapse.
Following the furrow of a path, I had
its opposite in my heart, inviting me;
maybe I needed the knife that lops,
the mind that decides and shapes itself.
I needed other books

besides your roaring page.
But I can regret nothing; your song
still dissolves interior snarls.
Your delirium climbs to the stars.

I'd like at least to be able to force
into this struggling cadence of mine
some little snatch of your raving;
to possess the gift to attune
all your voices to my stuttering speech—
I who once dreamed of seizing
those salty words
where nature and art commingle
in order to cry out more fully
my melancholy, that of an aging child
who should never have learned to think.
But all I have are the fusty
words from the dictionary, and the dark
voice of love growing feeble,
turning to literary lament.
All I have are these words
that offer themselves like streetwalkers
to anyone that will have them;
all I have are stale phrases
that students and the rabble
could steal from me tomorrow
to turn into true verse.
And your boom grows louder
and the new shadow, blue, expands.
My thoughts fall behind as if losing a race.
I have no senses,
no sense. I have no limits.

Dissolve it if you choose,
this little whining life,
the way a sponge will take
a chalk-scrawl off a blackboard.

I wait to return to your circle
when my scattered passage is complete.
My coming was a witness
to an order I forgot along the way.
My very words confirm
an impossible happening they can't fathom.
But always, as I listened to
your soft surf breaking on the shore
amazement seized me
like someone with almost no memory
come suddenly home to the past.
Having taken my lessons
less from your rapid glory, more
from that slow panting that makes
almost no sound on your desolate noondays,
I surrender now in humility. I'm only
a spark from a thyrsus: to burn—
that's my meaning, and nothing else.

(*FIELD, Contemporary Poetry and Poetics*)

HERE IS another example of the modernist sublime, matching Marianne Moore's octopus of a mountain. This time the overwhelming natural presence is the sea. It is less alien than Mount Rainier—the poem's speaker tells us that he grew up next to it—and its interaction with the human realm is both ancient and manifold. But its majesty and danger, along with the sheer difficulty of comprehending it fully, match it up nicely with the great peak in the American wilderness that so intrigued Moore.

Here, too, is another suite, a set of dances, variations, shifting pictures in a gallery. Its sections feel independent enough that they are often anthologized separately. The structural choice matches those of Yeats, Stevens, and Williams. This kind of form, in which the composer/artist can keep beginning again, can walk (or dance) all the way around an intriguing subject, is neither narrative nor pure lyric. It lies in a middle ground where the artist can shift perspective, imitating the simultaneous representations of Cubism, and alter tones abruptly, mimicking the restless activity of the consciousness. The form easily accommodates argument, anecdote, exclamation, and meditation. By its very nature it tends to imply unstable emotional weather and to feel nervous and incomplete, unwilling to settle into full closure or achieved coherence, preferring a modernist insistence on the unfinished, the ongoing, the multiple, and the tentative.

Here also is another vision in which the self is reborn to the world, rewedded to it, as in Rilke's ecstatic meditation and, sometimes more problematically, in those of all our other poets. Here is a vision of life that makes the inner and the outer worlds continuous with each other, seeing them as part of the same whole. This poem, like the others we have looked at, accumulates various memories, ideas, and experiences, adding up to a stirring account of the human relation to the natural world, one that argues for reciprocities of perception and existence. It is a map of the Ligurian coast superimposed on a map of the speaker's heart.

And here is yet another poem that creates and explores its own aesthetic as it goes. The artistic frustrations and ambitions of its maker are on full display. It seems to be born of a crisis of both representation and emotion: How is one to be a poet in the modern world, after World War I and in the midst of considerable public and private disillusion—about the self, the state of civilization and progress, and the possibilities of beauty and art? The modern need to demystify mortality in secular terms and to resolve the dilemmas of human self-consciousness is once again addressed and met.

All of this is accomplished with considerable subtlety and finesse by a poet who would make such qualities his trademark. He is clearly reluctant to overdramatize modern angst and alienation in the fashion of, say, *The Waste Land*. Montale's poetic persona is modest, tentative, skeptical, and ironic. He dislikes idealizing and he detests exaggeration. If he is to accomplish an identification of inner and outer worlds, a dissolving of the barrier between human and nonhuman, a thrilling continuity between landscape and observer, he insists on doing it with humility and understatement.

Furthermore, there is to be no ecstatic merging or transcendence. The nervous, melancholy, perceiving self will remain distinct from the world around it, even as it finds some of its best and fullest meanings there. That world will be problematic, too, complex and disturbing, full of mysteries and distresses, yet oddly beautiful. When the poem is finished, the speaker (and the reader) still face the dilemmas of selfhood and consciousness. However, while the poem is in progress, a kind of strange and wonderful relief is experienced, relief at recognizing how fully one's emotions, in all their complexity, are mirrored in the nonhuman realm if one is both candid and attentive. The result, in its cautious way, is all the more exhilarating for its modesty.

All of these factors were already present in Montale's first lyric, written when the poet was around the age of twenty and revised for inclusion in his first book, *Ossi di seppia* (Cuttlefish Bones):

> To spend the afternoon, absorbed and pale,
> beside a burning garden wall;
> to hear, among the stubble and the thorns,
> the blackbirds cackling and the rustling snakes.
>
> On the cracked earth or in the vetch
> to spy on columns of red ants
> now crossing, now dispersing,
> atop their miniature heaps.
>
> To ponder, peering through the leaves,
> the heaving of the scaly sea
> while the cicadas' wavering screech
> goes up from balding peaks.
>
> And walking out into the sunlight's glare
> to feel with melancholy wonder
> how all of life and its travail
> is in this following a wall
> topped with the shards of broken bottles.

The music of this poem, which I have tried to reflect in my translation, is dissonant, particularly in terms of the Italian poetic tradition. You can't in fact separate the harshness of representation from the way the sounds of words, clashing and high strung, reflect it. The sea is reptilian; the land is arid and stony, more hospitable to insects than other forms of life; the sun is fiery; the snakes and blackbirds are neither cute nor friendly; and the human additions to all this are signified and summed up by a wall with broken glass embedded in its top. You take in simultaneously an unappealing and troubling world along with a sense of beauty that stems partly from honesty of representation and partly from the skill at portraying experience through sounds and images. It's a young man's poem, no doubt, in its absolutism about melancholy—"all of life and its travail" reduced to the scraps of glittering, lethal glass. But it has a maturity of design and a confidence about its subject that justify its fame.

That confidence came from the poet's familiarity with the Ligurian coastline that is the setting of so many of his poems. Summer after summer his family returned to their villa near Monterosso, one of the five towns that make up the Cinque Terre, on Italy's Mediterranean coast. While this area is near the Italian Riviera, suggesting wealth and leisure, yachts and house parties, Montale was more interested in its dramatic geography and its austere, unfriendly feel. Rugged cliffs plunge to the sea, so that getting from one place to another means climbing and descending steep paths. Small fishing villages cling precariously to precipitous hillsides around tiny harbors. The sun beats down mercilessly, and the glare from the sea can be blinding. Fishermen eke out a living by their unpredictable catches, and the local population farms only with great difficulty, carving out small terraces to create gardens, vineyards, and orchards. Water is scarce and often has to be carried or piped great distances to irrigate tiny greenhouses, olive trees, grapevines, and vegetable patches.

And the sea dominates everything. Its giant presence is a constant reminder of the limits of human control. The best way to get from place to place, given the land's steep ruggedness, is by water, but it is extremely dangerous in sudden storms. The sea yields up delicious fish, squid, and even lobsters but not very predictably or abundantly. Moreover, it obscures even its own history, harboring in unseen depths the shipwrecks and corpses of those who have tried to traverse it at least since the time of the Etruscans and the Phoenicians. In the Montale lyric I quoted earlier, it is a dragon, dangerous even in sleep, its heaving scaly surface something to be watched and pondered. Perhaps the dragon guards a treasure; more likely, it just means destruction.

Montale's childhood by the sea gave him the deepest and most intimate kind of familiarity with its meaning and presence, the kind we have with our mothers and fathers, known from our first consciousness and infancy. No wonder he found he could turn to that sea and its coastline for the meditations of his poetry. Here was a place where questions about the human tradition and its uneasy place in the cosmic scheme of things posed themselves naturally. The bookish young poet had only to step outside and look carefully around him to have a form of discourse that felt both rich and natural.

He could also, just by using accuracy of description and candor of emotion, shift the course of Italian poetry away from romanticism and fin de siècle decadence toward a modernism that relied not on manifestos and shock, like the work of the Futurists and Dadaists, but on a modest and steady clarity of observation. One recent and influential predecessor, Gabriele d'Annunzio, had written ecstatic lyrics about the Italian landscape just a few years earlier, lyrics that reflected both romantic and symbolist notions about transcendent experience and self-extinction. His poems are studded with mythic references to give them glamor, and the nature they present has no place for snakes, anthills, or broken glass:

> Which of the Hours,
> which of the Sea-Hours,
> which of the occult joys
> you gave them,
> with the secret language
> you taught them,
> O Ermione,
> goes with you on your journey
> beyond the limpid rivers,
> beyond green hills,
> beyond the azure mountains,
> O Ermione,
> beyond the shining cottage,
> beyond oak-groves,
> beyond the glorious azure mountains?[1]

This kind of verse, which had aroused widespread admiration when it appeared in 1903, must have tempted the young Montale to a different model, one in which the natural world would be less mediated and idealized, more rugged, gritty, and disturbing. He would be less generic—no limpid rivers, green hills, and azure mountains—and more detailed. He would reject the rhetoric that implied classical models, ecstatic states of mind, and heroic personas.

More to his liking as a model would have been the fragmentary poems and prose writings of Dino Campana, the disturbed and wandering poet, eventually hospitalized for mental illness, who is sometimes characterized as the Italian Rimbaud:

> The fog has lifted: I go out. The good, homey smell of lavender and washing that small Tuscan villages have makes me happy again. The church has a portico of small squared columns made of whole stones, bare and elegant, simple and austere, truly Tuscan. Among the cypresses I notice other porticos. On one hillside a cross opens its arms to the vast flanks of the Falterona, dark booty, which in turn lays bare its own rocky structure. The grasses burn in the graveyard with a pale red-ochre flame.[2]

Not that much like Rimbaud, really. The tone is mildly ecstatic, but the passage is based entirely on what is actually seen, heard, smelled, and touched in the rustic environment. The prose medium helps the poet avoid the posturing and operatic gesturing that the Italian nineteenth century had produced, and its spirit of realistic observation and modest appreciation, imported back into Montale's poetic voice and style, gave him his own unique note:

> Listen, the poet laureates
> move only among those plants
> with special names: acanthus, boxwood privet;
> myself, I like the roads that lead
> to grassy ditches where an urchin
> reaching in meager puddles
> can catch a half-starved eel.

This same poem, "The Lemon Trees," ends on a note of cautious elation, hard won and tentative:

> But the illusion fails and time recalls us
> to noisy cities where the sky appears
> only in snatches, beyond the cornices.
> Rain wearies the earth; winter's
> tedium thickens upon the houses,
> light grows stingy, the soul goes bitter.
> And then, one day, through a half-shut gate,
> the yellow lemons catch our eye
> and the heart's frost thaws
> while somewhere within us songs
> begin to shower
> from golden trumpets of sunlight.[3]

Trusting both the seasons and our senses may get us through our dark times. This is more like what Williams was doing in America, rewriting Whitman's late romantic lyricism. It is based on a determination to make poetry out of the local and the mundane, seen clearly and without sentiment, and to present a world that is not falsified by myth, excessive allusion, or pompous reassurances. No limpid rivers, green hills, or azure mountains. Instead, just the boys who catch eels in puddles and the lemon trees of your neighbor's orchard. No wonder that when Montale felt ready to try a longer subject and a fuller declaration of his emerging aesthetic, he turned again to the Ligurian coastline and the awesome, unsettling presence of the sea.

A poem about the sea could be said to offer possibilities of invoking and redefining the sublime. If one is trying to differentiate one's work from the romantic and symbolist traditions, then addressing a privileged aspect of that tradition's aesthetic is an excellent way of making one's point. In that respect, Montale's subject is more like Moore's mountain than like Williams's Hudson River, Weehawken, and New York City.

The differences between Montale and Moore are informative as well. She was writing about a wilderness almost untouched by history, whereas he was addressing a deep historical presence. Moore was a tourist, relatively unfamiliar with the great mountain she had briefly visited, while Montale was writing about something he had known from earliest childhood. His long familiarity gives him a confidence that in turn sponsors a directness of manner and presentation Moore could not call upon. The ocean can be dragonlike, as it was in that early lyric, but it is also as familiar as a parent, and it can be addressed with intimacy and candor.

Montale had studied music. He had considered becoming a professional singer, and he very much admired the impressionistic "nature music" of Debussy. Once again we have a structure that visually emulates a gallery of pictures while aurally imitating a musical suite, a set of dances or variations. The openness of this structure invites the experimental approach to form that is characteristic of modernism while also proving hospitable to the self-divisions and ambiguities that were flooding into the modernist sensibility.

The opening lyric constitutes a vignette wherein the attentive speaker, whose personal history and social identity are not invoked, takes in his surroundings, experiencing their life and activity while he himself remains still, poised to see and listen rather than to act. By beginning abruptly and rather cryptically, the poem differentiates itself from romantic models. By remaining temporarily anonymous, this speaker/observer makes room for us to share his perspective. His meditative attention, the poem implies, could easily be duplicated by the reader, for whom he is an extension and a surrogate.

The noise above him at the opening turns out to be two jays, who close the episode by flying past him down to the sea. The events are entirely naturalistic—no myths are invoked; no "poetic" effects are stressed. The emphasis is on the intense presence of vegetation, sunlight, surf, and summer weather. D'Annunzio would have thrown in Pan, Demeter, or Dionysus to this mix. Montale is determined to make do with his actual surroundings.

That does not prevent him from adding some sly effects of his own. The little whirlwind that opens the lyric is a *vortice*, in Italian. The reference may glance at vorticism, the current movement related both to cubism and futurism. It's as if the speaker wishes to reflect his knowledge of these movements and manifestos while turning from them to an enduring world of nature. All of these movements had called for new ways of representing the world, particularly its dynamic energies. Montale is aware of them without joining them. The poet-observer, in other words, is not without self-consciousness and historical positioning. He must respond to both nature itself and the energies of the vorticists and futurists, deciding where his art is to be positioned in relation to them.

The exciting movement of this stanza, which after all represents a relatively tranquil scene, shows Montale's early mastery of a fluent free verse that is dense, evocative, and highly musical in its own right:

> The earth scorches, crosshatched
> by twisted pinetree shadows,
> and the sea's below me, veiled,
> partly by branches, also by haze
> that the ground itself, in gasps,
> gives off from time to time.

The intensity of this puts us in the scene, invoking all our senses and making us take note of surroundings we might not have found so exciting without the poem's instigation. The surf now becomes audible:

> Louder, then softer, the sound of boiling water
> strangling itself
> next to a stretch of shoals, comes up to me—
> or sometimes a bomb of spume
> explodes against the rocks.

The observer's consciousness, marked by the First World War, finds analogies in the human realm of violence that contrast with the relief of his pastoral setting. Montale had seen action at the front, as had so many of his contemporaries, and there was no need to write directly about the horrors of war. They were already significantly present to the consciousness of his whole generation. Those who had listened to strangling cries and exploding bombs would especially appreciate the presence of a natural world that made them distant echoes. It's as if the jays wish to emphasize the sea's superiority to human history by their movement, which emulates a kind of weapon that is older than the bombs and bullets of modern warfare:

> I raise my eyes, the braying stops
> above my head; and flung
> out and down toward the water's uproar
> arrowing blue-white, there go two jays.

There is the human realm, with its vortices, its weapons, and its oppressive history, and there is this strange, disconcerting other realm where one cannot predict what jays will do but where the absence of human control and self-assertion provides a sort of healing. It is far more subtle than *The Waste Land,* for example, but the issues are not dissimilar.

In the second section the speaker is ready to address the sea directly. Now his personal history—"The house of my far-off summers / was near you, you know, / in that country where the sun / scorches and mosquitoes cloud the air"—has a bearing on his meditation. The summers are not idealized (scorching sun and clouds of mosquitoes deflect any romanticizing of childhood in nature), but they provide an opportunity to measure past familiarity and present knowledge:

> Now as then you turn me to stone,
> sea, but I no longer
> hold myself worthy of the solemn
> admonition of your breath.

In both past and present the sea's majesty transfixes the observer, making him like a statue or someone confronting a Medusa or a basilisk, but the difference is that maturity has made him feel unworthy. He'd like to reconnect, recapture his closeness and innocence, and have the sea once more as a kind of parent:

> You taught me first
> that the tiny commotion of my heart
> was merely a moment of yours;
> that deep within me was

your perilous law: to be vast, diverse
and yet fixed—
and to empty myself of all filth
like you, who fling to your beaches
among seaweed   corks   starfish
the rubbish of your depths.

To be small was not only to recognize the size and power of the ocean but
also to experience a kinship with its "perilous law" and self-cleansing ritu-
als. Again we sense that the "modern" sensibility of the speaker, who has
experienced the interventions of war and technology between his childhood
self and present self, leads him to hope, cautiously, that reestablishing his
early bond with nature may heal him and restore his sanity and sensibility.
If we think again about Eliot's representation of this state of mind and near
despair, what strikes us most is Montale's quiet subtlety. Even as he avoids
the romantic overvaluing of childhood and nature, he also eschews the
melodramatic treatment of maturity and depression in the modern world.
The emphatic realism of the beach litter that closes the section grounds the
meditation in a firmly perceived material world. What began as a kind of
prayer ("Antico . . .") ends with the flotsam and jetsam a beachcomber
encounters, balancing the abstraction of the law ("esser vasto e diverso / e
insieme fisso") with the details of trash—corks, seaweed, and dead starfish.

Having taken stock of his past and present relation to the Mediterranean,
the speaker can begin to explore that present more fully, elaborating not on
his childhood experiences but on more recent memories:

Sometimes clambering down
these dry ravines, swollen just now
with autumn moisture,
I couldn't quite feel at heart the wheel
of seasons and the relentless
drip of time;

In a landscape characterized by change—dry at times, flooded at others—
the protagonist loses his sense of the temporal in terms of both its cyclic
character and its entropic effects. The sea comes in to fill the gap:

yet the inkling of your presence
panting in that air, so still before,

surprised me,
filling my spirit,
among the rocks that lined the path.

The speaker would seem to be on the edge of a transcendent experience. The rocks and plants around him all seem to yearn to join the sea and to become one with its vastness and liquidity. The dry world, still and baking hot, is counterbalanced by the activity and liquidity of the ocean. With rising excitement, sensing all this conjoining of meaning and purpose in the things around him, the protagonist continues his downward climb toward the waterline:

I climbed on down through heaps of rocks,
with salty gusts arriving
in my heart; the tense ocean
was like a game of ringtoss.
With this same joy
the lost plover
swoops through the narrow gorge
down to the shore.

The changeable nature of the sea has replaced the lost sense of the action of time, reconnecting the speaker to natural processes. Suddenly the great ocean is more like a carnival attraction, a game where winning and losing are of no great consequence. And the speaker's downward scramble reflects the instinctive swoop of the bird. This closing image recalls the jays of the opening section, modifying their mocking otherness with a claim of identification, but it also has a built-in ambiguity of its own. Can we really say that any bird is "lost" (*sperso* can also mean "dispersed" or "scattered")? What the plover or lapwing usually does is draw the observer away from its nest by its crying and pretense of injury. That "joy" then is somewhat deceptive, our misperception of instinctive behavior. Instead of a full sense of transcendence, the poem has arrived at a more typical Montalean "resolution," a cautious affirmation of the ocean's meaning and the observer's relation to it. The bird's flight may express joy, but we are left to ponder other possibilities—survival and deception—as well.

Now we move inside the earth, visiting the inner world of the sea itself. The grottoes have been carved by the action of the water, and their fantastic "architecture" seems to bring us to the ocean's home, where we can see its presence more fully and clearly:

> Out of your booming heart
> ethereal temples rose
> with spires flashing lights—
> in the lucent blue a city of glass
> rose slowly from the mist
> and its roar was more like a whisper.
> The dreamed country surfaced from the swell.
> Out of the hubbub came the evidence.
> The exile was back, in his uncorrupted home.

The first half of this section draws beauty and excitement from the sense of intimacy. The "exile" seems to be both the speaker and the sea itself. Both have arrived home, emulating Odysseus and the resolution of an epic journey.

Typically, the second half of this section qualifies this experience of unity and beauty. Now the intimacy becomes patriarchal: "So, father, to one who watches, / your unleashing teaches a heavy law. / And there is no escaping it." The law is the speaker's recognition of his personal mortality. He cannot be immortal like the ocean or renewable like the tides and seasons. If he were to deny this, even the stones would rise up to contradict him, as would the beach rubble, "a tangle of branches and straw." While this sharply qualifies the experience of transcendence that was developing in the sense of a shared home and intimacy, it, too, deserves qualification, lest it become too melodramatic: "In the destiny that's shaping / I may experience respite; / an end to fear, that's all." The speaker's death will not be a hellish afterlife of some kind. It's likely to be rest—and sleep. Death, then, does not represent a significant risk, given the absence of metaphysical structures. Seeing "respite" as the only "risk" one faces lightens the "heavy law" of mortality considerably. The ocean carries the same emphasis in both storms and calms: "*This*, says the surf in its mess and its rage, / and *this*, the calm swell says as well." The ocean's identical meaning when in apparently opposite states is particularly soothing, like consistent fairness and integrity in a parent or other authority. This section covers a considerable amount of emotional ground, but its final lines, while ambiguous, feel tranquil and reassuring.

In the fifth section the speaker investigates times when he has felt completely alienated from the sea:

> I arrive at unexpected moments
> when your inhuman heart, as now
> divided from mine, strikes terror.
> Then your music is all dissonance,
> your every move unfriendly.
> I fold back into myself, drained
> of strength, your voice seems lost.
> I gaze at the rockslide
> that stretches down toward you,
> at the cliff that juts above you,
> crumbling, yellowish, furrowed
> by rainwater channels.
> My life is this dry slope.

Alienated from the sea, the speaker tries to identify with the land. His own helplessness and confusion are mirrored in the jumbled rocks and the eroded cliff. The rock yearns toward the sea, and the cliff is furrowed by the water that wants only to join the ocean as well. He can still find his emotions configured and mirrored in the world around him, but they are arid and motionless, distinct from the life and vastness of the sea.

Again, though, there is a midway shift of emotional current. The speaker finds a small plant growing on the arid hillside, a daisy. Its defiant survival gives him courage. If his life is the dry slope, it is also what grows on that slope:

> And it's this as well, this plant
> born out of devastation
> facing the blows of the ocean
> and the unpredictable gusts of wind.
> This patch of soil where nothing grows
> has cracked itself to sprout a daisy.

Now a third shift comes. The daisy faces the ocean, a small life confronting an immensity, and the connection it tentatively arrives at is filial, a combination of love and distrust:

> In it I hesitate, facing the sea that assails me,
> still missing its silence in my life.
> I look at the glittering earth,
> at air so serene it grows dark.

What's welling up in me, sea,
could easily be the rancor
every son feels toward his father.

The wry acknowledgment glances at Freud, but mostly, given the surrounding sense of beauty and serenity, suggests that the rancor is eventually subsumed by filial piety and love, an acceptance of patrimony and relatedness.

The sixth section opens with a more traditional poetic diction. As one commentator notes, the tone is florid and courtly, as it was in the dreamy grotto passage.[4] We notice these ceremonial moments because they show that the poet is perfectly capable of a more familiar and plangent music and thus underline his choice of dissonant effects and grittier images. The series of conjectured futures sounds generic:

Nobody knows what's coming
tomorrow, dark or joyful;
maybe the road we take
will bring us to untouched glades
where youthful waters murmur endlessly;
or maybe a last descent
into a fatal valley,
down into darkness, no more morning light.
Maybe foreign shores
will welcome us again, we'll lose
our memory of the sun, our minds
will drop the jingling rhymes we knew.

The reference to "jingling rhymes" alerts us to the superficiality of the more traditional poetic diction, warning us not to be seduced by it. Montale drives the point home by speaking of the fictive imposition of narrative onto the richer texture of experience, and mortality becomes a comic effect, the story that the storytellers avoid: "The fable that, yes, / contained our very lives / will turn to the dark tale / no one wants to tell!"

By now we have learned that the sections generally shift tone and direction at the midway point, and this one is no exception:

One thing will still be passed along,
father, and it's this: a little bit of your gift
will always survive in these syllables

we bring along with us, these buzzing bees.
We'll journey far and still we'll keep
an echo of your voice, the way dull grass
in shaded courtyards between houses
never quite forgets the sunlight.

Against the uncertainty of the future and the artificiality of the fictive and mythic, the poet now places language itself, locating its sources in the sea's meaning and influence and equating it with two natural and modest things: the sounds that bees make and the persistence of grass even when it is deprived of sunlight. The bee metaphor is classically derived, tying poetry's authority to the sweetness and light that the honey and wax of bees can produce. The grass metaphor is more modern and urban, reflecting Montale's deliberate search for antiromantic images.

If something of the sea's patrimony can inhabit the language we use—as naturally as bees buzz and grass grows—and if it can survive the dulling effects of the modern and the urban, then a poet can hope that his medium will retain a use and validity that keep him in touch with what is essential. The emergent aesthetic, modest and cautious, is being articulated with increasing confidence:

And a day will come when these soundless words
that you engendered in us, nourished
on lassitude and silence,
will seem to some brother heart
to savor of Greek salt.

The words will be silent on the page, reflecting the silence in which they were conceived. Their flavor will be retained, that whiff of the ocean that recalls its brine and sea air and that makes food palatable, linking it with our own saline blood, sweat, and tears. The use of "Greek" would seem to invoke early civilization, seafaring, and a link even to Homer and Sappho and the origins of the poet's own tradition. If the speaker can hope that language will carry that savor of origins—the sea's fathering of us, our language's debt to its essence and antiquity, and our own community of human experience—then he need not feel defeated by his modern positioning and his rejection of the superficial images and jingling rhymes of poets like d'Annunzio. He is part of a continuity that is both human and artistic, invoking grass, bees, and the seasoning of food as analogues to his own activity.

The speaker is now able in the seventh section to sketch out an ideal for his own nature, based on the rock/sea tension that has been present in the poem's imagery throughout. Imagining himself as a stone shaped and scarred by the action of the ocean, he sees that as an ideal marriage between the yielding and the unyielding, a kind of balancing:

> I'd like to be pocked and essential
> as the salt-eaten pebbles
> you toss around;
> a timeless splinter, evidence
> of a cold, unyielding will.

The pebble's surface is roughened (*scabro*, cognate with "scabbed") by the salt water, where we usually think of water as smoothing stones. Its evidence of roughness is also the testimony to its "essential" nature, reduced to its essence and surviving over long periods. Thus it is both a chip, flake, or splinter (*scheggia*), and it is free of temporality (*fuori del tempo*) because it is such vivid testimony to the ocean's steadiness of purpose. Aspiring to be a pebble or splinter seems a very modest ambition, but in the poem's context, where the speaker consistently elects simple things—bees, grass, salt, birds, rocks, daisies—as the true locus of value and the source of aesthetic authenticity, it is not surprising at all.

The speaker is forced to admit that his own character is more complex, mixed, and divided:

> Instead, I've been one who watches intently
> in himself and others the boiling away
> of a fleeting life—a man who defers
> the act that no one then destroys.

This observer is Hamlet-like, the quintessential man who observes and hesitates. He watches life boil away, and he reflects that his actions, if he does not take them, can at least then not be undone. He has meant well, certainly:

> I wanted to find the evil
> which eats away at the world, the tiny flaw
> of a lever that throws the cosmic machine
> out of gear; and I saw all
> the events of the moment
> ready to separate and collapse.

This ambitious desire to locate the evils of modern life, this prescience about how "things fall apart, the center cannot hold," has been hampered, as in Yeats, Eliot, and Rilke, by an intense self-consciousness:

> Following the furrow of a path, I had
> its opposite in my heart, inviting me;
> maybe I needed the knife that lops,
> the mind that decides and shapes itself.

This kind of independence and decisiveness would have separated him from his sense of dependence and relative helplessness: "I needed other books / besides your roaring page." Again, the metaphor links language as a human instinct with the natural world we inhabit. The bookish speaker has studied one text, albeit a sacred one, for too long and too exclusively. He is far too attached to the ocean's book, but he is defiant about this attachment: "But I can regret nothing; your song / still dissolves interior snarls. / Your delirium climbs to the stars." There is such a strong accord of inner and outer when the speaker is in the ocean's presence that even snarls and delirium do not deter him. He is firm about his allegiance to the song that gives rise to his song and to the delirium that connects the ocean even to the cosmos, a wilderness of meaning that, despite the absence of metaphysical structure and reassurance, gives the speaker a kind of blind faith in its value and its connection to his shaping aesthetic. This section, an unfolding affirmation that begins with a rough pebble and ends with a mighty tempest at sea, destructive and sublime, bespeaks a confidence of allegiance and poetic inspiration that is central to the suite as a whole.

The penultimate eighth section continues the discussion of a poetics that has turned out to be the main thrust of the poem.[5] Having achieved a level of discourse that makes a conversation with the ocean feel natural, even inevitable, the fledgling poet as the sea's ephebe can confess his doubts and fears. He begins by describing his ambitions:

> I'd like at least to be able to force
> into this struggling cadence of mine
> some little snatch of your raving;
> to possess the gift to attune
> all your voices to my stuttering speech.

He dreamed, he continues, of finding "salty words" that would express his melancholy, "that of an aging child / who should never have learned to think." The current reality, however, is discouraging. The poet is left with "fusty / words from the dictionary" and "the dark / voice of love, growing feeble, / turning to literary lament." The next comparison, of words to prostitutes, characterizing artistic disillusionment in terms of urban squalor, is the most memorable and modern gesture of the section:

> All I have are these words
> that offer themselves like streetwalkers
> to anyone that will have them;
> all I have are stale phrases
> that students and the rabble
> could steal from me tomorrow
> to turn into true verse.

The sense of defeat, of falling short of an artistic goal, leads to a sense of extinction that resembles a romantic experience of oneness with nature but is, in this context, more negative and deadly:

> And your boom grows louder
> and the new shadow, blue, expands.
> My thoughts fall behind, as if losing a race.
> I have no senses,
> no sense. I have no limits.

This is a kind of drowning, a loss of self that is both positive and negative, for both the reader and the poet. To have no sense or senses is a danger; to have no limits is a kind of expansion and exhilaration. The ambiguous next-to-last line, "M'abbandonano a prove i miei pensieri," has been variously translated as "My ideas desert me at the test" (Galassi), "My thoughts fail, they leave me" (Arrowsmith), and "As if to test me, my thoughts abandon me" (Mazza). The sense is of failing in some kind of contest, losing out. And the loss of thought seems to leave the poet/speaker helpless and faint.

Why does Montale enact such a collapse of confidence at this point? One answer lies in the idea of deliberate contrast with the poetic persona of d'Annunzio.[6] That poet had shaped his career around the idea of being a man of action: a heroic lover, with famous affairs (e.g., with Eleonora Duse); a war hero who wrote poems in praise of things like torpedo boats; and a patriot who led an abortive expedition to recover Fiume, which Italy had lost at the treaty of Versailles. If Montale was to reject d'Annunzio's rhetoric and his falsification of the natural world, he was also choosing to see himself as an unheroic, even a Prufrockian, sort of figure. Following the older poet's path led to Fascism, already a strong presence when Montale was working on *Ossi di seppia*. Some alternative had to be explored, even if it sounded humiliating. The shy, bookish young man did not know how he could become a major artist, but he knew unquestionably what path he wanted to reject. If that made him appear helpless and faint-hearted, then he would see whether that possibility could be exploited. He would go ahead and admit to his smallness and his melancholy, hoping, like Yeats with his admissions of self-division and doubt, to turn apparent weakness to artistic advantage. In fact, the experience of losing and drowning, the extinction of self, allows the poet/speaker to emerge with greater strength and confidence in the final lyric of the sequence.[7]

He has given himself up to the sea, and he lets it stand for his fate. His individual identity is subsumed and negligible, no longer a subject for anxiety. If the sea wishes to, it can extinguish his life as a teacher might erase a blackboard. In addition, death, it turns out, would be welcome as a completion, a collecting of what has been dispersed. Faith in this process gives the speaker a sense of both resignation and peculiar strength:

> I wait to return to your circle
> when my scattered passage is complete.
> My coming was a witness
> to an order I forgot along the way.
> My very words confirm
> an impossible happening they can't fathom.

The poet's words point beyond themselves and beyond the self and personality of the poet. In this sense, d'Annunzio's cult of personal heroism is more than a little ridiculous. There is no way such an individual can be close to the meaning and presence of the sea. His egotism will always interpose itself. To the more modest artist, then, eschewing the heroic and the tragic, is given the truer and more enduring insight:

> But always, as I listened to
> your soft surf breaking on the shore
> amazement seized me

like someone with almost no memory,
come suddenly home to the past.

It was necessary to be silent and a good listener in order to pick up the sea's whispering backwash. When the connection occurs, it is like an amnesiac recovering his past, reconnecting to his own memory and that of others. In his confidence that the subtler motions and meanings of the sea can be available only to his brand of artistic humility, the speaker can close his sequence with a burst of abnegation that is paradoxically a full artistic realization:

Having taken my lessons
less from your rapid glory, more
from that slow panting that makes
almost no sound on your desolate noondays,
I surrender now in humility. I'm only
a spark from a thyrsus: to burn—
that's my meaning, and nothing else.

That the speaker is resigned to the brevity of his life and the inevitability of his death would seem to make the sequence rather downbeat and melancholy. However, the final image is of light and fire, an assertion of artistic splendor. It is also appropriately brief and small, a spark from a torch, but it feels defiant in its confident assertion. By using a thyrsus (*tirso*), Montale makes one deliberate raid on d'Annunzio's poetic world and diction. D'Annunzio's poems are filled with mythic references that confidently link him to the ancient world and Dionysian revels. A thyrsus is the wreathed staff, "ivy-wreathed and phallic," of the god and his initiates.[8] Making a torch of it brings both light and ephemeral fire into a scene of Dionysian celebration, and in the context of the poem it reconciles two opposed elements, fire and water.

By appropriating the kind of mythic reference d'Annunzio was fond of, Montale slyly inserts his own more modernist and realist poetics between d'Annunzio and nature, effectively dismissing the older poet even as he "surrenders" to the sea in his "humility." It is a brilliant move that combines abnegation with powerful self-assertion, and it makes what looks like a defeated closure into something of a brilliant artistic and rhetorical victory. It is hard to go back to a book like *Alcyone* after one has been reading the "Mediterranean" sequence and the rest of *Ossi di seppia.* None of it seems real or relevant.

In later years Montale moved away from the Ligurian coast, both literally and figuratively. Ahead lay Florence and an expanding horizon that led to difficult encounters with contemporary history (Fascism, Nazism, World War II) and Dantesque surveys of the century he found himself living through. Nonetheless, the aesthetic sketched out in this youthful sequence, emphasizing modesty, circumspection, and a poetics founded on realistic accounts of the natural world and of human limitations, would sustain Montale throughout an entire career, marking him as one of the greatest of the modernist poets. I might have chosen a more confused and embittered modernist "moment" from this period, a poem such as "Arsenio." Still, I feel that the Mediterranean sequence, wonderfully sustained and beautifully negotiated as it is, remains a powerful example of this poet's emergent modernism, one that links him to our other poets, to Rilke's exploitation of self-consciousness, to Yeats's making advantages out of weaknesses, to Stevens's resolve to kick away the scaffoldings and reassurances of metaphysics, to Williams's celebration of the local and the mundane, and to Moore's renegotiation of the romantic sublime on modernist terms. The poem reminds us that Montale's greatness was his own while it also links him to a remarkable artistic community that was transcending national borders and linguistic barriers in its search for new ways of expressing the human dilemma and the possibilities for art.

CONCLUSION

HAVING COME to the end of our examination of six poets and the moments of making that produced our six poems, it might be useful to survey briefly the territory traversed. What features stand out? What common strategies and shared understandings link the poems we have been exploring?

We might start with issues of poetic form. All six poets are using traditional aspects of poetic form while making sharp modifications. The line and the stanza, for example, are still features of their poetic medium, but they do not always behave recognizably.

Yeats might be called the most traditional since he uses rhyme and a regular stanza pattern that can be identified as *ottava rima*, the stanza form that Byron adapted from Boccaccio, Ariosto, Tasso, Pulci, and Frere and that, used in narrative poems like *Don Juan* and *The Vision of Judgment*, brings a comic snap to the storytelling, especially in the comical closures of the couplets. But Yeats's use of this rhyme scheme produces very different results. He signals his intentions to be less traditional by employing off-rhyme—the first stanza rhymes *questioning, sing,* and *everything,* but it also rhymes *replies, history,* and *eyes,* then *upon* and *man*—and by making the couplets quizzical rather than comical. He will not sound like Byron or Ariosto, though Byron's fluency and informality are attractive to him. And while his poem has comic flavorings, it is somber and meditative at its core.[1]

Stevens's line is familiar as well, based on the unrhymed iambic pentameter we associate with Shakespeare, Milton, Wordsworth, and Keats. The fact that he finds this a perfectly acceptable medium for his Sunday-morning meditation about the spiritual standoff between religion and art suggests that his essential modernism is to be found in choices other than the prosodic. His echoing of tradition is part of his way of marking his differences from it, a feature he shares with Yeats.

Rilke and Montale, although not particularly traditional, do not make war on traditional ideas about the line and stanza. They loosen and modify them for their own purposes, so we feel that their prosodic choices are driven by subject and by the speaker's emotional response rather than by rules, formulas, and precedents. Rilke could be said to be working with the classical elegiac manner and Montale with a variation of it. Their relation to meditative poems of a more traditional sort (e.g., "Tintern Abbey") is comfortable and evident.

Moore and Williams emerge as the most experimental of the group. Moore works close to prose, mixing poetic effects with deliberately prosaic movements and articulations, even causing readers to wonder why what she's doing should be called poetry. Williams commits himself to free verse and to a handling of line and stanza that is clearly intended to be "organic," dictated by the subject and unique to its particular moment of composition.

The technical spectrum of prosodic choices, showing a range of experimentation, is further evident when we inquire about genres and categories. Rilke, Moore, and Montale, it seems to me, are doing modern versions of the ancient form known as the ode. This was traditionally a poem of praise and celebration, ecstatic in manner and often centered on an event, an object, or a concept. It was sometimes cast in regular stanzas, but it could also be irregular in movement. The irregular ode, reaching back to Pindar, had unpredictable line and stanza lengths and thus felt more spontaneous and occasional, with form matching subject and occasion. The rapturous tone felt like a sustaining of high speech and bardic authority, the poetic frenzy of inspiration. The roses of Rilke, the mountain of Moore, and the sea of Montale in their own modernist ways extend and elaborate the ode tradition in ways that feel appropriate to the new art of the twentieth century.

But Montale is also associating himself with another old form. Like Stevens, Yeats, and Williams, he is writing a suite based on the idea of a series of dances, variations on a theme. Again, this is familiar to tradition, a gathering of lyric moments around a common subject. The idea of the dance, which may take you somewhere but will also bring you back, a kind of moving in place, seems essential to what each poet is trying to accomplish. Montale addresses himself to the sea nine times. Stevens comes back eight times to the subject of art's relation to theological dogma until he has aired it thoroughly. Williams wants to make sure that his voyage on a January morning, his crossing of a river that becomes a border between the ordinary and the extraordinary, a border that dissolves in joy, is a movement that has pattern and design, fifteen vignettes arranged and numbered with Roman numerals, a sense of ordering that exists in tension with the scattering of observation and the motion of exploration. Yeats, meanwhile, wants his meditation on change and aging to rise to a level of formality and exactness, eight rhymed and matching octaves that bestow dignity and symmetry on the disorderly histories of minds and bodies.

The ode and the suite, then, prove to be useful modernist forms because they are extremely adaptable to circumstance and subject. Their flexible possibilities are amply demonstrated by the different results they produce in the examples of each mode.

We must also take note of the problematic nature of poetic closure as a feature of modernism. Or perhaps we should say the lack of closure? Rilke ends with a giant question. Aren't all of us, he wants to know, like these roses? Well, possibly, although the fighting boys are not really like that, and a bitter aftertaste lingers from their vivid difference from the bowl of roses. We sense the pressure to relocate the human dimension, the ideality of a common sense of being, but we also see that the roses are roses and we are whatever we happen to be as we read and ponder the poem. If we can say "yes" to the question "Aren't all of us like that?" we bring the affirmative answer as much from our own response as we do from finding it firmly fixed in Rilke's portrait of the world.

Similarly, Yeats finds it useful to close with questions. That some have seen them as genuine and others as rhetorical once again signals the equivocal nature of modernist endings and resolutions. The debate that has surrounded the end of Yeats's poem is lively testimony to the difficulty of arriving at an agreement about what it means. The ending's ability to generate endless speculation shows that it is really no ending at all, any more than it is a beginning. The dance must—and will—go on.

Stevens closes his poem with magisterial and memorable images. He seems more inclined to assertions—"we live in an old chaos of the sun"—than to questions, but because his assertions cast off old beliefs in favor of new and "unsponsored" definitions of existence, they launch us into a future of uncertainty and flux, the "ambiguous undulations" of the pigeons' wings taking us and them "downward to darkness," to nightfall and skepticism as well as to wonder.

Williams's ending is a memorable openness about aesthetic purpose, an attempt to connect with an audience after first asserting art's solipsism and independence. It moves from a certainty of purpose ("All this—was for you, old woman") to a degree of doubt ("But you got to try hard") to a somewhat evasive analogy and question ("Well, you know how / the young girls . . .?") to a final word ("somehow") that leaves a great deal unresolved and up in the air.

Moore's poem closes with an avalanche that both asserts the mountain's splendor and dangerous otherness and feels like an arbitrary curtailment of the cataloging and celebrating that has gone on so long and could obviously go on much longer. Neatness of finish has been longed for and ridiculed so fully by the time we get to that closing moment that it is difficult to think of the ending as anything much in the way of a conclusion and resolution. This most open and most experimental of our group of six is faithful to its own choices, right to the final period.

Montale's closure is, as he says, a "surrender" that comes from his recognition of insignificance. He celebrates the sea, not himself, and if he can assert any mastery or any fire of inspiration and utterance, it is the momentary "spark" from a torch, part of a dark ceremony, a temporary flash that discloses the surrounding dark. The pessimism is rather like Stevens's brand, a courageous stoicism without petulance or self-pity. It leaves the reader the choice of how to respond and what, if anything, to believe.

Darkness is wonderfully summoned, we notice, by the close of each of these six poems, and the different forms it takes testify to their enormous variety. In Rilke it is "the darkening of the earth at evening" and "the vague command of the distant stars." In Yeats it is the midnight oil that burns to sustain the hard-won and "blear-eyed" wisdom, and it is the brightening glance of the dancer that suggests a surrounding dark as backdrop. In Stevens it is the famous sunset that sends the birds home to roost and brings the poem and the reader "downward" with them to an ambiguous rest and an equivocal lodging in the vast American wilderness. In Williams it is the fact that the girls are out on the avenue "after dark / when they ought to be home in bed," a lighthearted invocation of night and misbehavior. In Moore it is the last glimpse of the great mountain, "rain falling in the valleys and snow falling on the peak," before vision is cut off by the curtain of snow produced by the avalanche, a darkness produced by whiteness. And in Montale it is the spark from the thyrsus, glimpsed against a huge and surrounding night. I spoke in my introduction of walking into the brilliant light and profound shadow of modernist poetry. The theme of darkness helps illuminate the degree of skepticism and uncertainty that these poets naturalized as part of their new understanding of art, an art whose purpose is not to resolve or confirm but to question and to admit and face the failures that their century needed to confront and acknowledge.

At the same time, I think that their intense skepticism about the past, in particular the materialist, rationalist, humanist tradition of the Enlightenment, was giving birth to new insights that connected, for these poets, both to the deeper past, humankind's preliterate insights, and to the future, to a repudiation of history as tragic and experience as solipsistic. In place of these traditional views, they worked out models of being that posited a continuity between mind and world, spirit and matter, self and nonself. Rilke rises to an affirmation of our kindredness with the roses. Yeats faces—and then defaces—the tragic sense of self he has both cultivated and endured as a private and public agony. Stevens defies American Protestantism's stifling hegemony in order to embrace his environment and the ephemeral, unstable world of the senses that links him to it. Williams, too, makes a kind of paganism out of his bond with Whitman and his willingness to take on the world just as he sees it, hears it, smells it, and tastes it. Moore makes her mountain an implicit and explicit critique of human pride in human constructions and overconfidence. Linking her art to nature's vastness and strangeness also gives her common ground with Montale, who fashions an aesthetic born of his confidence in the greatness and power of the chaotic and beautiful ocean.

These gestures toward a new way of understanding being, rising from repudiations of traditional hierarchies and values, mark the hopeful and haunting side of modernism. They are the reason we need not see Eliot or Auden or Pound as perfect exemplars of modernist practice. In their separate ways, embracing Anglican Christianity in the first two cases and fascist dogmas in the third, all three were too unwilling, finally, to let go of traditional values they had invested in both as artists and as individuals. Totalizing systems of explanation and dogma are finally not compatible with the modernist spirit, at least as I understand it. The stories of such compromising may be tragic, but they need not provide the dominant narrative.

Diversity, finally, is the characteristic of these modernist moments that I find most striking. While some generalizations about attitudes toward form and subject are certainly possible, what also asserts itself again and again is the uniqueness of each of these texts. Since they proceed from a sense that modernist art pledges itself to uniqueness and to a discarding of assumptions, rules, precedents, and demands from outside structures and authorities, it is surely the most eloquent testimony, finally, that poems as hugely different as, say, "Among School Children" and "An Octopus" can be said to belong to the elastic category of modernist poetry. That helps illuminate, I think, the effort and testimony with which this book has involved itself.

NOTES

INTRODUCTION

1. "Tom Swift has vanished too / / Who worked at none but wit's expense, / Putting dirigibles together, / Out in the yard, in the quiet weather / Whistling behind Tom Sawyer's fence" ("Folk Tune").

2. Phenomenological psychology also explored these insights in the work of William James and Eugene Minkowski (Kern). Recent studies in the area of neuroscience (Damasio, 1995, 1999) have confirmed them as well.

3. Nabokov, 142.

CHAPTER 1. RAINER MARIA RILKE

1. Freedman (261–66). The three women were his hostess, Alice Faehndrich, Baroness Julie von Nordeck zu Rabenau, and Countess Manon zu Solms-Laubach. The cottage he was using was called the Rose Cottage ("Rosenhäusl"). The flowers in the poem, according to Freedman, "were modeled on the yellow rose the Countess Mary Gneisenau had presented to him as a farewell gift when she saw him in Berlin before his departure." Hobnobbing with countesses and baronesses doesn't necessarily square with the image of an innovative modernist, breaking ground and defying convention, but Rilke found their company thrilling and necessary. In a certain sense, they were roses, too.

2. In addition to Freedman, biographies and biographical studies include those by Leppmann, Prater, and Kleinbard.

3. "Living near Worpswede, having chosen painters as his closest companions, marked Rilke for life. The gradual development of the late 1890s now gained momentum during the early 1900s: he gave himself more and more completely to a passion for the visual arts, including the desire to view visual objects in the light of their historical role. In the spring of 1902, during his final months as a householder, Rilke completed the first of his important monographs on art, his *Worpswede*, preceded by an additional essay about Heinrich Vogeler's work" (Freedman 158).

4. See Torgerson, *Dear Friend*. See also Torgerson, "You Must Change Your Art," and Carol Muske, "Retrieving the Lament: Red Shadows, Red Echoes between 'Requiem' and 'Self-Portrait, 1906,'" in *FIELD* 63.

5. Bernstein (11ff).

6. Edward Snow observes, in his Introduction to Rilke, *New Poems* [1907], that "Seldom is visual perception an end in itself, and often it is the focus of a poem's deconstructive energies: a gazelle dissolves into the stream of discontinuous metaphors that evoke it; a marble fountain becomes a complex microcosm of fluid interchanges and secret relations" (xi).

7. There is a tendency to see the "extinction" at the end as the animals'. For example, consider Freedman: "Vibrancy within is canceled by uncomprehending perception that kills each spark of recognition as it reaches the core of himself. . . . The panther has become wholly *thing*" (172). But this preserves the subject/object dichotomy that Rilke is trying to subvert. Being seen by the thing you are seeing is, as this and other poems demonstrate, crucial to the revolution of consciousness that the *New Poems* seek.

8. This insight is anticipated in "Früher Apollo" (Early Apollo), which opens the *Neue Gedichte*. There the god's gaze, which is also early spring sunlight, means that "nothing in his head / could hinder the radiance of all poems // from hitting us with almost deadly force" because "there's still no shadow in his gaze." Sunlight as something that sees us, in other words, can be both thrillingly beautiful and dangerous to our own precarious identity.

9. For an account of Husserl's breakthrough, see Edwards, especially the chapter titled "Heidegger and the Overcoming of Subjectivity." See also Abram, *The Spell of the Sensuous*.

10. *Letters on Cézanne* (34).

11. Later poets (e.g., Stevens and Williams) would make excellent use of the still life. However, I have not found a significant example that predates Rilke. It might be argued that "object poems" by romantic and symbolist poets constitute a precedent, but they do not invoke the still life as a genre in and of itself. Other still life examples in the *New Poems* include "Blaue Hortensie" (vol. 1) and "Rosa Hortensie" (vol. 2). Rilke also did short studies of the rose interior, the opium poppy, and the heliotrope. These are like sketches compared to the large canvas, "The Bowl of Roses."

12. Gass misses this fact in his *Reading Rilke*: "Bullyboys, actors, tellers of tale tales, runaway horses—fright, force and falsification—losing composure, pretending, revealing pain and terror: these are compared to the bowl of roses" (4–5). But the point is contrast, not comparison. Gass has missed the cue "But now you know how that's forgotten." No wonder he finds the opening "oddly violent and discordant."

13. I owe this insight to a suggestion by Peter Schmidt.

14. While "visionary power" is a correct translation of "innern Sehkraft," it should be noted that "innern" connects with "lauter Inneres" ("pure inwardness") in line 20 and "eine Hand voll Innres" ("a handful of inwardness") in line 72, the next-to-last line. Thus the German does a better job of connecting the visionary and the inner than does the English.

15. Snow translates the line "And aren't all that way: simply self-containing" (197),

and Bernstein offers the following: "And aren't all [the roses] that way, containing just themselves" (13).

16. Nov. 19, 1925. Cited in Rilke, *Sonnets to Orpheus,* tr. M. D. Herter Norton (131–36). The fact that the fighting boys are acting as if "attacked by bees" is another instance of their wrong relation to both nature and poetry. They have trespassed, in effect, on sacred territory.

17. Freedman 270.

CHAPTER 2. WILLIAM BUTLER YEATS

1. For an account of *The Tower,* with attention to its organization and themes, see my *Troubled Mirror.*

2. Yeats was embroiled in frequent controversy with the Catholic press at this time. He kept pointing out that the church was given to interference in the affairs of the state, and they in turn attacked him as dirty-minded and pagan for supporting divorce and publishing poems like "Leda and the Swan." See Cullingford 185f.

3. That poem became the title poem for a volume that is strangely mixed, combining poems in his romantic and symbolist manner with poems that edge toward his modernist phase. See my essay "The Living World for Text."

4. The mixture of symbolism and modernism in *The Tower* and its relation to the issue of self-presentation are discussed in my essay "High Talk: The Voice from *The Tower.*"

5. I think that Yeats's marriage to Georgie Hyde-Lees in 1917, along with his purchase of the tower, Ballylee, near Lady Gregory's estate, helped significantly in recasting his artistic self-conception. He was responding to the war, of course, and to the pressures of history, but he saw the tower and the marriage as a new page in his life, and it is telling that poems related to the tower and the marriage, like "The Phases of the Moon," are among those in which he fully exploits the possibility of self-ridicule as a dramatic and rhetorical device. By the time he writes "The Tower" and "Nineteen Hundred and Nineteen," he is fully in control of this new rhetoric. A good account of Yeats's exploration of modernism, in conversations with Ezra Pound, can be be found in Longenbach's *Stone Cottage.*

6. This keeps happening throughout *The Tower.* We think that the protagonist has addressed and resolved the issues of old age, for example, only to find it resurfacing intact in the next poem. I take up the effect of this on the collection as a whole in *Troubled Mirror.*

7. The nun's presence in fact argues its relation to more traditional forms of education (as it also suggests that Ireland's modernity, rooted in Roman Catholicism as it is, has definite limits).

8. In fact, the historical Yeats knew quite a bit about Montessori education, as Torchiana demonstrates. Moreover, he had found himself much in sympathy with the reformist educational ideas of Gentile, as I later demonstrate. The point here is

simply that the poem's reader gets an impression of superficial communication and deflected sympathies, as part of the rhetorical and narrative strategy.

9. The egg also comes from Aristophanes, who notes that Zeus divided the spheres as a hair might bisect a cooked egg. But I think Yeats associates such intense empathy with motherhood and prenatal states, so that Leda and Helen come into it, too. Helen was a twin to Clytemnestra, and Leda also produced another pair of twins, Castor and Pollux. That makes either two double-yolked eggs or four, hatched two at a time.

10. The blending of their natures is somewhat suspect, given these two images. The images that the "Yeats" of the poem chooses are open to criticism for their failure to address issues successfully, and we must be alert for the way that "Yeats" the author may use them to characterize his persona's failings.

11. The word "wild" serves, among other things, to evoke other Yeats poems, most notably "The Wild Swans at Coole," "Easter 1916," and "Leda and the Swan," with its violent rape scene.

12. It was Brooks who noticed that Yeats is probably using Hans Christian Anderson's story "The Ugly Duckling" as his inspiration for the idea of the baby swan among ducklings, one kind of paddler mistaken for another. The allusion would seem to sharpen both the comedy and the pathos.

13. The best candidate, in my view, for something hollow of cheek that looks as though it drinks wind and eats shadows is Donatello's *Penitent Magdalene*, an extraordinary image carved of wood, with gold and polychrome. The Magdalene is striking for its realistic depiction of someone who has experienced the ravages of age and suffering. It has Maud's strong chin, high cheekbones, and piercing eyes. What makes the Donatello link problematic is the existence of earlier drafts. One has "As da Vinci crayon fashioned it," and another has "What Quintocento finger fashioned it." See Parkinson (95). In any case, the unspecified "Quattrocento finger" gives the reader a good deal of leeway in imagining the appropriate image. Brooks, for example, picks Botticelli because he is interested in stressing the sharp contrast between scarecrow and a Maud who is still swanlike: "It is as ideal as if a painter like Botticelli, say, had fashioned it" (167).

14. In "Sailing to Byzantium," written around the same time, Yeats had explored the scarecrow image—"An aged man is but a paltry thing, / A tattered coat upon a stick"—and had tried to displace it with an automaton—a mechanical bird of "hammered gold and gold enameling"—that was more attractive but also scarcely a full solution to the problem. See Tiffany (17–21).

15. When we read "honey of generation had betrayed" we face a choice: Either "shape" or "lap" could be the subject of the verb "betrayed." Yeats obviously wants us to take it both ways, though the syntax goes on to resolve the choice in favor of "shape."

16. I thought for a long time that "shape" was intended to suggest the fetus, apparent only as a bulge on the pregnant mother, a child not even born yet. The betrayal of

the soul would occur at conception, which summons and entraps it, rather than at the actual birth. It seems more likely that Yeats has an infant in mind. Earlier drafts of the poem include "What mother with a child upon her breast" and "What youthful mother, rocking on her lap / A fretful thing that knows itself betrayed." See Bradford (9–11). Still, the draft should not constrain the final text, and "shape" is deliberately more ambiguous than "child" or even "thing," so readers can imagine a fetus if they so choose.

17. They feel almost interchangeable at times. One can imagine a stanza with "Is labour dancing or blossoming?" and "you are the leaf, the blossom and the bole," although that would keep the poem from ending on the note of interrogation.

18. In that sense it is something of a reprise of the issues treated in an earlier symbolist poem, "Adam's Curse," as Dawson points out. The curse that is discussed in that poem is the fact that nothing can be achieved without labor in this world. At the end the protagonist and his companions fall silent, and he feels they have all grown weary hearted from the effort involved in making beauty and art. Thus, the conclusions of the two poems are opposite in effect and meaning.

19. Ideas about dance were shifting, of course, from the prescribed and notated choreography of the ballet to the improvisatory dances of Loie Fuller (whom we know Yeats admired) and Isadora Duncan. Those changes made knowing the dancer from the dance even more difficult.

20. I say "reincarnation" because the Platonic theory underlying the idea that honey of generation draws immortal souls into life also contains the idea that this can happen to a soul more than once. In "The Phases of the Moon" Yeats outlines an entire theory whereby souls journey through a progressive set of selves from which they may or may not eventually be able to escape completely.

21. *Allegories of Reading* (11). Sokolsky characterizes de Man's reading as follows: "De Man's persuasive analysis of the closing lines argues that the final question must be read both rhetorically and literally. Thus its irreconcilable meanings as triumphant assertion of unity and despairing uncertainty endlessly undo one another, putting meaning *en abyme*" (77). This insight, although I would express it differently, seems mostly to confirm the poem's modernism.

22. Sokolsky (78). A fetish, for Sokolsky, is "an erotically charged and displaced figure for a larger, unattainable desire" (i.e., the dancer stands for Maud Gonne).

23. Sokolsky (68). She may have in mind a reading like Parkinson's: "With this last stanza the problems posed by the poem were transported into a world of transcendent possibilities, successes beyond the reach of the divided life embodied in the first four stanzas of the poem and in the aspirations of great intellects" (108).

24. Brooks (171).

25. Ibid. (174).

26. De Man (12). Stanley Cavell points out that de Man is reading the verb "know" as if it means "tell" or "distinguish." He goes on: "But knowing from, in Yeats' line,

goes altogether beyond telling. The line asks how we know the dancer from, meaning by means of, the dance; how it is that the dance can reveal the dancer. (If the dance and the dancer were, as it were, the same thing then this would be no question. As things are, the question is simultaneously one of epistemology and of aesthetics.) But the line equally asks how we can know from, meaning know apart from, the dance; meaning know the dancer *away* from the dance" (Cavell, 195). So "know" can mean "distinguish," "know by means of," and "know apart from." At least no one has proposed its biblical sense, at least not yet.

27. Sokolsky (69).

28. Sokolsky (68).

29. Brooks (174–75). And Parkinson adds to the passage quoted earlier, "Two of Yeats's favorite icons standing for unity of being, the tree and the dancer, represent an integrity of parts so welded as to make any abstraction from them impossible, dramatizing . . . the flow of flesh under the impulse of passionate thought" he so admired (108).

30. Parkinson notes: "The poem flirts with the danger of casting doubts on its own resolutions, largely because it exhibits in its dramaturgy a multiple poetics" (51).

31. Margaret Mills Harper notes that "Gentile locates the real in the act" and that in his writings "disciplines that follow Aristotle in regarding the individual mind as separate from the reality it considers are criticized" (110).

32. *Letters* (922).

33. The way in which these key words interact in the poem is discussed in Dawson. For example, "If one considers labor to be that which achieves salvation as the true achievement, and spontaneous participation in present joy as the only salvation, then, in the activity of these two final images of 'Among School Children,' 'labour' and 'play' are one" (295). "Play" comes into the poem through Plato's spume, Aristotle's "taws," and Pythagoras's fiddling.

CHAPTER 3. WALLACE STEVENS

1. Several commentators remark on this, most notably Michel Benamou: "The best example of Stevens' pictorial method of composition is to be found in the structure of 'Sunday Morning,' his most celebrated long poem" (12). MacLeod discusses this as well. See also Buttel, who is almost persuaded that Stevens had set out "to abolish the distinctions between poetry and painting" (148).

2. Robert Frost and Hart Crane, while not treated in this study, present further examples of the way that American modernism, on the ground, developed around a more specific response to place and local culture.

3. I find myself connecting it with American painters like Marsden Hartley, Stuart Davis, Georgia O'Keeffe, and Charles Burchfield, as well as with those nature writers who can be seen as descendents of the transcendentalists—John Muir, John Burroughs, and Henry Beston.

4. See especially Voros's study and her second chapter, "'The Westwardness of Everything': Stevens's Ktaadn." Excerpts from the journal Stevens kept in British Columbia during August 1903, are to be found in *L* (64–67).

5. For accounts of this period see Richardson and MacLeod.

6. Sidney Feshbach argues for the close correspondence between "Sunday Morning" and Santayana's *Interpretations of Poetry and Religion* in "A Pretext for Wallace Stevens' 'Sunday Morning.'" I stress Santayana's importance to Stevens's thought in "A Skeptical Music."

7. Emily Dickinson had struggled with similar issues in her life and poems: "Some keep the Sabbath going to church—/ I keep it, staying at Home—/ With a Bobolink for a Chorister / And an Orchard, for a Dome." The poem concludes with a phenomenological insight: "So instead of getting to Heaven, at last—/ I'm going, all along."

8. Her uneasiness led to a shortened and reorganized version, dropping stanzas II, III, and VI and reordering the poem I-VIII-IV-V-VII. Richardson notes: "In excluding Sections II, III, and VI from the poem as it was published in *Poetry*, Harriet Monroe . . . heard in her mind the censorious comments of the commonsense society were the excised stanzas to appear" (436). On June 6, 1915, Stevens had written Monroe: "Provided your selection of the numbers of *Sunday Morning* is printed in the following order: I, VIII, IV, V, I see no objection to cutting down. The order is necessary to the idea" (*L* 183). On June 23 he agreed to add stanza VII as an ending and to a change of the phrase "on disregarded plate," even though his explanation had clarified its meaning.

9. Readers have wondered whether the bird might be an image woven into the rug rather than a real pet, but that does not really account for "green freedom" satisfactorily.

10. Or dishabille: "A loose negligee; also the state of being dressed in a loose or careless style; undress" (*Webster's Second Unabridged*).

11. Ezra Pound had written a poem with a peignoir in it the year before, in 1914, "Albatre":

> The lady in the white bath-robe which she calls a peignoir,
> Is, for the time being, the mistress of my friend,
> And the delicate white feet of her little white dog
> Are not more delicate than she is,
> Nor would Gautier himself have despised their contrasts in whiteness
> As she sits in the great chair
> Between two indolent candles.

This is both painterly and aesthetic enough to have given Stevens a precedent. Its whiteness recalls Whistler's aesthetics and suggests that Stevens is deliberately invoking the newer painting styles (e.g., Fauve) by means of his bright and contrasting colors. Stevens's poem can be seen in part, then, as a vigorous rewriting of the indolence and decadence Pound was borrowing from Whistler and Gautier.

12. The choice of "measures" of course reinforces the preference for art over the-ology. It invokes poetic measure as well as the idea of music and dancing. The emphasis on pleasure led Yvor Winters to accuse Stevens of hedonism, along with dandyism, but as numerous commentators have demonstrated, the poem is Epi-curean rather than hedonist, and the dandyism, a kind of verbal clowning that Stevens was prone to use as a protective mask, is put aside for the most part.

13. Feshbach, in "Elegy Rebuffed by Pastoral Eclogue," summarizes the position nicely: "The doctrinal implication of his argument is that if she will rid herself of a desire to escape this, the only world and her desire to cling to moments essentially and necessarily subject to natural change, his Epicurean philosophy allows her to retain her pursuit of pleasure and, most importantly, to perceive beauty in nature and in the laws of nature. She should sacrifice sacrifice" (245).

14. Stevens had written to Elsie in 1907: "I am not in the least religious. The sun clears my spirit, if I may say that, and thinking of blue valleys, and the odor of the earth, and many things. Such things make a god of a man; but a chapel makes a man of him. Churches are human" (L 96). An earlier letter is similarly explicit: "An old argument with me is that the true religious force in the world is not the church but the world itself; the mysterious callings of Nature and our responses" (L 58).

15. I have in mind especially the lines "She dwells with Beauty—Beauty that must die; / And Joy, whose hand is ever at his lips / Bidding adieu."

16. Death is often masculine (e.g., the Grim Reaper), but in Italian, for example in Petrarch, death is feminine, partly by virtue of the language itself.

17. This may be what leads Helen Vendler to remark that "The exquisite cadences of *Sunday Morning* are in fact corpse-like, existing around the woman's desires in a waxy perfection of resignation" (57).

18. Shades of Yeats, who of course had not yet written "Among School Children."

19. *Le Danse*, painted in 1909, was already justly famous. Its ring of naked women seems to be an enlargement of a group Matisse had put at the center of *Le bonheur de vivre* (1905–1906, owned by Gertrude and Leo Stein), probably after a composition by Ingres called *L'age d'or*. If Stevens knew of this, the transformation from "Golden Age" to "the happiness of life" would have both amused him and reinforced his views.

20. It was Anne Tashjian who first suggested this to me. The Stravinsky had pre-miered on May 29, 1913, in Paris, and the performance had an instant notoriety. The Arensberg circle would no doubt have been discussing it, perhaps from eyewitness accounts by some of its members, right around the time Stevens wrote "Sunday Morning." The coincidence of primitive dancing and modern art, along with the date, make the event and music, as a source for Stevens, too great to ignore. (This doesn't mean that Stevens had actually heard the music; the U.S. premiere wasn't until 1922 in Philadelphia, by Stokowski.) For a useful account of Stravinsky's piece and its place in the modernist preoccupation with spring, primitivism, and renewal,

see the "Spring, Sacred and Profane" chapter in Conrad, *Modern Times, Modern Places* (381–99).

21. Longenbach (1991, 65–66) feels that the death of so many young men in World War I contributed to the feeling of the fellowship among men that perish. The historical circumstance makes that plausible, but it is important to recognize that for Stevens the democracy of mortality is universal, not dependent on wars, plagues, or any other special forms of loss.

22. Jacqueline Vaught Brogan feels that Stevens often suppresses "what *he* perceives to be his feminine voice, or, more accurately, that part of his poetic voice that is feminine metaphorically in the way the idea of 'feminine' itself is metaphorical" (4). She adds that "while Stevens would always suffer from a schism within himself, one that ultimately derived from cultural biases against women (and which would affect his poetry in a number of important ways), he would also come as close as it was possible for a person in his time and circumstance to 'curing' himself."

23. Bates (112): "[S]he concludes that we live on a physical and temporal island, at once free of divine despotism and shackled to a world of flux and death." In 1928 Stevens answered a query about the poem as follows: "This is not essentially a woman's meditation on religion and the meaning of life. It is anybody's meditation" (*L* 250). This surely confirms the wish to lessen the speaker's authority and open the poem to speculation and creativity from the reader.

24. Vendler feels that the particulars that follow the generalizations "are allegorical instances of the abstract formulation. . . . The scene, in short, is being used largely as an instance of a thesis, not surrendered to in and for itself"(49). While I see her point, I can only propose that that is not how the lines feel to me when I read them. For me, the particulars *balance* the generalizations.

25. Our hunting them will affect them adversely, however. The last passenger pigeon, one symbol of the American wilderness and the human depredations on it, had died in the Cincinnati zoo the year before Stevens wrote his poem. The event was widely reported in the press.

26. *L* (73), quoted in Voros (44–45).

27. Bethea stresses this in a discussion of "Peter Quince at the Clavier": "For Stevens blurs the historical distinction between soul and body, noumenon and phenomenon; in his view spirituality is composite with, not separate from, corporeality, and it is *through* sensuality that we augment the soul. . . . Real *existence* constitutes a composite of the imaginary and the actual, the spiritual and the material, the ideal and the real" (215–16).

CHAPTER 4. WILLIAM CARLOS WILLIAMS

1. The volume was published in 1949, with an introduction by Randall Jarrell, and was, as Williams envisioned it would be, the standard textbook used to introduce his work to students for many years. In 1985 it was replaced by a new *Selected Poems*,

edited by the British poet Charles Tomlinson. "January Morning" is not included in that volume, with the result that it has now become one of Williams's less known and seldom discussed poems.

2. Pound sensed this, too, of course. He wrote the perfect Imagist poem and then went on to newer territories, as I later confirm.

3. Both Futurism, which came out of Italy, and Vorticism, which Pound and Wyndham Lewis had created in England, tended to stress energy and movement in a way that modified the principles of Imagism and Cubism.

4. This reading disagrees with that of Peter Schmidt, in his excellent study, and concurs with Magowan, who describes "a dawn journey to the ferry and across the Hudson to Manhattan" (30). Schmidt surmises that "The poem is about a ferry trip Williams took home to New Jersey after apparently staying up all night on duty in a New York hospital" (65). I base my reading on the fact that we begin by seeing the domes of the Church of the Paulist Fathers in Weehawken against a smoky dawn. That suggests that we are facing east and heading toward the river and the ferry slip at Weehawken (Weehauken). Later in the poem we are on the ferry, where, among other things, we can turn to look back at the Palisades. However, the fact that the direction of the journey is somewhat open to conjecture is significant, too. As with Whitman in "Crossing Brooklyn Ferry," Williams is not that concerned with whether he is coming or going. Or he may wish to imply that he is crossing in both directions, as my discussion of the later phases of the poem indicate. Still, I argue that going toward the light—the rising sun—in the dead of winter is crucial to Williams's sense of the journey's meaning. Biologically speaking, the poem is heliotropic.

5. Perhaps the best account of this aesthetic and the ways in which it involves readers in the creative process is to be found in David Walker's study *The Transparent Lyric*. For example, "Replacing the poet (or the lyric speaker, a poet-surrogate) with the reader as the center of dramatic attention, the poem becomes a transparent medium, a *process* of poetic activity rather than its product" (18).

6. Various critical attempts have tried to describe this relinquishing of authority and control in Williams. Riddel, for instance, invokes Foucault's adaptation of a Nietzschean idea, the *refus du commencement*: "the refusal to believe that one can trace a present thing or occurrence back to some remote, distant origin. . . . Rejecting this search for some lost center, authority, presence, or plenitude, Williams turns to the local as a centerless center" (12–13). Hillis Miller suggests that Williams turns himself inside out, becoming the world he contemplates and interacts with, disappearing into it, in effect. Both of these descriptions may go too far in reacting to what is new and different in Williams's handling of an author's traditional role and behavior. Walker's approach is more to the point. The idea that New Jersey is a "centerless center" would have amused Williams, though.

7. Dijkstra's account of this, in his first chapter, is particularly useful.

8. *CP*, notes (480).

9. *SL* (40).

10. The seductive rhythm of travel is suggested by an initial regularity, a certain dactylic jog that is brought up sharply at a key phrase: "I have discovered that most of / the beauties of travel are due to / the strange hours."

11. "Dirt-colored," while it may refer to the dark and even muddy clothing of construction workers, is likely to denote the men as African American. Since the glimpse is quick and the emphasis visual, this detail should probably not be overinterpreted.

12. Three of the poems in *Al que quiere!* are titled "Pastoral."

13. Lowney, citing Jonathan Culler, notes that apostrophe "functions in post-Enlightenment poetry as a strategy for overcoming the alienation of subject from object . . . by making the object function as a subject" (35). This is one function, certainly, and we could say that Williams is "overcoming alienation" from history and from English literature as well as from nature as he apostrophizes the "white gulls" to make Touchstone into a captain resembling Henry Hudson. Having started apostrophizing, he finds it difficult, subsequently, to stop, and his apostrophes culminate and collapse as he addresses the "old woman" in the final section.

14. Doyle notes the connection of the dance to the idea of a "suite": "The whole 'suite' is a dance of images, and also of all immediately observable phenomena in the universe. Their discreteness is an essential element in this dance. The young doctor, for the moment, is their dancing-master, the intensity of his relationship to them preventing a centrifugal tendency in the poem as a whole. The dance becomes openly identified with the technique of exact observation, the measuring, the imposition of order" (11).

15. "The Wanderer" ends, it might be noted, with a mystical marriage of man and river, in which the protagonist takes "the filthy Passaic" into himself and absorbs its full meaning. It is old and very dirty, but he is young and full of hope and possibility. Together they face the future possibilities of America.

16. *CP* (489).

CHAPTER 5. MARIANNE MOORE

1. This version is based on the 1935 *Selected Poems*, although I have normalized the spelling and punctuation, which are British in that edition, in accord with more recent editions that convert them to American. I have also numbered the lines for ease of reference in my discussion and corrected obvious typographical errors.

The version in Moore's 1924 volume, *Observations*, does not differ significantly from this text, although there are a few interesting variants. The version of the poem in Moore's so-called *Complete Poems*, until very recently the only edition in print, was cut by the author in 1951, primarily removing lines 129–61. My position is that most of Moore's late revisions were unfortunate and distortive. Until we have a variorum edition, readers are advised to seek out the 1935 *Selected* as the best source for Moore's poems up to that date.

2. Two commentators, Willis (*RP*) and Schulze, have professed to find two separate ascents of the mountain over the course of the poem. If this helps them organize their readings, fine; it's not especially distortive. However, the structure is more their imposition of it on the poem than something the poem tries to enact itself.

3. Or perhaps we should say twenty-eight, since one of them—"Neatness of finish!"—is an exact repetition, and Moore may have been conscious of matching the "twenty-eight ice fields from fifty to five hundred feet thick," the variation in glacier thickness, with the variation in sentence lengths.

4. The other poems from this period that I have in mind are "People's Surroundings" (75 lines), "Sea Unicorns and Land Unicorns" (82 lines), and the notoriously difficult "Marriage" (290 lines). Moore worked on several poems simultaneously in this period and took her time about finishing them. The question of her revisions and the harm they did her work are addressed in Walker, *Poets Reading*, particularly in the essays about "The Frigate Bird" (Young) and "Nine Nectarines and Other Porcelain" (Walker). I wish I could say that the new *Poems of Marianne Moore*, edited by Grace Schulman (2003), addresses these issues adequately; it does not.

5. It was only fairly recently that photography had enabled people to see things underwater—the Ward article Moore cites is preceded by a remarkable series of underwater photos of an octopus in action—and to have aerial views like the one depicted on the pamphlet's map, which shows Rainier to be strikingly octopus-like when viewed from high above.

6. This is from one of the articles she cites, by W. P. Pycraft, in the column called "The World of Science" in the *London Illustrated News*, June 28, 1924. She also cites articles from August 1923, in the *London Illustrated News* and the *London Graphic*. Her relishing of detail and phrasing from these articles—"spider fashion," "Picking periwinkles"—allows her to dismantle the casual comparison and salute the uniqueness of octopuses before she turns to a concentration on the uniqueness of the mountain.

7. This is discussed in the Ward article she cites from the *London Illustrated News* of August 11, 1923, p. 71.

8. "Slender, dark-brown worms live in countless millions in the surface ice. Microscopic rose-colored plants also thrive in such great numbers that they tint the surface here and there, making what is commonly called 'red snow.'" U.S. Department of the Interior, *National Parks Portfolio*, "In an Arctic Wonderland."

9. It seems appropriate to quote her note here: "*Glass that will bend*. Sir William Bell, of the British Institute of Patentees, has made a list of inventions which he says the world needs: glass that will bend; a smooth road surface that will not be slippery in wet weather; a furnace that will conserve 95 per cent of its heat; a process to make flannel unshrinkable; a noiseless airplane; a motor-engine of one pound per weight per horsepower; methods to reduce friction; a process to extract phosphorus from vulcanized indiarubber, so that it can be boiled up and used again; practical ways of utilizing the tides" (*SP* 120). That Moore assumes this list will interest her readers

(which indeed it should) breaks down the normal barriers between lyric poetry and other forms of knowledge and discourse. It's also interesting, many years later, to consider which of these items have been successfully produced.

10. It is characteristic of commentators that they feel that Moore's own attitudes become elusive as she disappears behind her quotations. Randall Jarrell wrote in 1952: "But the most extreme precision leads inevitably to quotation; and quotation is armor and ambiguity and irony all at once—turtles are great quoters. Miss Moore leaves the stones she picks up carefully uncut, but places them in an unimaginably complicated and difficult setting, to sparkle under the Northern lights of her continual irony" (201). This is about half correct. Making Moore into a turtle, armored and slow, does not do her justice. And "carefully uncut" does not reflect the way she shapes, revises, and sometimes deliberately misattributes her quotations (e.g., her attribution of "pride-producing language" to Trollope's *Autobiography* appears to be incorrect). The northern lights metaphor is brilliant, but it makes her poetic world colder and more consistently predictable than is really the case.

11. Moore seems to move toward prose as a way of escaping traditional notions of the poetic and reinventing poetry out of a new encounter with prose. She wrote to Yvor Winters in 1922: "For the litterateur, prose is a step beyond poetry, I feel, and then there is another poetry that is a step beyond that" (*SL* 192). Margaret Holley comments: "The quotation marks are a visible threshold, a boundary dividing poetic discourse from the ordinary discourse which it borrows. Quotation opens a window in the poem onto language from outside it, language now included but demarcated. . . . Poetic and practical language are thus made to collaborate openly in the production of the poem. . . . By means of this open collaboration the tacit intertextuality of the literary product is made visible" (68–69).

12. Grace Schulman argues that Moore evolves a poem of inner debate or dialectic, "a rhetorical scheme that approximates the mind in its growth by change" (54).

13. Cf. Molesworth: "'An Octopus' can be read, in part, as a poem about Warner, and about the choice of Christian over Greek values, and hence a poem about religion as much as about cultural values" (184). I agree with the first part of this assertion and am more dubious about what follows. Molesworth's reading assumes that "neatness of finish" is both good and Christian and that Moore is openly advocating it.

14. There is a 1922 photograph of a climbing party, including Marianne and Warner, in Willis (1987, 39). It is also included on the Willis website.

15. "I have been rather lackluster about speaking of work that I have been doing off and on for two years, but Mother has goaded me into completing it, so I am again at work on it—two poems, 'Sea Unicorns and Land Unicorns,' and 'An Octopus,' which is descriptive of Mt. Rainier in Washington." Letter to Bryher, Sept. 9, 1924 (*SL* 208).

16. It's worth noting in passing that her review of Williams's *Kora in Hell* singles out for praise the poem that was the subject of my preceding chapter: "How many

poets, old or new, have written anything like 'January Morning' in *Al que Quiere!*" (*CPr* 59).

17. All of this is long before an identifiable movement known as ecofeminism, but I am obviously suggesting that Moore anticipates its insights.

18. It is also an anomalous presence. Moore lifted it from descriptions of Lake Agnes and Lake Louise in Wilcox's book on the Canadian Rockies, thus asserting her right to collage actual landscapes as well as assorted quotations. See the Willis website.

19. The Moore family used special names for each other in their correspondence. Marianne had once been "Fang," but after they all read *The Wind in the Willows*, she became Rat, while her mother was known as Mole and her brother was Toad in his less official mode and, more frequently, Badger in his new life as pastor, military man, and husband. Early Moore poems are filled with rats, which are always, among other things, sly self-references that encode her family romance. She confutes badgers with marmots in the manuscript versions of "An Octopus," changing it finally for publication (Willis, *RP* and website).

20. The phrase "thoughtful beavers" is dropped from the list attributed to *What to See in America* in CP, which automatically misattributes it to the Parks pamphlet since the covering footnote reads "Quoted lines of which the source is not given are from The Department of the Interior Rules and Regulations, *The National Parks Portfolio* (1922)." The phrase Moore *should* have cut is "bristling, puny, swearing men" since that is removed by her cuts. This and other such errors suggest that the cutting of the poems and the related changes in the notes were not done with any great care or consistency.

21. Weatherhead notes that "Some of the difficulty of the poem is due to its lack of recognizable structural form. . . . Many of Moore's poems have form—form gained from rhymes, rhythms, and patterned arrangements of lines. But she avoids form that results from the organization of parts—a process in which details are selected, shaped, and ordered to contribute to a general picture that is contrary to her characteristic practice. . . . When she does subordinate details, she does so to provide a foil for the kind of perception which appreciates them" (website).

22. Probably their temperature, as they seem to have been inspired by the ice caves that Marianne and Warner climbed up to.

23. "The Steeple-Jack," in *SP* (1).

24. According to Taffy Martin, the poem displays "joyful appreciation of the indecipherable density of Mount Tacoma's glacier. Every specimen of disarray offers a form of delight, precisely because of its inherent and unfathomable contradiction" (25).

25. Nietzsche's Dionysian side of Greek thought, which dealt in contradictions and accessed the mysteries of nature, was not acknowledged, and I rather doubt that Moore had read *The Birth of Tragedy*.

26. It is also related, as Willis's examination of the notebooks and manuscripts suggests, to Greek claims about their origins and racial purity, material Moore came across while reading Cardinal Newman (*RP* 8). Schulze adds, "A people of conclusions rather than curiosity, the Greeks closed themselves off from nature's chaos and mentally resolved the mysteries of existence that are, for the truthful poet, unknowable quantities" (website).

27. This view is also argued in Joyce (81f).

28. We know that Moore had been reading *The Golden Bowl* during this period. She would have been conscious of admiring the reach of James's art while never forgetting the immense differences between a poem and a novel. The poets she was reading included Shelley, Eliot, Pound, and H.D. Willis, Schulze, and Hubbard all discuss Moore's reading in this period, drawing often on her notebooks.

29. I would also relate this to the "cavalcade of calico," which celebrates the particolored and the multiple in a way that associates them with feminine sensibility.

30. Margaret Holley notes: "This unusual combination of the observer's close perceptual concentration and the sprawling lists of observed things, of namings and qualifications, notations and asides—this blend of exactitude and endlessness is a self-challenging text par excellence. . . . Moore here acknowledges the limits of the phenomenological enterprise on which she has embarked. . . . Thus the poem consents to be transcended by its subject, the mountain" (57).

31. On Dec. 20, 1922, Moore wrote to Yvor Winters: "*The Waste Land* is, I feel, macabre; it suggests that imagination has been compressed whereas experience should be a precipitate. I, too, question the rhythmic cohesiveness. 'Demotic French,' the bats and tower and bursts of imagination do, however, set up 'an infectious riot in the mind' and the impression long after reading justifies the poem to me, I think, as a creative achievement" (*SL* 191).

32. Department of the Interior, *National Parks Portfolio*, "Presentation."

33. John Slatin notes that "the specifically American setting of 'An Octopus' implies a challenge to Eliot's insistence on the primacy of the European literary tradition" (156).

34. As cited in Willis (1987, 38).

35. Paradise Park was and still is the name of the upper-meadow region next to one of the largest glaciers at Rainier. There is a lodge there, where the Moore family stayed. The name Paradise seems especially related to the way in which wildflowers flourish there in remarkable abundance. Several commentators mention Moore's possible responses to the name, for example, Slatin: "[T]he mountain ultimately becomes not only a synecdoche for America but also an image of America as Paradise" (157). Hubbard concludes that "'An Octopus' invites visitation, not residency. . . . Paradise Park is not Paradise, but a later edition, one written over with human history, and allowing, unlike that first paradise, both 'a way out and a way in'" (website).

36. In a study published since the completion of this chapter, *Shifting Ground: Reinventing Landscape in Modern American Poetry*, Bonnie Costello corroborates many of my points here, for example, "'An Octopus' tries to convey the immediate experience of the wilderness. It does so, paradoxically, by calling attention to our mediations. Moore presents a reality that is never circumscribed, which cannot be reduced to an image or a use, and cannot be mastered by a single perspective" (97).

CHAPTER 6. EUGENIO MONTALE

1. Trans. J. G. Nichols, from *Halcyon* (189).

2. Written around 1913. Campana (53).

3. Trans. David Young. Unpublished.

4. Cary, as quoted in Montale (1992, 231). Galassi cites Mengaldo, making a similar observation (Montale 2000, 463).

5. Galassi cites Jacomuzzi's characterization of it as "the most easily individualizable, and individualized, area of declarations of poetics in Montale's poetry" (Montale 2000, 462).

6. The d'Annunzio connection is discussed in Becker (4–6 and 25–26) and Cary, in Montale (1992, 232–33).

7. Cambon notes: "The paradox of poem 8 leads to the qualitative leap of poem 9, the conclusive one, where literature has been left definitely behind and what is in question is the meaning of the speaker's entire existence" (25). I agree, except that I don't think literature is ever "left behind." The fiery spark at the end is a sign of creation and inspiration, the aspiring artist rewarded.

8. Cary, quoted in Montale (1992, 232).

CONCLUSION

1. It should be noted that Keats explored this stanza, too, in the strange narrative poem *Isabella*, a poem Yeats would of course have known. But Yeats may have more or less stumbled upon ottava rima since he had earlier been fond of an eight-line stanza that rhymed *aabbcddc*, and he may have liked this variation, which occurs first, and then quite frequently, in *The Tower* and then remains a favorite right through to the end (e.g., "The Circus Animals' Desertion").

WORKS CITED

Abram, David. *The Spell of the Sensuous: Perception and Language in a More-than-Human World*. New York: Pantheon Books, 1996.

Bates, Milton J. *Wallace Stevens: A Mythology of Self*. Berkeley: University of California Press, 1985.

Becker, Jared. *Eugenio Montale*. Boston: Twayne, 1986.

Benamou, Michel. *Wallace Stevens and the Symbolist Imagination*. Princeton, N.J.: Princeton University Press, 1972.

Bernstein, Michael André. *Five Portraits: Modernity and the Imagination in Twentieth-century German Writing*. Evanston, Ill.: Northwestern University Press, 2000.

Bethea, Dean Wentworth. "'Sunday Morning' at the Clavier: A Comparative Approach to Teaching Stevens." In *Teaching Wallace Stevens: Practical Essays*, edited by John N. Serio and B. J. Leggett. Knoxville: University of Tennessee Press, 1994.

Bradford, Curtis. *Yeats at Work*. Carbondale: Southern Illinois University Press, 1965.

Brogan, Jacqueline Vaught. "Sexism and Stevens." In *Wallace Stevens and the Feminine*, edited by Melita Schaum. Tuscaloosa: University of Alabama Press, 1993.

Brooks, Cleanth. *The Well-Wrought Urn: Studies in the Structure of Poetry*. New York: Harcourt Brace, 1947.

Buell, Lawrence. *The Environmental Imagination: Thoreau, Nature Writing, and the Formation of American Culture*. Cambridge: Harvard University Press, 1995.

Buttel, Robert. *Wallace Stevens: The Making of* Harmonium. Princeton, N.J.: Princeton University Press, 1967.

Cambon, Glauco. *Eugenio Montale's Poetry*. Princeton, N.J.: Princeton University Press, 1982.

Campana, Dino. *Orphic Songs*, translated by Charles Wright. FIELD Translation Series 9. Oberlin, Ohio: Oberlin College Press, 1982.

Cary, Joseph. *Three Modern Italian Poets*. New York: New York University Press, 1969.

Cavell, Stanley. "Politics as Opposed to What?" In *The Politics of Interpretation*, edited by W. J. T. Mitchell. Chicago: University of Chicago Press, 1984, 181–202.

Conrad, Peter. *Modern Times, Modern Places*. New York: Knopf, 1999.

Costello, Bonnie. "The Effects of Analogy: Wallace Stevens and Painting." In *Wallace Stevens: The Poetics of Modernism*, edited by Albert Gelpi. New York: Cambridge University Press, 1985.

————. *Shifting Ground: Reinventing Landscape in Modern American Poetry*. Cambridge: Harvard University Press, 2003.

Cullingford, Elizabeth Butler. *Gender and History in Yeats's Love Poetry*. Syracuse, N.Y.: Syracuse University Press, 1996.

D'Annunzio, Gabriele. *Halcyon*, translated by J. G. Nichols. New York: Routledge, 2003.

Damasio, Antonio. *Descartes' Error*. New York: HarperCollins, 1995.

————. *The Feeling of What Happens: Body and Emotion in the Making of Consciousness*. New York: Harcourt Brace, 1999.

Dawson, L. M. "'Among School Children': 'Labour' and 'Play.'" *Philological Quarterly* 52 (1973): 286–95.

de Man, Paul. *Allegories of Reading*. New Haven: Yale University Press, 1979.

Dijkstra, Bram. *Cubism, Stieglitz, and the Early Poetry of William Carlos Williams: The Hieroglyphics of a New Speech*. Princeton, N.J.: Princeton University Press, 1969.

Doyle, Charles. *William Carlos Williams and the American Poem*. New York: St. Martin's, 1983.

Edwards, James C. *The Plain Sense of Things: The Fate of Religion in an Age of Normal Nihilsm*. University Park: Pennsylvania State University Press, 1997.

Feshbach, Sidney. "Elegy Rebuffed by Pastoral Eclogue in Wallace Stevens' 'Sunday Morning.'" *Analecta Husserliana* 62: 231–46.

————. "A Pretext for Wallace Stevens' 'Sunday Morning.'" *Journal of Modern Literature* 23 (1999): 59–78.

Freedman, Ralph. *Life of a Poet: Rainer Maria Rilke*. Evanston, Ill.: Northwestern University Press, 1996.

Gass, William. *Reading Rilke: Reflections on the Problems of Translation*. New York: Knopf, 1999.

Gentile, Giovanni. *The Reform of Education*. New York: Harcourt Brace, 1922.

Harper, Margaret Mills. "The Authoritative Image: 'Among School Children' and Italian Educational Reform." *Studies in the Literary Imagination* 30 (1997): 105–18.

Holley, Margaret. *The Poetry of Marianne Moore: A Study in Voice and Value*. New York: Cambridge University Press, 1987.

Hubbard, Stacy Carson. "The Many-armed Embrace: Collection, Quotation, and Mediation in Marianne Moore's Poetry." *Sagetrieb* 12 (Fall 1993). Excerpted on the Willis website.

Jacomuzzi, Angelo. *La Poesia di Montale*. Turin, Italy: Einaudi, 1978.

Jarrell, Randall. *Poetry and the Age*. New York: Knopf, 1953.

Joyce, Elizabeth. *Cultural Critique and Abstraction: Marianne Moore and the Avant-Garde.* Lewisburg, Penn.: Bucknell University Press, 1998.

Kay, George. *The Penguin Book of Italian Verse.* London: Penguin Books, 1958.

Kearney, Richard. *Poetics of Imagining: Modern to Post-Modern.* New York: Fordham University Press, 1998.

Kern, Stephen. *The Culture of Space and Time, 1880–1918.* Cambridge: Harvard University Press, 1998.

Kleinbard, David. *The Beginning of Terror: A Psychological Study of Rainer Maria Rilke's Life and Work.* New York: New York University Press, 1993.

Leppmann, Wolfgang. *Rilke: A Life.* New York: Fromm International, 1984.

Longenbach, James. *Stone Cottage: Pound, Yeats, and Modernism.* New York: Oxford University Press, 1988.

———. *Wallace Stevens: The Plain Sense of Things.* New York: Oxford University Press, 1991.

Lowney, John. *The American Avant-garde Tradition: William Carlos Williams, Postmodern Poetics, and the Politics of Cultural Memory.* Lewisburg, Penn.: Bucknell University Press, 1987.

MacGowan, Christopher J. *William Carlos Williams' Early Poetry: The Visual Arts Background.* Ann Arbor: UMI Research Press, 1984.

MacLeod, Glen. *Wallace Stevens and Modern Art: From the Armory Show to Abstract Expressionism.* New Haven, Conn.: Yale University Press, 1993.

Mallarmé, Stephane. *The Poems,* translated and introduced by Keith Bosley. London: Penguin Books, 1977.

———. *Selected Poetry and Prose,* edited by Mary Ann Caws. New York: New Directions, 1982.

Martin, Taffy. *Marianne Moore: Subversive Modernist.* Austin: University of Texas Press, 1986.

Mengaldo, Pier Vincenzo. *La tradizione del novecento.* Milan: Feltrinelli, 1980.

Miller, J, Hillis. *Poets of Reality.* Cambridge: Harvard University Press, 1965.

Molesworth, Charles. *Marianne Moore: A Literary Life.* New York: Atheneum, 1990.

Montale, Eugenio. *The Bones of Cuttlefish,* translated by Antonio Mazza. Oakville, Ontario, Canada: Mosaic Press, 1983.

———. *Collected Poems, 1920–1954,* translated and annotated by Jonathan Galassi. New York: Farrar, Straus, Giroux, 1998, 2000.

———. *Cuttlefish Bones,* translated by William Arrowsmith. New York: Norton, 1992.

———. *Selected Poems,* translated by Jonathan Galassi, Charles Wright, and David Young, with an introduction by David Young. FIELD Translation Series 26. Oberlin, Ohio: Oberlin College Press, 2004.

———. *The Storm and Other Poems,* translated by Charles Wright. FIELD Translation Series 1. Oberlin, Ohio: Oberlin College Press, 1978.

Moore, Marianne. *The Complete Poems of Marianne Moore.* New York: Macmillan, 1981 (abbreviated *CP*).

——. *The Complete Prose of Marianne Moore,* edited by Patricia C. Willis. New York: Viking, 1986 (abbreviated *CPr*).

——. *Observations.* New York: Dial Press, 1924.

——. *The Poems of Marianne Moore,* edited by Grace Schulman. New York: Viking, 2003.

——. *The Selected Letters of Marianne Moore,* edited by Bonnie Costello, Celeste Goodridge, and Cristianne Miller. New York: Knopf, 1997 (abbreviated *SL*).

——. *Selected Poems of Marianne Moore.* New York: Macmillan, 1935 (abbreviated *SP*).

Muske, Carol. "Retrieving the Lament: Red Echoes Between 'Requiem' and 'Self-Portrait, 1906.'" *FIELD* 63 (2000): 40–58.

Nabokov, Vladimiv. *Strong Opinions.* New York: McGraw-Hill, 1973.

Oelschlager, Max. *The Idea of Wilderness: From Prehistory to the Age of Ecology.* New Haven: Yale University Press, 1991.

Parkinson, Thomas. *W. B. Yeats: The Later Poetry.* University of California Press, 1966.

Prater, Donald A. *A Ringing Glass: The Life of Rainer Maria Rilke.* Oxford: Clarendon, 1986.

Reynolds, Dee. *Symbolist Aesthetics and Early Abstract Art.* New York: Cambridge University Press, 1995.

Richardson, Joan. *Wallace Stevens: The Early Years.* New York: William Morrow, 1986.

Riddel, Joseph. *The Inverted Bell: Modernism and the Counterpoetics of William Carlos Williams.* Baton Rouge: Louisiana State University Press, 1974.

Rilke, Rainer Maria. *The Book of Fresh Beginnings: Selected Poems of Rainer Maria Rilke.* FIELD Translation Series, 20. Oberlin, Ohio: Oberlin College Press, 1994.

——. *The Duino Elegies: A New Translation,* translated by David Young. New York: Norton, 1978.

——. *Letters on Cézanne,* translated by Joel Agee. New York: Fromm International, 1985.

——. *New Poems [1907]: A Bilingual Edition,* translated by Edward Snow. Berkeley: North Point Press, 1984.

——. *Sonnets to Orpheus,* translated by M. D. Herter-Norton. New York: Norton, 1938.

Schmidt, Peter. *William Carlos Williams, the Arts, and Literary Tradition.* Baton Rouge: Louisiana State University Press, 1988.

Schulman, Grace. *Marianne Moore: The Poetry of Engagement.* Urbana: University of Illinois Press, 1986.

Schulze, Robin Gail. *The Web of Friendship: Marianne Moore and Wallace Stevens.* Ann Arbor: University of Michigan Press, 1995. Also excerpted on the Willis website.

Slatin, John M. *The Savage's Romance: the Poetry of Marianne Moore*. University Park: Pennsylvania State University Press, 1986.

Sokolsky, Anita. "The Resistance to Sentimentality: Yeats, de Man, and the Aesthetic Education." *Yale Journal of Criticism* 1 (1987): 67–86.

Stevens, Wallace. *Collected Poems*. New York: Knopf, 1954 (abbreviated *CP*).

———. *Letters of Wallace Stevens*, edited by Holly Stevens. New York: Knopf, 1966 (abbreviated *L*).

Tiffany, Daniel. *Toy Medium: Materialism and Modern Lyric*. Berkeley: University of California, 2000.

Torchiana, Donald T. "'Among School Children' and the Education of the Irish Spirit." In *Critical Essays on W. B. Yeats*, edited by Richard J. Finneran. Boston: G. K. Hall, 1976, 81–100.

Torgerson, Eric. *Dear Friend: Rainer Maria Rilke and Paula Modersohn-Becker*. Evanston, Ill.: Northwestern University Press, 1999.

———. "You Must Change Your Art." *FIELD 63* (2000): 59–66.

U.S. Department of the Interior. *The National Parks Portfolio*. Washington, D.C.: GPO, 1915. No page numbers.

———. *Rules and Regulations: The Mount Rainier National Park*. Washington, D.C.: U.S. National Park Service, 1915, 1922.

Vendler, Helen. *On Extended Wings: Wallace Stevens's Longer Poems*. Cambridge: Harvard University Press, 1969.

Voros, Gyorgyi. *Notations of the Wild: Ecology in the Poetry of Wallace Stevens*. Iowa City: University of Iowa Press, 1997.

Walker, David. *The Transparent Lyric: Reading and Meaning in the Poetry of Stevens and Williams*. Princeton, N.J.: Princeton University Press, 1984.

———, ed. *Poets Reading: the FIELD Symposia*. Oberlin, Ohio: Oberlin College Press, 1999.

Weatherhead, A. Kingsley. *The Edge of the Image: Marianne Moore, William Carlos Williams, and Some Other Poets*. Seattle: University of Washington Press, 1967. Also excerpted on the Willis website.

Wilbur, Richard. *The Beautiful Changes*. New York: Harcourt Brace, 1947.

Wilde, Oscar, "The Soul of Man Under Socialism." In *Collins Complete Works of Oscar Wilde*. Centenary edition, edited by Merlin Holland, Vyvyan Holland, and Owen Dudley Edwards. Glasgow: HarperCollins, 1999.

Williams, William Carlos. *The Collected Poems, vol. 1, 1909–1939*, edited by A. Walton Litz and Christopher MacGowan. New York: New Directions, 1986 (abbreviated *CP*).

———. *The Selected Letters*, edited by John C. Thirlwall. New York: New Directions, 1957, 1985 (abbreviated *SL*).

———. *Selected Poems*. Introduction by Randall Jarrell. New York: New Directions, 1949.

————. *Selected Poems,* edited with an introduction by Charles Tomlinson. New York: New Directions, 1985.

Willis, Patricia C. "On 'An Octopus.'" http://www.english.uiuc.edu/maps/poets/m_r/moore/octopus.htm (contains excerpts from Weatherhead, Willis, Martin, Margaret Dickie, Lynn Keller, Laurence Stapleton, Schulze, Hubbard, and Celeste Goodridge).

————. "The Road to Paradise: First Notes on 'An Octopus.'" *Twentieth Century Literature* 30 (1984): 242–66 (abbreviated *RP*). Also on the Willis website.

————. *Vision into Verse.* Philadelphia: Rosenbach Museum and Library, 1987.

Yeats, W. B. *The Letters of W. B. Yeats,* edited by Allan Wade. London: Rupert Hart-Davis, 1954.

————. *The Poems: A New Edition,* edited by Richard J. Finneran. New York: Macmillan, 1983.

Young, David. "High Talk: The Voice from *The Tower.*" *Kenyon Review* 11 (1989): 64–76.

————. "The Living World for Text: Life and Art in *The Wild Swans at Coole.*" In *The Author in His Work: Essays on a Problem in Criticism,* edited by Louis L. Martz and Aubrey Williams. New Haven: Yale University Press, 1978.

————. "A Skeptical Music: Stevens and Santayana." *Criticism* 7 (1965): 263–77.

————. *Troubled Mirror: A Study of Yeats's* The Tower. Iowa City: University of Iowa Press, 1987.

INDEX

metaphor, 15–16, 17–18, 99–100, 101–102

modernism, xii, 50–51, 53, 74–75, 98–99

Modersohn-Becker, Paula, 4, 7

Möbius-strip effect, 23, 28

Monroe, Harriet, 54, 66–67, 157

Montale, Eugenio, ix, xii, 145, 146, 148, 149; "The Lemon Trees," 129–30; "Mediterranean," 118–24; "To Spend the Afternoon," 126

Moore, Marianne, ix, x, 50, 144, 146, 148, 149; "An Octopus," 91–97; textual issues, 161

Moore, Warner, 103, 116

Nabokov, Vladimir, xiii

Nijinsky, Vaslav, 62

Oelschlager, Max, xiii

paintings, 66, 80

passenger pigeons, 159

Petrarch, Francis, 28

phenomenology, xi, 11–12, 23

Plato, 31, 34, 35, 59

poetic sequences, 72, 124

poetic speaker technique, 3, 10, 26, 27–29, 32, 42, 55–56, 58, 60, 63–64

Pound, Ezra, xi, 50, 72, 75, 115, 157

Pythagoras, 34–35, 44

questions, 33, 34, 37–38, 39, 60–61, 155

Rainier, Mount, 99

Raphael, "Madonna della Seggiola," 36

Reynolds, Dee, x

Rilke, Rainer Maria, ix, x, 42, 67, 89, 125, 143, 145, 146, 147; "Archaic Torso of Apollo," 10–11, 151; and aristocratic patrons, 4, 6–7, 151; and artistic maturation, 6–7, 151; *The Book of Pictures*, 8; "The Bowl of Roses," 1–3, 9–10, 67; *The*

Duino Elegies, 5, 8, 20–22; early work, 6, 7; *New Poems*, 8, 20, 22; new sense of being, 20–23, 42; "Orpheus. Eurydice. Hermes," 20; "The Panther," 9, 151; and Paris, 4, 7, 12; as symbolist, xii

Rodin, August, 7, 8, 12

romanticism, 7, 51

Santayana, George, 53–54

Schmidt, Peter, 152, 160

sentimentality, 3

Shakespeare, William, 27, 60, 79, 84, 89

Shelley, Percy, 100

Snow, Edward, 152

Sokolsky, Anita, 41–42, 155–56

Stein, Gertrude, 50, 75

Stevens, Wallace, ix, 71, 73, 76, 82, 144, 145, 146, 147; "The Comedian as the Letter C," 60; "Earthy Anecdote," 52–53; and English romanticism, 51; *Harmonium*, 52, 67; and paintings *en deshabille*, 55; picture gallery effect, 50; religion as a specifically American issue, 50–51, 53; "Sunday Morning," ix, 46–49, 71; use of iambic pentameter, 50–51

still life, 13–15, 17

Stravinsky, Igor, 62, 158

sublime, 66, 97, 100–101, 124

symbolism, xi, 6, 7

Tashjian, Anne, 158

transcendentalism, 51

translation issues, xiii–xiv, 19, 152–53

Vendler, Helen, 159

visual arts, xi, 6–7, 8, 12–14, 18, 32, 36, 50, 53, 54–55, 62, 66, 72, 84–85, 152, 154, 156

von Hoffmannsthal, Hugo, 22

Voros, Gyorgyi, 65, 157

vorticism, 73, 131, 160

BERLITZ®

COSTA DORADA
and BARCELONA

By the staff of Berlitz Guides

10th edition
(1992/1993)

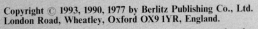

How to use our guide

- All the practical information, hints and tips that you will need before and during the trip start on page 98.

- For general background, see the sections Barcelona and the Costa Dorada, p. 6, and A Brief History, p. 10.

- All the sights to see are listed between pages 17 and 70. Our own choice of sights most highly recommended is pinpointed by the Berlitz traveller symbol.

- Entertainment, nightlife and all other leisure activities are described from pages 71 to 83 and 92 to 97, while information on restaurants and cuisine is to be found between pages 84 and 91.

- Finally, there is an index at the back of the book, pp. 126–128.

Although we make every effort to ensure the accuracy of all the information in this book, changes occur incessantly. We cannot therefore take responsibility for facts, prices, addresses and circumstances in general that are constantly subject to alteration. Our guides are updated on a regular basis as we reprint, and we are always grateful to readers who let us know of any errors, changes or serious omissions they come across.

Text: Ken Bernstein
Photography: Ken Welsh; cover: SPECTRUM COLOUR LIBRARY, London
Thanks to Sophy Morland and Mark Skeet for their research and assistance.
4 Cartography: Falk-Verlag, Hamburg

Contents

Cover photo: Columbus Monument; photo pp. 2–3: View from Parc Güell.

Barcelona and the Costa Dorada

The fine golden sand which gave the Costa Dorada its name extends almost without a break along more than 150 miles of this calm Mediterranean shore.

Technically it starts north of Barcelona at the River Tordera, at the point where the more famous Costa Brava ends, and runs down, including as it goes the Costa del Maresme, to Barcelona. South of Barcelona, it begins again and stretches all the way down the coast of Catalonia to the delta of the mighty River Ebro. The Costa Dorada encompasses the great city of Barcelona and fishing villages too obscure to rate a post office. All along the coast, the swimming, boating and a bustling outdoor life continue uninterrupted under the dependable Spanish sun —until the moon and stars take over with the nightlife.

Sheer holiday fun is just one part of the Costa Dorada's invitation. This is a land of magnificent ancient churches and castles. Inland, beyond the vineyards, you can visit the

Ebro

St. Carles de la Rápita

Cambrils

Tarragona

Vilanova i la Geltrú

COSTA DORADA

unique mountain monastery of Montserrat—or less celebrated but unsurpassed treasures of architecture and faith. And wherever you may find yourself along the Costa Dorada, you'll sense the dynamism of Catalonia.

Spaniards in general may cherish their siesta, but the Catalan people can take it or (like the big department stores) leave it. Most Spaniards keep their women at home; in Catalonia, women enter the professions and direct traffic. Spaniards may dance the fiery flamenco; Catalans hold hands for the stately, measured *sardana*.

The people are bilingual. They speak Catalan, a derivative of Latin, as well as (and often better than) the official language of Spain, Castilian. They are more adept with foreign languages than other Spaniards. In the Middle Ages, the Catalans ruled a great sweep of the Mediterranean, including at one time or another Sicily, Sardinia, Corsica and parts of Greece. The language and culture which flourished in those imperial times still bind the Barcelona industrialist to the Sant Pol fisherman and the Amposta rice farmer.

Modern Catalonia has produced an inordinately bounti-

ful crop of original artists, such as Joan Miró and Salvador Dalí and, something of an adopted son, Picasso. But centuries earlier, brilliant Catalan architects designed stunning Romanesque churches, decorated with frescoes full of colour. With a bit of time, a tourist can see the best of everything, ancient and modern, either housed in the superlative museums of Barcelona or on the spot.

The metropolis of Catalonia, Barcelona, is a vital and very European city of flower stalls and tree-lined boulevards. The glory of its medieval architecture complements the audacity of its modern buildings. The citizens, renowned for their industriousness, work hard in 19th-century factories with huge brick chimney-stacks, or on the docks, or behind the counters of a proliferation of banks. They read more books, see more operas, and cling even more fiercely to their old traditions than the people of any other Spanish city.

The other major coastal city, Tarragona, was a provincial capital of imperial Rome. Imaginative landscaping and dramatic floodlighting at night enliven its archaeological splendours. And, in a city said to have been converted to Christianity by St. Paul himself, the cathedral—begun in the 12th century—fills the visitor with a sense of awe.

On the political map of Spain, the Costa Dorada belongs to Barcelona and Tarragona provinces. (Lleida and Girona are Catalonia's other two provinces.) In this important wine-producing district, the carafe on your table will probably be a tasty local vintage. Fishing is also a big industry, so you can be certain of fresh-from-the-net seafood. Other principal industrial activities are textile manufacture and—obviously—tourism.

The Catalans may be realists and individualists, but they are wild about singing in choirs and playing in bands and dancing the graceful *sardana*. A more eccentric aspect of their folklore is an earnest enthusiasm for climbing upon each others' shoulders to create dangerously swaying pyramids. Teams of trained castle-makers *(castellers)* travel the countryside for contests; the newspapers run articles; and, of course, the peculiar music of Catalan woodwind instruments accompanies each climax.

You'll like the cooking. From typical Catalan farm soup (loaded with sausage, beans, and a slice of meat-loaf) to nuts (local almonds, of course), the food is good and wholesome.

And before your holiday ends, you'll want to squeeze in some shopping. Local artisans and regional factories produce gifts and souvenirs both corny and sophisticated, shockingly cheap or, alas, hopelessly expensive. In a word, something for every taste.

In a Barcelona square, Catalans hold hands to dance the sardana.

A Brief History

Catalonia's long road from colony to imperial power and back to provincial status zigzags through extremes of idealism and cruelty, triumph and disaster. Characters as colourful as the Caesars, Charlemagne, and Ferdinand and Isabella left their mark on its history.

So did a 9th-century warrior named Wilfred the Hairy (Wifredo el Velloso), Catalonia's first-ever hero, who threw his noble if shaggy support behind a Frankish king called Charles the Bald. Charles was trying to expel the Moors, a recurring project in the Middle Ages. When Hairy Wilfred fell wounded, the legend goes, the king asked what reward he desired. The request—independence for Barcelona—was granted. The year was 878. But to begin at the beginning

takes us far into prehistoric times. Paleolithic and Neolithic relics have turned up in Catalonia. While little is known of those early people, we are however sure that Phoenicians and Greeks brought commerce and culture to Catalonia; and the Carthaginians are said to have given Barcelona its original name, Barcino, in honour of General Hamilcar Barca, father of the legendary Hannibal.

In the 2nd Punic War (3rd century B.C.), the Romans defeated Carthage and ruled Iberia for the next six centuries. Spain gave birth to four Roman emperors. One of the capitals of the Roman empire was Tarragona, then called Tarraco. All over Catalonia, from the seashore to lonely mountaintops, the stamp of Rome remains: walls and roadways, villas and monuments, vineyards and the Catalan language, an expressive descendant of Latin.

By the 5th century A.D., Rome's grip had slackened and Spain was overrun by Vandals and Visigoths. The next in-

Aqueduct near Tarragona recalls Catalonia's role in Roman empire.

10

vasion began in 711, when Moorish forces from Africa assailed the Iberian peninsula. Muslim civilization was imposed, but the Christian efforts to reconquer Spain never ceased. The subsequent Moorish influence on Christian Spanish art and architecture, was, nonetheless, profound.

An early but indecisive defeat of the Moors was the re-capture of Barcelona by Charlemagne's forces. Catalonia paid generously for its liberation, becoming a Frankish dependency called the Spanish March. Then came our heroic Count Wilfred the Hairy, who earned Barcelona its freedom.

Catalonia's Golden Age

In the Middle Ages, Catalonia prospered commercially, poli-

tically and intellectually. Count Ramón Berenguer I of Barcelona drew up a sort of constitution, the *Usatges,* in 1060. Ramón Berenguer III (1096–1131) turned Catalonia towards imperial enterprises; he formed a union with an independent Provence (the languages are very similar) and established trade relations with Italy. Ramón Berenguer IV (1131–62) married a princess of Aragon, a brilliant expansionist tactic which created a joint kingdom of great substance. The count of Barcelona became king of Aragon, and "greater Catalonia" flourished.

Jaime I (James the Conqueror) dislodged the Moors from their stubborn hold on the Balearic Islands, installing in their stead Christianity and Catalan law. His son, Pedro III the Great, through military action and a few twists of fate, added the throne of Sicily to the dynasty's collection. By the 14th century, Catalonia's fortunes had soared to breathtaking heights, with the addition of two dukedoms in Greece, the seizure of Sardinia, and the annexation of Corsica. For a time the kingdom of Catalonia was Power No. 1 in the entire Mediterranean.

This was the era, too, of great art and architecture—original designs for churches with vast naves and tall, slim columns and the striking sculptures and paintings which glorified them. And this was a heyday for the language. Ramón Llull of Majorca (1235–1315), known as Raimundus Lullus in Latin, saint and scholar, enhanced medieval culture in

Catalan. At the same time, Catalonian cartographers, especially Majorcans, were drawing the maps that were to guide the first great navigators on their journeys beyond the known horizon.

The next Catalonian figure to make history was Ferdinand (Ferran II in Catalan), who married Isabella of Castile and became Ferdinand V of Spain.

ages of discovery proved disastrous for Catalonia. The Mediterranean lost much of its importance as a trading zone, while the south-western ports of Cadiz and Seville won the franchise for the rich transatlantic business.

Giant effigies (opposite) *honour Ferdinand and Isabella. In Barcelona port, a replica of Columbus' ship.*

Ferdinand and Isabella, known as the Catholic Monarchs, conquered the last Moorish bastion, Granada. They also took joint credit for two other big events in 1492: they ordered the expulsion of Spain's Jews, and they sponsored Columbus on his voyage of discovery to America. Ironically, the Columbus project and other voy-

Times of Troubles

Seventeenth-century Catalonia was a troubled land, rebelling against Philip IV of Spain, putting itself under the protection of the king of France. Violent struggles went on for a dozen years. Finally a besieged Barcelona surrendered. Catalonia renewed its allegiance to the Spanish crown, but man- **13**

aged to preserve its treasured local laws.

But all was lost in the War of the Spanish Succession, in which Catalonia again demonstrated its marked difference from the rest of Spain and joined the wrong side. With the triumph of the Bourbon king Philip V in 1714, Barcelona was overrun. Official punishment followed, including the dismissal of the Catalonian parliament and the banning of the Catalan language from official use. Striking historical parallels were to follow the Spanish Civil War of 1936–39.

In the second half of the 18th century, Charles III—usually characterized as an enlightened despot—rescued Catalonia from its slump, opening up the region's ports to the very profitable Latin-American trade. He also had a visionary idea for a superport on the edge of the Ebro Delta, but the metropolis of Sant Carles de la Rápita (see page 63) never amounted to much more than an extravagant mirage.

For Catalonia as well as the rest of Spain, the 19th century seemed to be just one war after another, starting with the War of the Third Coalition in 1805 and ending with the Spanish-American War of 1898. Both were disasters. In the first, the British, under Nelson, destroyed the Spanish and French fleets at Trafalgar. In the last, Spain lost its key remaining colonies—Cuba, Puerto Rico and the Philippines.

Lauros-Giraudon

After finding America, Columbus sailed triumphantly to Barcelona.

Thirty-three years after the empire faded away, King Alfonso XIII went into exile, as Republicans gained control in several Spanish cities. National elections later in 1931 favoured the Republicans, who advocated socialist and anti-clerical policies. As conservative resistance began to crystallize, Catalonia was proclaimed an autonomous republic.

The Civil War

But confusion and disorder were growing in Spain. The conflict between left and right became more irreconcilable. Spain's youngest general, Francisco Franco, came to the head of a military insurrection. The whole world watched the three-year struggle; outside forces helped to prolong it.

Military reverses forced the Republicans to move their capital from Valencia to Barcelona in late 1937 where there had already been an outbreak of bitter fighting between two factions of the Republican side, Anarchists and Communists. There followed repeated bombings of Barcelona by Italian planes based on Majorca and a year of hardship for the population. The city fell at last in January, 1939, and Catalonia was reabsorbed into Spain—four provinces out of the nation's 50. Within two months the Civil War was over. It had cost the lives of hundreds of thousands of Spaniards.

Modern Times

Spain was able to stay neutral in the Second World War. In the postwar years, the tough law-and-order regime of Franco set in motion the nation's recovery. Then came the phenomenon of mass tourism, with profound effects on the economy and the people.

Franco's designated successor, the grandson of Alfonso XIII, was enthroned on the death of the dictator in 1975. To the dismay of Franco's followers, King Juan Carlos I flung open the gates to full parliamentary democracy. In the flush of freedom, old and new problems competed for attention. After the years of repression, the languages and cultures of Catalonia and the Basque Country flourished anew, and regional autonomy was granted.

Firmly back in the mainstream after its long isolation, democratic Spain hitched its hopes to the European Community. **15**

Where to Go

no longer sprawling suburbs, have self-contained identities. The beaches go on for mile after mile of ideal sand and clear sea, with impressive mountains in the distance. Every fifth hilltop seems to be occupied by a castle or at least a medieval watch-tower. These relics are so common that only the best preserved or most historic are signposted.

The Coast North of Barcelona

The Costa Brava is known for its rugged cliffs and small inlets, but the Costa Dorada is downright cowardly. Rarely is the lie of the land more daring than a few miles of broad sand beaches nuzzling against a clear, gentle sea.

Let's begin by a survey of the coastline, first heading north-east from Barcelona up to the Costa Brava frontier. Technically, this stretch of the coast between Barcelona and Blanes is known as the Costa del Maresme (maresme meaning a low-lying coastal region susceptible to flooding).

The voyage starts with BADALONA (population 230,000), a last reminder of big-city rush and industrial necessities.

Beyond Badalona the countryside gradually takes on a more rural cast. The towns,

Costa Dorada consists of miles of lazy beaches interspersed with towns as fair as Sitges (opposite).

The first real beach centres, in a countryside noted for flower-growing, are EL MASNOU and PREMIÁ DE MAR. These beaches run right alongside the railway line.

This was the first railway in Spain, built under British technical direction and inaugurated in 1848 between Barcelona and MATARÓ, now an industrial city of about 100,000. It's all work and no play in Mataró; a tourist with a tan attracts stares from the pale local residents. Mataró was called Iluro by the ancient Romans, who left many priceless sculptures and mosaics. Most of these archaeological finds went into the municipal museum, which was shut down in 1975 when more than 200 items were found to be missing. The museum curator resigned.

CALDETES, also known as Caldes d'Estrac, is an appealing old town with villas set among the pines on its hillsides. The Romans bathed in its fine 102° Fahrenheit mineral waters; so do some of today's visitors. This unspoiled spa also has plenty of seashore.

Since the 16th century, when the village church was built, ARENYS DE MAR has been a seafaring town. Nowadays the fishing fleet is greatly outnumbered by pleasure boats; Arenys's impressive modern marina makes it an international sailing and yachting centre. The town itself climbs from the shore along a stately tree-lined main street. The parish church contains a sumptuous baroque altarpiece which tourists may appreciate better by depositing money in a coin slot to switch on a spotlight.

A good place for camping along the seafront is the busy village of CANET DE MAR. Here you can visit the medieval castle of Santa Florentina.

Sant Pol de Mar, a fishing village with charm, has only about 2,000 inhabitants. Narrow, winding streets lead to an ancient watchtower on top of the promontory. Unlike many a coastal town, it has been able to preserve its character.

Calella, also called Calella de la Costa to distinguish it from Calella de Palafrugell (Costa Brava), bustles with tourist development. Eleven-floor blocks of flats and more than 80 hotels house the thousands of visitors who converge here for what the local tourist board calls "cosmopolitan gaiety". Among distinguishing characteristics are a white lighthouse atop a knoll at the south edge of town; an 18th-century church; and a tree-shaded promenade along a very wide sand beach. Its many streets of souvenir shops, bars and restaurants prove Calella's importance as one of the coast's most popular international resorts.

Nearly 2 miles of beaches and unpolluted seawater have made the village of Pineda de Mar a delightful tourist attraction.

Next, Santa Susanna is a farming village which has been developed for tourism, with all the modern amenities.

Malgrat de Mar is an industrial town of about 10,000. With its 3 miles of beach, it provides the ingredients for a pleasant seaside holiday.

The Costa del Maresme runs out beyond Malgrat. Officially the Costa Brava begins on the other side of the River Tordera. The actual boundary, of scant interest to anyone but a map-maker or tax collector, is a river-bed a couple of hundred yards wide. In summer it's normally bone dry and desolate. In winter, though, water rushes down from the Serra de Montseny in search of the sea. That's when the Tordera turns into a raging flood. It has been known to overflow its banks and even wash away a bridge or two.

Tourists along this stretch of the coast are in a good position to sign up for sea excursions beyond the jurisdictional frontiers. The boats normally call at such celebrated resorts as Blanes, Lloret, Tossa and Sant Feliu de Guíxols. The Costa Brava's spectacular scenery, admired from the sea, justifies its claim to world renown.

Barcelona

Catalonia's capital is a very big city with muscle and brains. Close on two million people live within the boundaries of this design-obsessed centre of banking, publishing and industry. Another million live in the surrounding area.

Its main attractions for visitors are renowned—the mighty cathedral, the port, gracious promenades and distinguished museums. You have to be alert for the smaller delights: a noble patio hidden in a slum, a tiled park bench moulded to the anatomy, a street-light fixture lovingly worked in iron, a sculpted gargoyle sneering down from medieval eaves.

The lively people of Barcelona know how to make money. They spend it on flowers and football, music and books, and gooey pastries for their children. They enjoy the fireworks and dancing in the street. They go to gourmet snack-bars and sexy floor-shows, and wear formal evening dress to the opera house.

In the Middle Ages Barcelona was the capital of a surprisingly influential Catalonia. Thirteenth-century Barcelona, ruling distant cities of the Mediterranean, was building big ships in what is today the Maritime Museum, and living by Europe's first code of sea law.

The next great era, economically and artistically, came with late 19th-century industrialization. Politically, the 20th century witnessed a brief revival. In 1931, Barcelona became the capital of an autonomous Catalan Republic, that came to an end in 1939, when the Nationalist forces triumphed. During the Franco era, Catalonia's proud sense of identity was firmly suppressed. But now the language and culture flourish anew, and Barcelona is the hotbed of the region's renaissance.

Gothic Quarter

To walk through 15 centuries of history, through the so-called Gothic Quarter *(Barri Gòtic),* we start, arbitrarily, at the city's present-day hub, the **Plaça de Catalunya** (Catalonia Square). Most of the

"Aerial ropeway" over Barcelona's port offers panorama of lively city.

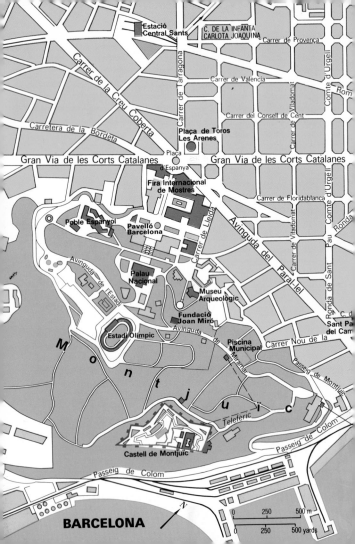

Estació
Central Sants

C. DE LA INFANTA
CARLOTA JOAQUINA

Carrer de Provença

Carrer de Tarragona

Carrer de València

Carrer de la Creu Coberta

Comte d'Urgell

Rom

Carrer del Consell de Cent

Carretera de la Bordeta

Comte de Viladomat

Plaça de Toros
Les Arenes

Plaça
d'Espanya

Gran Via de les Corts Catalanes   Gran Via de les Corts Catalanes

Fira Internacional
de Mostres

Carrer de Floridablanca

Poble Espanyol

Pavelló
Barcelona

Carrer de Lleida

Avinguda del Paral·lel

Comte d'Urgell

Palau
Nacional

Ronda de Sant Pau

Sant Pa
del Cam

Museu
Arqueològic

Avinguda de l'Estadi

Fundació
Joan Miró

C. d

Estadi Olímpic

Avinguda de

Piscina
Municipal

Carrer Nou de la

M
o
n
t
j
u
ï
c

de

Miramar

Passeig de Montjuïc

Telefèric

Passeig de Colom

Castell de Montjuic

Passeig de Colom

Passeig de Colom

N

0   250   500 m

0   250   500 yards

BARCELONA

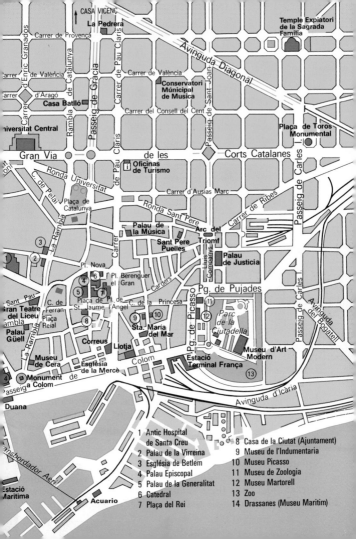

CASA VICENÇ
La Pedrera
Temple Expiatori de la Sagrada Familia
Carrer de Provença
Avinguda Diagonal
Carrer de València
Carrer de València
Conservatori Múnicipal de Musica
Carrer d'Enric Granados
Carrer de València
Rambla de Catalunya
Passeig de Gracia
Passeig de Pau Claris
Passeig de Sant Joan
Carrer d'Aragó
Casa Batlló
Carrer del Consell del Cent
Universitat Central
Plaça de Toros Monumental
Gran Via
de les
Corts Catalanes
Passeig de Carles I
Ronda Universitat
Oficinas de Turismo
C. de Pelai
Carrer d'Ausias Marc
Carrer de Ribes
Passeig de Carles I
Plaça de Catalunya
Ronda Sant Pere
La Rambla
Palau de la Música
Arc del Triomf
Sant Pere Puelles
Palau de Justicia
Pl. Nova
Carrer
Pl. Berenguer el Gran
Carders
Pg. de Pujades
Sant Pau
C. de
4 6
5 7
Plaça de Pl. de l'Angel
St. Jaume
Princesa
11
12
Parc de la Ciutadella
Avinguda del Bogatell
Gran Teatre del Liceu
Ferran
Pl. de la
Plaça Reial
8
9
10
Pg. de Picasso
Palau Güell
Sta. Maria del Mar
Correus
Llotja
Colom
Museu d'Art Modern
Museu de Cera
Església de la Mercè
Estació Terminal França
13
Monument a Colom
Passeig de Colom
Duana
Avinguda d'Icária
Transbordador Aeri
Estació Maritima
Acuario

1 Antic Hospital de Santa Creu
2 Palau de la Virreina
3 Església de Betlem
4 Palau Episcopal
5 Palau de la Generalitat
6 Catedral
7 Plaça del Rei
8 Casa de la Ciutat (Ajuntament)
9 Museu de l'Indumentaria
10 Museu Picasso
11 Museu de Zoologia
12 Museu Martorell
13 Zoo
14 Drassanes (Museu Maritim)

bus, metro and railway lines converge here.

At the south-eastern edge of the plaza begins a short but important street intriguingly named **Portal de l'Àngel** (Gate of the Angel). As it descends from Plaça de Catalunya, the street narrows; for most hours of the day, it's a pedestrians-only sanctuary, with convenient benches for tired feet.

Gothic Quarter: delights of medieval architecture at every turn.

Avinguda Portal de l'Àngel leads to **Plaça Nova** (New Square), not new at all. In the 13th century, this was a major market area. Now there is an outdoor market on Sundays.

Incongruously, the modern building of the College of Architects overlooks this ancient square. At first glance, you might think the façades of the College had been decorated by children. On second glance, you'd be right in guessing that the author of these huge graffiti could be none other than Pablo Picasso, who contributed these sketches on the theme of Catalan folklore.

From here the spires of the cathedral are already in sight. We'll take a closer look shortly. But first, notice the two stone towers straight ahead. Known as Portal del Bisbe (Bishop's Gate), they were part of the 4th-century Roman wall, raised higher eight centuries later.

Walk between the towers, that is, between the Palau Episcopal (Bishop's Palace), and the Archdeacon's House, and you will immediately feel the other-worldliness of Barcelona's Gothic Quarter. Take a look at the Romanesque patio of the Bishop's Palace, the first of many majestic courtyards to be seen in Barcelona. Very little connection could be claimed between the elegance of these columned precincts and the idea of a Spanish patio of whitewashed stucco.

The patio of the **Casa de l'Ardiaca** (the Archdeacon's House) is more intimate and appealing, with its slim palm tree and moss-covered fountain. The 11th-century building was restored in the early 16th century.

And so to the **Catedral de Santa Eulalia** (St. Eulalia Cathedral), dedicated to a legendary local girl who was tortured and executed for her fervent Christian faith in the 4th century.

The cathedral's construction was begun at the end of the 13th century and lasted for about 150 years. At the end of the 19th century, new work was undertaken thanks to a subsidy from a rich industrialist. Some critics complain that he spoiled the pure Catalan Gothic effect. But don't worry about the critics. Come back one night when the delicate spires are illuminated and light inside glows through the stained-glass windows. It's a pulse-quickening sight by any standards.

The interior of the cathedral is laid out in classic Catalan Gothic form, with three aisles neatly engineered to produce an effect of grandeur and uplift.

Look into the side chapels, with their precious paintings and sculptures. In the chapel of St. Benedict, the lifelike **Altarpiece of the Transfiguration** is the work of a great 15th-century Catalan artist, Bernat Martorell.

The **choir,** in the geometric centre of the cathedral, con-

1 Palau Episcopal
2 Casa de l'Ardiaca
3 Catedral
4 Palau de la Generalitat
5 Casa de la Ciutat (Ajuntament)
6 Saló del Tinell
7 Capella Reial de Santa Agata
8 Museu d'Història de la Ciutat
9 Museu Frederic Marés

centrates dazzling sculptural intricacies. The 15th-century German sculptor Michael Lochner carved the splendid **25** canopies over the choir pews.

A wide stairway leads beneath the high altar to the crypt of the aforementioned St. Eulalia. Notice the rogue's gallery of small stone-carved heads around the stairway and entry arch. The saint's carved alabaster sarcophagus dates from 1327.

For a change to a cheery atmosphere, step into the

cloister, a 15th-century Gothic classic. All cloisters are supposed to be tranquil, and so is this—except for the half dozen argumentative geese who rule the roost here, as have their ancestors for centuries.

The **Museu de la Catedral** (Cathedral Museum) displays religious paintings and sculpture from the 14th century onwards.

Before leaving the cathedral, step into the **Capella de Santa Llucia** (St. Lucy's Chapel), a spartan 13th-century sanctuary built by the bishop whose sepulchre is on view. Notice the 13th- and 14th-century tombstones in the floor. Every step, as they say, touches a bit of history.

Now a few other highlights near the cathedral in the Gothic Quarter:

Museu Frederic Marés. The museum houses an ambitious collection of statues from the 10th century on.

Museu d'Història de la Ciutat (Museum of the History of the City). The average visitor may choose to neglect Barcelona's old maps and documents, collected in this pleasant palace, but the scene below ground is unforgettable. Subterranean passages follow the admirable tracks of Roman civilization. Houses, waterworks, statues and ceramics have been excavated. In search of ballast for the ancient city's defensive towers, they threw in anything at hand including tombs, plaques and upside-down columns. Now archaeologists are tunnelling under the very cathedral to uncover relics of the Visigoths.

The museum faces Barcelona's most historic square, **Plaça del Rei** (King's Square). According to unconfirmed tradition, Columbus was received on this very spot when he returned a hero from his first voyage to the New World. Ferdinand and Isabella, the Catholic Monarchs, may have sat on the great steps of **Saló del Tinell** (Tinell Hall). They're shown thus, sitting in a famous stylized painting in which American Indians brought back by Columbus fairly swoon with ecstasy at the sight of their new masters.

Whether or not Columbus climbed the ceremonial stairs,

Cathedral tower looms over façade by Picasso. Plaça del Rei (below) is a splendid medieval ensemble.

Tinell Hall would have been a fine spot for his "welcome home" reception. Built in the 14th century, it consists of one immense room with a wood-panelled ceiling supported by six arches. Above the hall is an architectural afterthought of the mid-16th century, the **Torre del Rei Martí** (King Martin's Lookout Tower). This curious accumulation of porticoed galleries rises five storeys above the hall—just the place to mount a spy-glass to see the sea.

The square is also bounded by the **Capella de Santa Agata** (Chapel of St. Agatha), a 13th-century royal church with a slender tower. The far side of the chapel, facing the modern city, rests on the ancient Roman wall. You can see it all in detail from the **Plaça de Ramón Berenguer el Gran,** a sort of sunken garden right against the wall.

Plaça Sant Jaume (St. James's Square) lies right in the heart of the city, and in the heart, too, of the Barcelonese, for the square is graced by Barcelona's two most recognizable, symbolic buildings: the city hall and the Generalitat.

On the north side of the square is the **Palau de la Generalitat,** home of Catalonia's autonomous government. This ceremonious 15th-century structure hides a surprise or two: the overpowering ornamentation of St. George's Room and an upstairs patio with orange trees.

Across the square, the **Casa de la Ciutat** or Ajuntament (city hall) is even older. A sumptuous highlight of this 14th-century political centre is the **Saló del Consell de Cent** (Chamber of the Council of One Hundred), restored to its original glory worthy of any assembly.

But medieval life in Barcelona was not all pomp and majesty. Just to the west of the Generalitat, narrow streets with names like Call and Banys Nous mark the ancient Jewish Quarter. In the 11th, 12th and 13th centuries, it was a centre of philosophy, poetry and science. The Jews were money-lenders, also, and financed King Jaime I in his Mediterranean conquests. In 1391, as anti-semitic passions gripped Spain, the Barcelona ghetto was sacked.

La Rambla, relaxed but always dynamic, charms young and old.

La Rambla

Barcelona's best-known promenade, La Rambla, descends gradually but excitingly from Plaça de Catalunya to the port, a distance of about a mile. Like the sun and the shade, the tawdry and shabby share space with the chic and charming all the way down La Rambla. Almost every visitor succumbs to the attraction of this boulevard, thronged day and night with a fascinating crowd of people, animals and things. When you can't walk another inch along the undulating paving designs in the central walkway, watch the parade of the passing crowd from an outdoor café or rent a chair from a concessionaire.

Every couple of cross-streets the Rambla's character subtly changes. So does its official name, five times in all—but that needn't concern us. It may explain why the Rambla is often referred to in the plural as Les Rambles.

The start of the Rambla at the Plaça de Catalunya ought to be its most elegant area, but this is not really so. The air of animation here might baffle or mislead an outsider. Those groups of men spiritedly arguing are not forming political **29**

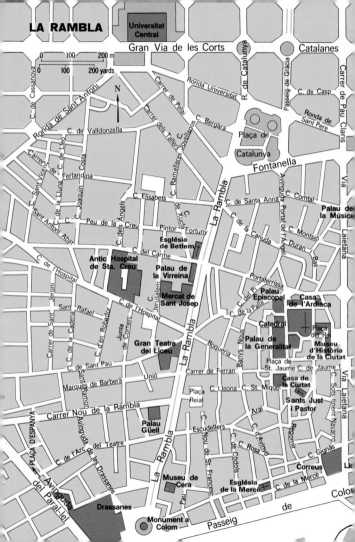

parties or disputing dogma. They are football fans conducting post-mortems after a match.

Here, too, you can buy a newspaper, magazine or book from the international choice displayed at the news-stands. The Rambla is also the kind of place where you can buy a lottery ticket or one cigarette from a very small businessman.

Not far beyond the Hyde Park Corner of football experts there used to be a university centre. In the 16th and 17th centuries, students congregated here; the name — Rambla dels Estudis — remains.

The huge old **Església de Betlem** (Church of Bethlehem), on the right, looks as if it might be an important attraction. But not in this city of so many truly exceptional churches, big and small.

You can buy a bird or a monkey along here, or just stand and stare at one of many stands dealing in canaries, doves, parrots and pigeons. Beyond the bird zone come the flower kiosks with their year-round colour: local carnations, Canary Islands bird-of-paradise flowers, and potted cacti.

The **Palau de la Virreina** (a reference to the Spanish vice-reine in 18th-century Peru) is one of the most sumptuous buildings on the Rambla. It houses the city hall Department of Culture, as well as the Postal Museum and the Numismatic Cabinet, of great interest to specialists. Other floors of the palace are used for topical exhibitions.

The **Mercat de Sant Josep** (popularly known as *La Boqueria*), one of those classic iron-covered and colonnaded markets of the 19th century, faces the Rambla. You have to wander among the eye-catching displays to appreciate the wealth of fresh fruit and vegetables, meat and seafood available here.

Just behind the market, in the Plaça del Doctor Fleming (honouring the discoverer of penicillin), a profession of bygone centuries endures. In the mornings, four men sit in adjacent small booths, filling the ancient role of scribes. With increasing literacy among the population they now offer a more sophisticated range of services — typing business letters, translating, expediting official forms. But they're still known to ghostwrite a love letter or two.

31

Travels with Sancho

An early tourist, Don Quixote de la Mancha, had never seen the sea until he visited Barcelona. The most universal fictional hero of all time also toured a publishing house.

In chapter 60 of Book Two of Cervantes' immortal novel, Quixote sums up the rough-tough atmosphere of 16th-century Barcelona, where "they hang outlaws and bandits 20 by 20 and 30 by 30". Running into the macabre aftermath of a mass execution in a forest, Quixote anticipates an old joke and says, "I reckon I must be near Barcelona".

A further detour from the market goes to the **Hospital de la Santa Creu,** now a formidable combination of buildings including the Library of Catalonia and the 18th-century Royal Academy of Medicine and Surgery. See the old operating theatre lit by a great crystal chandelier. A pilgrims' hospital stood here from the beginning of the 13th century.

Back on the Rambla, the main entrance to the **Gran Teatre del Liceu,** the Opera House, almost goes unnoticed. Behind a discreet façade is hidden one of the largest and most majestic auditoriums in the world. (The opera season in Barcelona lasts from December to May.)

Just off the Rambla in Carrer Nou de la Rambla stands one of the grand houses that Gaudí built: Palau Güell. The fortress-

like residence was designed for a Catalan aristocrat (see p. 42).

(see p. 42).

Carrer Nou de la Rambla and the Rambla itself make up the unofficial boundaries of a district of ill repute called the **Barri Chino** (Chinatown). Prostitution was outlawed in Spain in 1956 but you'd never know it in this part of Barcelona. From midday to dawn the narrow old streets call to mind the darkest corners of Marseilles. You have to be on guard against petty thieves here—bag snatchers in particular.

One more diversion, on the opposite side of the Rambla:

Charming old Spanish-style street transplanted to Poble Espanyol.

the **Plaça Reial** (Royal Square) is Barcelona's most perfectly proportioned square. Try to see it on a Sunday morning, when the stamp- and coin-collectors turn the arcaded square into a market-place. Watch grim-faced professionals, equipped with their own magnifying glasses and tweezers, facing each other across coin trays or stamp albums like so many champion chess players.

Towards the bottom of the promenade you'll find Barcelona's **Museu de Cera** (Wax Museum). In what was once a bank building, the lifelike images of all manner of celebrities are displayed, with special attention to famous murderers.

The Rambla leads on down to the Columbus monument and the port (see p. 37). Whether you stay in the shade of the tall plane trees on the promenade or cross the traffic to window-shop along the edges of the street (where you can buy anything from a guitar to a deep-sea diving-bell), you'll want to walk the Rambla from beginning to end and back again. For better or worse, this is surely where it's all happening.

Montjuïc

The site of the Olympic stadium. Whether you reach it by foot, taxi, bus or funicular, you could spend a whole day there and not see everything you ought to.

Montjuïc is a modest mountain less than 700 feet high. Until relatively recently, it had only military significance. But Barcelona's World Exhibition of 1929 saw hundreds of buildings planted upon its hillsides. The best are still there.

The name, Montjuïc, seems to refer to an ancient Jewish cemetery on the site. Or it may be even older, from the Latin Mont Jovis—Jupiter Mountain.

Montjuïc begins, more or less officially, at Plaça d'Espanya, a huge and frightening traffic roundabout. From here, you can look up the hillside, past the commercial exhibition grounds to a great **fountain,** one of Barcelona's prides. On weekend and holiday evenings, the waters are inventively illuminated. The central jet rises as high as 165 feet; water roars up at 642 gallons per second.

Next to the fountain stands the German Pavilion designed by architect Mies van der Rohe for the 1929 Fair and demolished shortly afterwards. Recently reconstructed in a burst of civic pride, it's now known as **El Pavelló Barcelona.**

Looming above all this, with a dome reminiscent of the U.S. Capitol building in Washington, is a palace built as recently as 1929—also for the World Fair. Architecturally, the Palau Nacional won't win any prizes for originality, but it houses the **Museu d'Art de Catalunya** (Museum of Art of Catalonia), one of the world's greatest collections of medieval art. Sixty-eight exhibition halls follow chronological order in this exceptionally well organized museum; but check that it's not closed during extensive renovations.

The 10th- and 11th-century Catalan religious paintings bear a striking resemblance to ancient Byzantine icons. See the beautiful 12th-century wood carvings from church altars, and magnificent frescoes of the same period, rescued from crumbling old churches.

Another leftover from the World Exhibition of 1929, the Palace of Graphic Arts, has been turned into the **Museu Arqueològic** (Archaeological Museum). The prehistoric items come mostly from Catalonia and the Balearic Islands. Many Greek and Roman relics come from Empúries (Ampurias), the Costa Brava town first settled by the Phoenicians in the 6th century B.C. There are also architectural displays from Barcelona's Roman days.

The **Museu Etnològic** (Ethnological Museum) of Montjuïc is devoted to specimens gathered by expeditions to exotic far-off places.

The newest museum on the mountain, opened in 1975, goes under the name of **Fundació Joan Miró.** This complex of original concrete and glass, the work of architect Josep M. Sert, is a tribute to the great Catalan artist Joan Miró, and the intense Catalanism of the place extends to the titles of the works, given in Catalan and occasionally also in French, but never in Spanish. What with the bright architecture and the riot of Miró paintings, sculptures, drawings and tapestries, this is as happy a museum as you're ever likely to see anywhere in the world.

Most conducted tours of Barcelona stop at **Poble Espanyol** ("Spanish Village"), a five-acre exhibition of Spanish art and architecture in the form of an artificial village, which shows the charms and styles of Spain's regions in full scale and super-concentration.

When Don Quixote came to Barcelona, he watched a naval force set out to do battle with pirates thanks to a signal from the lookout point on Montjuïc. This early-warning system by means of flags or bonfires had been operating as early as 1401. But the fortress which stands atop Montjuïc today wasn't built until 1640. It was handed over to the city in 1960 and fitted out as the

La Sagrada Familia: spires of Gaudí church inspire pride in Catalans.

Museu Militar (Military Museum).

From the roof of the fortress, you get a sweeping 360-degree panorama of the metropolis of Barcelona and the sea. You can also look straight down onto the port, with its many fascinations.

For visitors with time to spare, Montjuïc has more attractions in reserve—a Greek amphitheatre, sports installations, meticulously landscaped terraced gardens, and an amusement park with the full complement of roller-coaster, Ferris wheel and other thrilling rides, plus a special children's amusement park.

The Waterfront *

The boosters of Barcelona always seem to be searching for superlatives. They call this the biggest city on the Mediterranean shore. They also claim that the **Monument a Colom** (Columbus Monument), between the port and the Rambla, is said to be the tallest monument to Columbus in the world. There is a lift inside

the column, which takes you to the upper platform, from where there is an extraordinary view out over Barcelona and the sea.

Glass-and-steel commercial buildings may come and go, but the **Reials Drassanes,** or medieval shipyards, are most special. The first work on what became this sprawling construction began in the 13th century. This is the only structure of its kind in the world today—an impressive testimony to the level of Catalan industrial architecture in the Middle Ages.

From these royal dockyards were launched the ships which carried the red-and-yellow Catalan flag to the far corners of the world as it was known before Columbus. Since 1941 the **Museu Marítim** (Maritime Museum) has occupied these appropriate quarters.

The most engrossing display is a full-sized reproduction of the galley *Real*, victorious flagship in the Battle of Lepanto of 1571, where a combined Hispano-Venetian fleet faced the Turks. Elsewhere you can inspect models of fishing boats and freighters, and glamorous ship figureheads. In the cartography department, look for an **37**

---

* The only thing the next items have in common is the geographical coincidence that they are on or near the Barcelona waterfront. They cover a wide swath of the city and a broad range of interests—perhaps something for everybody.

atlas drawn in 1439, which once belonged to Amerigo Vespucci.

Across an extremely wide and heavily congested thoroughfare, an unexpected annexe of the Maritime Museum is moored at the wharf of Portal de la Pau (Gate of Peace). This is a replica of the *Santa María,* Columbus's own flagship—full-sized and said to

Sightseeing tours of Barcelona's busy port include cooling breezes.

be authentically fitted out. You may board the floating mini-museum any time during the day.

Like all big ports, this area of Barcelona is strong on atmosphere. Longshoremen rub shoulders with amateur rod-and-reel-fishermen; guitar-

strumming tourists lie back on their knapsacks waiting for the ferryboat to Ibiza. Tugs nudge a huge white cruise liner to a soft berthing. Sightseeing boats, romantically called *go-londrinas* (swallows), stand by to show tourists the port.

From the Colom the imaginatively redesigned **Moll de Fusta** (still called Moll de Bosch on some maps) provides the perfect setting to eat tapas and watch the harbour.

A largely artificial peninsula protecting the port area from the open sea is called **La Barceloneta** (Little Barcelona). The residents are something like the local equivalent of Cockneys—certainly "characters" different from the rest. Barcelona's most popular seafood restaurants are found in this old fishermen's district. As an 18th-century experiment in urban planning, Barceloneta's street plan is worth a closer look. The blocks are long and uncommonly narrow so that each room of each house faces a street.

Several bus lines terminate at the Passeig Nacional, Barceloneta, site of the city's **Aquari** (Aquarium). Unlike the fishy section of the Barcelona Zoo (see p. 45), this aquarium con-

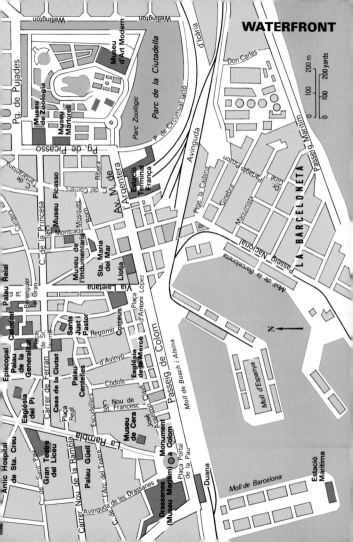

WATERFRONT

Wellington

Museu d'Art Modern

Don Carles

d'Icària

Pg. de Pujades

Museu de Zoologia

Museu Martorell

Parc de la Ciutadella

Parc Zoologic

P. de Circumval·lació

Avinguda

Passeig Marítim

Pg. de Picasso

Estació Terminal França

Av. de M. de l'Argentera

del Comerç

Ribera

Passatge Pizarro

Dr. Giné

Ginebra

LA BARCELONETA

C. de Fontanella

Museu Picasso

Mosques

Born

Pge. la Cadena

Maquinista

C. de la Princesa

C. de Montcada

Museu de l'Indumentaria

Sta. Maria del Mar

Llotja

Passeig Nacional

Cardes

Palau Reial

Pl. Berenguer le Gran

Via Laietana

Plaça d'Antoni López

Moll de la Barceloneta

Episcopal

Catedral

Sants Just i Pastor

Correus

Moll d'Espanya

Palau de la Generalitat

Regomir

Plaça de St. Jaume

Passeig de Colom

Palau Centelles

Església de la Mercè

Moll de Bosch i Alsina

Casa de la Ciutat

Carrer de Ferran

d'Avinyó

Còdols

Palau del Pi

Plaça Reial

C. Nou de St. Francesc

Escudellers

Josep A. Clavé

Anselm Clavé

Antic Hospital de Sta. Creu

C. de Sant Pau

Gran Teatre del Liceu

Palau Güell

Carrer Nou de la Rambla

Museu de Cera

L'Arc del Teatre

Monument a Colom

La Rambla

Drassanes (Museu Marítim)

Plaça Portal de la Pau

Duana

Moll de Barcelona

Estació Marítima

Avinguda de les Drassanes

200 m
200 yards
100
100
0
0

N

cerns itself only with the sea life of the Mediterranean. The lighting is gloomy—for the benefit of the fish, not the people.

Railway yards separate Barceloneta from the Parc de la Ciutadella (see p. 44). The terminal is called Estació de França because trains from France arrive here.

La Llotja is the Barcelona stock exchange. Since the 14th century, a *bolsa* (exchange) of one sort or another has oper-

ated on this spot.

The cornerstone of the **Església de Santa Maria del Mar** (Church of St.Mary-of-the-Sea) was laid in 1329. More than any other edifice in Barcelona, this one sums up the real grandeur of 14th-century Catalan churches. The stark beauty of the interior is heightened by the proportions of its soaring arches. The impression of immensity comes, in part, from the uncluttered lines. In addition to its religious functions, Santa Maria del Mar is often used as a concert hall for programmes of classical music or jazz. It faces the site of medieval tournaments, carnivals processions... and the executions of the Inquisition.

Carrer de Montcada just beyond would make a worthwhile visit even if it didn't contain one of Barcelona's most popular museums. As early as the 12th century, noble families of Catalonia had begun to build their mansions in this street. You can see their crests carved in stone alongside great portals. Better still, wander into the courtyards of the palaces and relive the glory of those medieval achievements.

The **Museu Picasso** is located in three contiguous 13th-century palaces in Carrer de

Montcada. Though Pablo Ruiz Picasso was born in Málaga, he came to Barcelona at the age of 14 to study art. Those days are documented by drawings and paintings in a style evidently imposed on the young genius by unimaginative teachers. But his true talents, from an even earlier age, are strikingly clear in informal sketches, cartoons and doodles. His large oil painting *Science and Charity,* could have been the work of a master; he was 15 at the time. One large exhibition is devoted to a series of 58 paintings which Picasso donated to the museum in 1968. Of these, 44 are bizarre variations on the theme of *Las Meninas,* the famous Velázquez painting in Madrid's Prado Museum.

An important collection of prints—over 100 artist's proofs spanning the decades from the 1920s through the '60s—has gone on view.

Across the street, in another lovely palace, the city of Barcelona has opened the **Museu de l'Indumentaria** (Costume Museum). Fashions for men, women and children as far back as the 16th century are exhibited according to period and use.

Spain's best-known modern sculptor, Antoní Tapiès, pays homage to Picasso in an eccentric fountain sculpture installed on the nearby Passeig de Picasso. Water gushes in and around a glass cube enclosing some old chairs and a sofa—bound with rope, bristling with steel beams and draped with a cloth. Picasso would have been amused.

Gaudí and "Eixample"

"Eixample" means extension or enlargement. In Barcelona, it means the new city which grew beyond the medieval walls in the 19th century. The expansion, several times the area of the existing city, was well planned. Its fine boulevards—the Passeig de Gràcia and Rambla de Catalunya, for instance—are expressions of elegance. The very long, wide **Avinguda Diagonal** is not only the main traffic artery from the motorway (expressway) into the city, but an eminently stately avenue with palm trees and interesting architecture.

The "Eixample" contains some of the most creative buildings ever designed, the work of Barcelona's inspired *art nouveau* architects at the **41** end of the 19th and beginning of the 20th centuries. The greatest of them all was Antoni Gaudí, a controversial genius born in the Catalonian market town of Reus in 1852. He died in Barcelona in 1926, run down by a tram.

Here are half a dozen typical Gaudí projects you could see in one outing, starting in Old Barcelona and working your way out through the "Eixample":

The **Palau Güell**, one of several buildings Gaudí designed for his friend and patron, Eusebio Güell, a British-educated Barcelona industrialist, civic leader and nobleman. This palace, just off the bustling Rambla (see p. 33), keeps its biggest innovations out of public view: its front façade, decorated with imaginative ironwork, lacks Gaudí's wit and colour. The rooftop chimney array is so original that it relieves some of the severity.

Casa Batlló. People emerging from the Metro (underground railway) here in Passeig de Gràcia may be startled to come face to face with Gaudí's sensuous curves in stone and iron, and his delicate tiles. The house next door, the Casa Amatller by the brilliant Cata-

lan architect Puig i Cadafalch, conflicts with Gaudí's effort so aggressively that this group of houses is often called the Block of Discord (in Spanish, this involves an ironic play on words).

Casa Milá ("La Pedrera").

One of Gaudí's classic buildings: Casa Batlló, in Passeig de Gràcia.

On the corner of Passeig de Gràcia and Carrer de Provença, this big block of flats stirs strong feelings. Some say it's too heavy, a stone monstrosity; Gaudí fans love its undulating façade, adorned with original wrought-iron-work, and the famous roof-terrace with its weird formations covering chimneys and ventilators.

Casa Vicenç. This was designed more than 20 years earlier than Casa Milá, when Gaudí was still groping for his style. In fact, Casa Vicenç, a summer home for a rich tile merchant, was Gaudí's first big job as an architect. The distinctive ironwork, the bright ideas with tile may rate admiration, but the overall effect seems incoherent.

Parc Güell. This incomparably inventive park started out as a suburban real estate development which failed. Count Güell and Gaudí wanted to create a perfect garden city for 60 families. But only two houses were sold (Gaudí bought one of them). The happy originality of Güell Park, bought by the city of Barcelona in 1926, delights young and old. See the ginger-bread-type houses, the cheery use of tiles, the huge serpentine bench bordering the main plaza. Explore the grounds and discover that the plaza is in fact the roof for what would have been a market-place supported by a thicket of 96 mock-classical columns. The last column in each regiment is playfully askew. Along the woods, walk under the perilously tilted arcade.

Temple Expiatori de la Sagrada Familia (Holy Family). Gaudí's eternally unfinished "sandcastle cathedral" must be seen; you may not believe it. Wild and wonderful, it is an extravagant hymn to one man's talent and faith. In his first four towers, was Gaudí consciously or unconsciously echoing the filigree of the classic cathedral in the Gothic Quarter? Or the shape of "human castles" of Catalan folk-lore? If he had lived, would he have continued in the same way? Can one building, however immense, ever success-fully combine so many disparate styles? Gaudí's cathedral produces puzzlement and awe. Many Catalans see this stupendous church as an extension of their own faith and strivings; their donations keep the construction work going. **43**

Don't be afraid of the huge cranes hauling pillars and streamlined arches into position. Where else can you stand inside a roofless cathedral and watch it being built? Before your eyes descendants of the great Catalan stonecutters are shaping the faces of angels.

Ciutadella

The residents of Barcelona greatly appreciate the Parc de la Ciutadella (Park of the Citadel) because it is a big, green refuge from the congestion of the city. They also appreciate it for symbolic reasons going back to the early 18th century.

In those days, the area, called La Ribera, was a pleasant residential suburb of perhaps 10,000 people. Because Barcelona fought on the losing side in the War of the Succession, a vengeful Philip V ordered Ribera levelled. Then he conscripted all the carpenters and masons of Barcelona to build a fortress on the spot.

In the middle of the 19th century, this building of bitter memories was at last demolished. And, characteristically, in its place, the city built a park

with gardens, lakes and promenades.

The great fountain is one of those monumental excesses typical of the period. This titanic mass of sculpture looks like a work of a committee, and indeed it was. One of the contributors was Gaudí, then a student of architecture.

The **Museu d'Art Modern** is actually devoted to Catalan

Beloved Barcelona fountain keeps statue of lady dry under umbrella.

art of the last 100 years. Outstanding here are the works of such great painters as Isidre Nonell, Ramon Casas and Mariano Fortuny, the latter a native of Reus, Gaudí's home town near Tarragona. Notice the wealth of astutely recorded detail in *The Vicarage*, and you can't miss *The Battle of Tetuán*, an action-packed panorama which fills a whole wall. Fortuny knew whereof he painted; he was the 19th-century equivalent of a combat photographer in Morocco.

Looking Down

Barcelona is crazy about views from on high.

A modern, modified cable-car built with Swiss technical assistance, floats high above the city between the Estació Funicular and Montjuïc. An elaborate "aerial ropeway" *(transbordador)* strung from towers 426 feet high serves a similar purpose between the port and Montjuïc.

If you have a queasy stomach, try the less daring cog railway running up to Tibidabo.

For a superb panorama of Barcelona, go up to the fortress high on the summit of Montjuïc (see pp. 36–37 or to the temple of Tibidabo (p. 46).

If time's short, ascend the pillar supporting the Columbus Statue in the port.

Upstairs the museum shows a hotch-potch of modern art, sculpture and *art-nouveau* furnishings.

A sizeable corner of the park is devoted to the **Barcelona Zoo,** an admirable modern version of the conventional collection of animals. Under a reform programme of the 1950s the zoo eliminated fences, using instead moats or

Star of the show at Barcelona zoo: albino gorilla thrives in captivity.

lakes to separate the public from the fauna. Young and old can enjoy six well planned departments: African animals, felines, monkeys, reptiles, birds and fish. A great attraction of the zoo, especially for children, are the dolphin and the killerwhale shows. **45**

Pedralbes

Barcelona's richest residential area, Pedralbes, consists of fashionable blocks of flats, earlier *art nouveau* buildings, and villas discreetly guarded by ornamental fences. (One of those fences—by Gaudí—in Avinguda Pedralbes, is a first-class work of art in itself.)

The **Palau de Pedralbes,** set in a charming park, looks quite livable. The palace was built in the 1920s as a municipal gift to King Alfonso XII. Most of the furnishings and works of art were imported from Italy. The king didn't get to enjoy it much, as he was forced to abdicate in 1931.

The palace houses a charming museum of carriages and the **Colecció Cambó,** a magnificent collection of paintings by the greatest Italian, French, Spanish and Dutch artists, assembled by a Catalan named Francesc Cambó.

The other important sight of Pedralbes, one of Barcelona's finest historic buildings, is the **Monestir de Pedralbes.** It was founded in 1326 by Elisenda de Montcada, the queen of Jaime II; she is buried in the monastery's Catalan Gothic church. Several dozen nuns live here today.

The cloister, with 25 arches on each side, rises three storeys high. You can meditate (briefly) among the poplars and orange trees in the quadrangle. But don't miss the monastery's greatest artistic treasure, in a cramped little chapel lit by two fluorescent tubes. The murals here were painted by Ferrer Bassa, the greatest 14th-century Catalan artist.

Tibidabo

For a first, or last, look at Barcelona no place excels Tibidabo, a mountain about 1,650 feet above the city. On an average of once a month, when visibility is flawless, it's said you can see the mountains of Majorca from here. On an ordinary day you can look down on all Barcelona and a slice of the Costa Dorada as well. Tibidabo can be reached by car, or by an adventurous combination of train, tram and cable car. It's a very popular excursion for the people of Barcelona, especially on a Sunday.

The shrine at the summit is the Templo Expiatorio del Sagrado Corazón (Expiatory Temple of the Sacred Heart of Jesus), a neo-Gothic extravaganza erected in 1911. A huge statue of a Christ with outstretched arms stands upon the topmost tower.

Just beneath the church is a big amusement park with a roller coaster, an old-fashioned aeroplane-go-round, and other rides for children or light-hearted adults. The **Museu d'Autòmats** (Mechanical Dolls Museum) contains one of the most enchanting collections of those 19th-century toys. There are also hotels on Tibidabo, as well as restaurants, snack-bars, sports facilities, an observatory and a TV tower.

Nothing shy about the pigeons in Plaça de Catalunya at lunch time.

Sitges and the Coast South of Barcelona

The coastal landscape on the south side of Barcelona has its share of cliffs and coves, but consists mainly of broad sand beaches. For variety there are appealing fishing villages, and even a stretch of green paddy fields. Along with the scenery

near outskirts hold practically no interest for tourists. (A vital exception is the international airport, close by the sea at El Prat de Llobregat.)

The first resort town following El Prat, CASTELLDEFELS, enjoys an extremely long sand beach. Low-rise hotels, apartment houses and villas exploit the coastline, while the town centre looks inland. In the 13th

and water sports the region is rich in history and culture.

Leaving Barcelona towards the south-west the suburbs can't seem to decide whether they are agricultural or factory towns—or just half-hearted resorts. Whatever the label, the

century, when Castelldefels first entered the history books, the sea was a danger. Watch-towers, some still standing, guarded against pirates. The castle which gave the town its name, impressive enough from afar, has become dilapidated since its last renovation in 1897.

A small **museum** is maintained in a restored mansion below the castle. The exhibits in the Casa de Cultura include prehistoric tools and 19th-century farm implements.

Beyond Castelldefels the railway line cuts through mountains, while the road winds around them the hard way, often skirting cliffsides dramatically. Two villages appear at unexpected inlets. GARRAF, an industrial town, has a marina and unobtrusive villas. VALLCARCA, with its own cargo port, is not a tourist town at all.

By the time the coastline begins to level out, the scene changes dramatically. **Sitges,** an internationally admired resort, combines natural beauty, liveliness and dignity.

Sitges is one of the rare Spanish coastal resorts which has maintained its identity, avoiding the monstrosities of tourist architecture while still encouraging tourism. This is one town without repetitive high-rise hotels. The swinging "downtown" area lives one life; further along the seafront promenade, the "other half"—largely wealthy families from Barcelona—enjoys a quieter

existence in villas hidden behind high, trimmed hedges. The beach is nearly three miles long—enough for crowd-lovers and seekers of serenity as well. Bathing is safe for children, as it tends to be all the way from here to Tarragona and beyond.

The parish church, on a promontory, was built between the 16th and 18th centuries,

Surfboard plus sail equals exciting sport, only for the well-balanced.

but sacked during the Civil War. It may not be an architectural gem, but its dramatic setting makes up for that; at night, it is skilfully illuminated **49** against the sky. Just behind the church, two museums contribute to the cultural atmosphere which helps explain the town's long-standing appeal to artists and intellectuals. The **Museu Cau Ferrat** (Cau Ferrat—or "iron lair"—Museum) contains a moving El Greco portrait, *The Tears of St. Peter,* as well as a blazingly colourful early oil by Picasso, *Corrida*

After an exhausting day of tanning, tourists stroll beneath the palms of Sitges and plan the night's agenda.

de toros. Here you can also see many works by Santiago Rusiñol (1861–1931), the Catalan artist and writer who gave the building to the town. Nextdoor, the **Museu Mar i Cel** (Sea and Sky Museum), in a 14th-century palace, displays medieval sculpture and religious paintings. A few streets inland, another museum is aimed at people who don't normally go to museums, least of all at a resort. The **Museu Romàntic** (Romantic Museum) of Sitges is an old aristocratic home lavishly decorated in 19th-century style and full of the fascinating *things* of the era—furniture, clocks and music boxes that work.

With its whitewashed houses facing narrow hilly streets, its gourmet restaurants, pizza parlours and flamenco nightclubs, and its mild climate, Sitges attracts holiday-makers over many months of the year. A very special time, however, comes every spring. At the fiesta of Corpus Christi the streets are covered with fresh flowers—a quarter of a million of them, in inventive patterns. The beauty couldn't be more fleeting, for the flower carpets last just one day.

A few miles down the coast

the city of VILANOVA I LA GELTRÚ has an extensive sand beach but much less tourist development than Sitges.

Befitting a town of about 45,000 people, there is a serious museum—the **Museu Balaguer** —devoted mainly to 19th-century paintings by Catalan artists.

Vilanova i la Geltrú also has its non-serious museum, a first cousin of the Romantic Museum in Sitges. **Casa Papiol,** an 18th-century mansion, re-creates a vanished way of life— right down to the stables and wine-cellar, and a trim garden in which swans reside along-side magnificent peacocks.

The only excitements be-tween the villages of CUBELLES and CUNIT are the River Foix and the boundary line dividing the provinces of Barcelona and Tarragona.

Slightly further down the coast, CALAFELL is much more of a tourist centre. With its two-mile long beach, Cala-fell was a natural choice for exploitation.

Shortly inland from Cala-fell lies EL VENDRELL, an impor-tant wine town and shopping centre and the birthplace of cellist Pablo Casals (1876–1973).

COMARRUGA, with nearly three miles of sand beach, has been transformed into a fash-ionable holiday resort with big hotels to supplement its com-fortable villas. It's a spa and sporting centre as well.

The coast road along here— usually jammed in summer— follows the Roman highway to Tarragona. A startling remind-er of this confronts motorists not far beyond Comarruga. In the middle of the road stands a triumphal arch—not one of those ugly neo-classical models commemorating some recent war, but the real thing. This well-proportioned monument, tall as a three-floor building has been there since the 2nd century A.D. The **Arc de Berà** (Arch of Berà), as it's called, now stands in a position of honour in a small island of green; instead of going under the arch, as it did for hundreds of years, the road now makes a detour around it.

TORREDEMBARRA, the next big resort centre, is expanding along its wide sand beach with new hotels, villas and flats. The local castle, until recently in private hands is restored by the government.

The next castle down the road, in the inland town of

ALTAFULLA, is said to have been begun in the 11th century. Altafulla is the kind of village where the children wave at foreigners. Its medieval back streets are as quiet as a museum.

TAMARIT Castle, visible from afar, juts out above the sea. Even though holiday-makers swim from beaches on either side of Tamarit, the castle looks thoroughly invulnerable. It may have been built in the 11th century, but has been considerably restored since then.

Finally, three notable historical sites as the traveller approaches the Tarragona area.

El Medol, a Roman stone-quarry, is right along the motorway *(autopista)* at the last service area before Tarragona. This man-made crater provided some of the stone for the Roman developments in Tarragona. You can almost see the same grain in the rock as in the great blocks of the city wall.

Right at the edge of the old coast road (N.340), the so-called **Torre de los Escipiones** (Tower of the Scipios) was a Roman funeral monument. Little can be said with assurance about this structure, probably a 1st century A.D. tomb. The sculpted figures of two men in Roman military dress can still be distinguished, but time has erased most other details.

The considerate highway engineers provided parking space and sightseeing facilities in honour of another ancient structure along the route,

Seaside apparition near Tarragona: austere, daunting Tamarit Castle.

known locally as **Pont del Diable** (Devil's Bridge). This perfect Roman aqueduct, a double-decker of stone, carried Tarragona's water supply from the River Gayá. No viaduct of today is more sound or practical—or more graceful.

Tarragona

Pop. 120,000
(Barcelona, 98 km.)

In the 3rd century B.C., the Romans landed at Tarragona and set up military and political headquarters. They liked its strategic location, mild climate and wine. So will you.

Tarraco, as the town was called, became the capital of Rome's biggest Spanish province. It grew to a population of 30,000 and coined its own money. It was one of the formidable imperial capitals of Antiquity. So much was built, and so much remains, that Tarragona sometimes feels like a time machine. Turn a corner and you flip from the 20th century to the 15th, or the 1st.

For example: **Plaça de la Font,** an apparently unexceptional spot to begin a walking tour of Tarragona. The middle of this elongated oblong plaza is now a municipal car park. The city hall occupies one end. But Plaça de la Font is built on the site of the Roman Circus, the 2nd or 3rd century A.D. precursor of a bullring.

Just behind the city hall, a modern avenue called Vía de l'Imperi skilfully recreates the grace of Roman times. The

Romans constructed amphitheatre overlooking the sea in Tarragona.

mosaics are reminiscent of the walks of Pompeii. The Roman column is authentic. This short street climbs to one of Tarragona's outstanding features: the **Passeig Arqueològic** (archaeological promenade), a close-up tour of the ancient city wall.

Nothing here is more than

53

about 2,100 years old—even the foundation of the wall, composed of titanic uncut stones weighing up to 35 tons each. They are often referred to as "cyclopean" because of their enormity and irregular shape.

Not only is the wall, with its towers and gateways, a notable historical and architectural attraction, there are also fine panoramas of the countryside and the sea. But don't be misled when you discover, just down the hill, a well preserved open-air Greek theatre. It's a municipal auditorium, built in 1970.

The Passeig Arqueològic, among other impressive ancient sites in Tarragona, is revealed in all its glory on summer nights, when it's bathed in illumination.

Leaving the last gateway, we follow the Passeig Torroja outside the wall as it curves toward the sea. A small park surrounding the Creu de Sant Antoni (St. Anthony's Cross) erected in 1604 faces one of the main gates of the walled city. The Portal de Sant Antoni (St. Anthony's Gateway) leads into the labyrinth of medieval Tarragona, a markedly Mediterranean city with flowerpots in the windows, laundry hanging out to dry and canaries in cages on the walls.

If you can resist wandering at random through this splash of local colour, stick to the Vía Granada until you reach the Plaça del Rei (King's Square). The **Museu Arqueològic** here is a modern, well designed exhibit of delicate mosaics, ancient utensils, pre-Roman, Roman and Spanish coins.

Adjoining the museum, the building once known as the King's Castle is now called the **Pretori Romà** (Roman Pretorium). This much-restored 2,000-year-old fortress contains more archaeological items, including a beautifully sculpted marble sarcophagus found in the sea. You can follow underground passages which linked the castle with the circus (now Plaça de la Font). The vaults served as dungeons in Antiquity, and again during the Spanish Civil War.

Walking from here toward the sea, you can look down upon the Roman **amphitheatre** built into the hillside. During excavations in 1953, an early Christian church was found on the site of the amphitheatre. Presumably, the primitive basilica was a memorial to a bish-

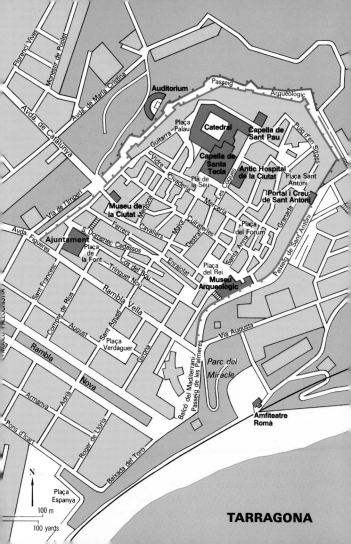

TARRAGONA

Florenci Vives
Monestir de Poblet
Avda. de Maria Cristina
Avda. de Catalunya
Auditorium
Passeig Arqueològic
Plaça Palau
Guitarra
Catedral
Capella de Sant Pau
Puig d'en Sitges
Vidre
Capella de Santa Tecla
Antic Hospital de la Ciutat
Plaça Sant Antoni
Civaderia
Pla de la Seu
Cortes
Portal i Creu de Sant Antoni
Via de l'Imperi
Museu de la Ciutat
Mercería
Granada
Avda. Figueres
Ferrers
Medina
Cavallers
Mayor
Cuiratería
Plaça del Forum
Passeig de Sant Antoni
Ajuntament
S. Domenec Cedassos
Plaça de la Font
Destral
Santa Anna
Cos del Bou
Enrajolat
Plaça del Rei
Sant Francesc
Trinquet Nou
Museu Arqueològic
Comte de Rius
Rambla Vella
Via Augusta
Sant August
Plaça Verdaguer
Girona
Rambla Nova
Parc del Miracle
Armanyà
Adrià
Balcó del Mediterrani
Passeig de les Palmeres
Pons d'Icart
Roder de Lúria
Amfiteatre Romà
Barxada del Toro

N

Plaça Espanya

100 m
100 yards

op and two deacons burned to death there in A.D. 259.

Here, above the ruins and the sea, begins what's called the **Balcó del Maditerrani** (Balcony of the Mediterranean), a cliffside promenade, Tarragona's pride. The view of the sea is unbeatable.

Tarragona's **Rambla** runs uphill and ends at the Balcony of the Mediterranean. Otherwise, it's reminiscent of Barcelona's famous promenade, with many trees, outdoor cafés and a great variety of shops all along it. The statue at the top end of the Rambla honours Admiral Roger de Lauria, a swashbuckling 13th-century hero of the Kingdom of Catalonia and Aragon.

Two other important ancient sites—beyond the area of the walking tour—must be mentioned before we turn to medieval Tarragona.

Near the central market and post office, with its entrance in Carrer Lleida, the remains of the **Roman Forum** have been unearthed. Unlike most archaeological excavations, this one is *above* the level of the present-day city, so two halves of the forum are now connected by a footbridge above Carrer Soler. You can

wander around the area at will, visualizing the layout of houses, shops and other amenities. This well-kept open-air museum is completely hemmed in by a modern city, yet keeps a stately calm.

On the edge of the city, overlooking the River Francolí, an extraordinary museum has been established in an unlikely place. The **Necròpoli i Museu**

Paleocristià (Necropolis and Paleo-Christian Museum), a cemetery for Tarragona's early Christians, is about as big as three football fields. The site has been left essentially as it was. You can walk along the observation platforms looking down upon hundreds of graves, urns and even bones lying where they were uncovered. And in the adjoining museum you can see the best of the finds. Several 5th-century sarcophagi are sculpted with astounding skill.

Medieval Tarragona

Walking up Carrer Sant Agustí from the Rambla, the old city soon closes in. By the time the street's name has changed—to Major—you can feel the throb of real main-stream Mediterranean life. The road turns a bend and suddenly the **Cathedral** comes into view, strangely cropped at the edges by its elevation and the narrowness of the street.

A flight of 19 steps leads from the end of Carrer Major to the Plà de la Seu, an attractive, almost intimate square before the church. But don't overlook the last cross-

street before the cathedral— the Mercería (Haberdashery Street) with its medieval porticoes. A shop here advertises canaries; a female costs half the price of a male (presumably because females can't sing).

Ancient tomb sculpture (opposite) *is one facet of Tarragona beauty. Streets, cathedral add to mood.*

Surrounding walls and tricks of perspective may distort your estimation of the cathedral's size. The area of the façade is deceptive. But the great Gothic doorway, and one of Europe's largest rose windows above it, provide a clue.

Follow the arrows to the tourist entrance, far around the church to the left, via the cloister. Construction of this cathedral, on the site of a Roman temple to Jupiter, was begun in 1171, and it was consecrated in 1331. The architectural styles inside the cathedral mix Romanesque and Gothic; the overall effect, looking up at the great vaulted ceiling, is austere majesty.

The **main altarpiece,** carved in alabaster by the 15th-century Catalan master Pere Johan, shows splendid lifelike detail. It is dedicated to St. Thecla, the local patron saint. She is said to have been converted to Christianity by St. Paul, who, according to legend, preached in Tarragona.

To the right of the high altar is the tomb of Prince Don Juan de Aragón, an archbishop of Tarragona who died in 1334 at the age of 33. Note the sensitive carving on the sepulchre. The artist's identity is un-

known; the influence seems to be Italian.

Nineteen chapels fill the sides of the church. Their design and decoration tend to extremes—either unforgettably beautiful, or unexpectedly 19th-century kitsch. Don't miss **three chapels:** Capella de Nostra Senyora de Montserrat (Chapel of Our Lady of Montserrat), with its 15th-century altarpiece; the filigreed sculpture in the 14th-century Capella de Santa Maria dels Sastres (Chapel of St. Mary of the Tailors) and the 18th-century Capella de Santa Tecla (Chapel of St. Thecla).

And if the art appreciation and sheer foot-slogging become a bit too much, just take a seat in the congregation and look up at the sunbeams piercing the filters of the rose window.

Outside, again, the **cloister** offers some surprises. First, its size—some 150 feet down each side. The quadrangle is so big that there is little shade, and perhaps less feeling of serenity than in other cloisters of the 12th and 13th centuries. But notice the sculptural innovations and details. Everyone stops to figure out the relief known as the Procession of the

Rats, a wry fable carved 700 years before the invention of Mickey Mouse. Built into one of the walls is another unexpected feature—a Moslem monument of marble. The date on its inscription works out to A.D. 960. This *mihrab* or shrine is believed to have arrived in Tarragona as a battle trophy.

The cathedral's **Museu Dio-**

Fishermen back from sea assign repair of nets to their womenfolk.

cesà (Diocesan Museum) possesses prehistoric and Roman archaeological relics, medieval religious paintings, and a large and valuable collection of tapestries.

Tarragona-on-Sea

For a drastic change of pace, take a bus or taxi, or a very long walk, down to the Tarragona waterfront district unaccountably known as **El Serrall** (the harem). This is clearly an important fishing centre, a radical escalation from the usual quaint port found elsewhere along this coast. In the afternoon the big trawlers come back from the open sea. Trays of ice and big refrigerated lorries are waiting on the quayside. Before disembarking, the tanned fishermen clean and separate the different species of fish in the hold. They swallow the last trickle of wine from the ship's *porrón,* then step ashore to bargain with wholesalers over prices. Elsewhere along the quay, half a dozen women seated under parasols mend the huge fishnets bound for sea before the next dawn.

For local colour, and aroma, El Serrall is hard to match. If you have half a chance, eat in one of the nearby fish restaurants. Tarragona cooking is known far and wide in Catalonia, and the ingredients couldn't be fresher. **59**

South-West of Tarragona

While Tarragona has its own municipal beaches, the nearest resort of international renown is **Salou,** about 10 kilometres down the coast. This cosmopolitan centre calls itself Playa de Europa (beach of Europe). Salou's good fortune is due to its two-mile-long beach, bor-

The town of Salou (pronounced Sal-OH-oo) distinguishes itself with almost universal good taste: the villas and blocks of flats maintain high architectural standards, the gardens are well kept and even the modern monument to James I the Conqueror fits right into place. The beach at Salou was the port of embarkation for James' armada which

dered by a lavish promenade with solid rows of stubby palm trees and masses of colourfully arranged flowers. What's more, swimmers who need more adventure can desert the beach and opt for half-hidden coves around rugged Cape Salou.

Real life along the coast: fishermen crouch over nets, while shoppers exchange strong opinions.

wrested Majorca from the Moors in 1229.

Salou's suburb of VILAFORTUNY, with another long beach, consists primarily of exclusive villas protected by high fences or hedges. The landscaping is exceptional.

CAMBRILS, often described as a "typical seafaring village", is a standard fishing port which happens to interrupt the solid line of beaches down the coast. Its charm centres on the large fleet of *bous*—small fishing boats carrying over-sized lamps for night duty. Cambrils can claim to be something of a gourmet town. Its waterfront counts more fine seafood restaurants than many a metropolis. Enthusiasts drive there from miles around, not for the water sports nor the scenery, but just for a meal.

MIAMI PLATJA has plenty of sand and sea, yet doesn't quite live up to the glamour of its name. It's just a quiet resort community of villas and apartments and family hotels. But the setting is dramatic—hills and cliffs push right onto the beaches.

The small resort of L'HOSPITALET DE L'INFANT (Hospice of the Prince) is built alongside the ruins of a 14th-century hospice for pilgrims, after which the town was named.

Between L'Hospitalet and the next resort on the coast, L'Ametlla de Mar, the shore is almost undeveloped, with one startling exception. The nuclear power station of Vandellós looms up like a science-fiction spaceport. At any rate, the titanic red and white main building looks as if it would be

more comfortable at Cape Canaveral than on this beachfront. Power lines fan out into the countryside.

L'AMETLLA, by happy contrast, is a no-nonsense, picture-postcard fishing village. Four nearby beaches make it something of a tourist centre, but this hasn't marred the town's picturesque charm. With its solid sea-wall, Fishermen's Guild, ice factory and a few cafés, it remains a genuine fishing port.

Just past the small port of L'AMPOLLA, the remarkable **Ebro Delta** begins. This lush, tropical peninsula—more than 100 square miles—was created from the mud travelling down the River Ebro all the way from Zaragoza. The river continues its land reclamation work and the delta expands quite perceptibly each year. A rich rice-growing district, it's all so flat that sometimes, with the reeds growing tall along the back roads, the level of the canals seems higher than the road. The delta is a rallying point for migratory birds—and for bird-watchers with binoculars or cameras.

AMPOSTA, a town of nearly 15,000 people, dominates the delta. It is considered a key centre for sports fishing. In earlier times, Amposta guarded the river route and charged a toll on ships heading inland.

TORTOSA (population 50,000) commands both banks of the Ebro, which explains its strategic importance since ancient times. Julius Caesar awarded Tortosa the title of independent municipality. The elaborate fortress at the top of the town belonged to the Moors, who held out there at length during the Christian Reconquest in 1148. The castle of San Juan is still known by its Arabic name, La Zuda.

Tortosa's **cathedral,** now a national monument, appears at first sight to be abandoned and menaced by the town around it. But you can enter through the cloister, which is well shaded by tall pines. The cathedral, built during the 14th, 15th and 16th centuries, is a classic example of Catalan Gothic. Don't miss the 14th-century triptych, painted on wood, and the two 15th-century carved stone pulpits.

Attempts to make the River Ebro a major navigational channel—Aragon's age-old dream of an outlet to the sea—have been dormant for 50 years. But the river still permeates everyday life in Tortosa. It looks as if it's carrying all the soil of Spain out to the Mediterranean—not the sort of river you'd want to swim in

The last town of any note along the coast, before the provincial boundary marks the

end of the Costa Dorada and the beginning of the Costa del Azahar, is SANT CARLES DE LA RÁPITA. Its huge natural harbour, supplemented by man-made sea-walls, serves a prosperous fishing fleet. A good deal of ship-building activity may be seen here, as well. But what makes Sant Carles (population about 10,000) different from all the other towns is its **main square.**

This gigantic plaza looks just the place for a coronation parade. It is so enormous, and the town itself so small, that there aren't enough shops and offices to fill its perimeter; many of the buildings are just private houses. The square was a city-planning brainstorm of Charles III, an eccentric 18th-century ruler who pictured Sant Carles as a port of international significance. The grandiose project died with him in 1788, but the legacy of his street plan and the melancholy square remain. Impertinently, the main road to Valencia goes right down the middle of Charles's freakish plaza.

Traditional fishing fleet occupies waterfront in Cambrils but tourists coexist and exploit nearby beaches.

Inland Excursions

Montserrat
(Barcelona, 62 km.)

For 700 years, pilgrims have been climbing the mighty rock formations to the monastery of Montserrat. Now that donkeys have been replaced by cable cars and excursion coaches, about a million people make the trip every year. The statistics don't say how many are pilgrims and how many are just sightseers, but one way or the other, visitors feel uplifted in this mountain redoubt.

Geographically and spiritually, Montserrat is the heart of Catalonia. The ancient Benedictine monastery, tucked into the rock, houses the patron of the Catalans—a 12th-century polychrome wood image of the Virgin Mary called **La Moreneta,** the little brown Madonna. Notice her nose: long, thin and pointed; it's the same nose you'll see on half the faces in the congregation. It's a thoroughly Catalan nose.

The brown madonna is so avidly venerated here that you may have to queue for 15 minutes for a look. The statue, in a niche above the basilica's high altar, is protected by glass. But a circle cut out of the shield permits the faithful to touch or kiss the image's outstretched right hand. Your visit may be delayed a minute or two while formally dressed newly-weds are ushered to the head of the line to pray and be photographed alongside La Moreneta (an unusual number of weddings take place in the pompous basilica, often witnessed by thousands of foreign tourists).

Tour companies run half-day and full-day excursions to Montserrat from Barcelona and all the major resorts of the Costa Dorada.

A highlight of any visit to Montserrat is its choir. The young choristers of the Escolanía, thought to be the oldest music-school in Europe, perform in the monastery at midday. The angelic voices sing as inspiringly as advertised.

A guided tour of the monastery concentrates on its **museum,** devoted to works of art and history. Several rooms cover "the Biblical East" through relics thousands of years old from Mesopotamia, Egypt and Palestine. Gold and silver chalices and reliquaries are on view. And the museum's art gallery owns a number of notable paintings, including a striking *Portrait of St. Jerome* by Caravaggio.

The monks here are rarely in view, busy as they are elsewhere with prayer, meditation, study in a 200,000-volume library, and down-to-earth labour. They make pottery, run a goldsmith's workshop and a printing plant, and distill a pleasant herbal liqueur called *Aromas de Montserrat.*

For a few pesetas, you can sample *Aromas* in the monastery's tourist bar, which also dispenses coffee and soft and hard drinks. It is one of a disconcertingly mundane array of shops and services for visitors. Montserrat has a hotel, a hairdressing salon, self-service restaurant and a souvenir supermarket.

The brisk commercial atmosphere disillusions some pilgrims, but the overall effect of Montserrat and its eerie mountains remains powerful.

In the basilica, with its eight-ton stone altar made of the mountain itself, sit and listen to the boys sing the *Virolai,* Montserrat's hymn. Perhaps you'll be able to distinguish some of the words—*Montserrat* and *la catalana terra.* The Catalan land and Montserrat have been inseparable

Symbol of Catalanism, Montserrat monastery is tucked into the rock.

for centuries. You'll begin to understand how when you hear the congregation join the choir in this anthem. **65**

Poblet
(Barcelona, 132 km.)

When you've seen one monastery, you have definitely not seen them all. The medieval fortress-monastery of Poblet contrasts sharply with Montserrat. Few tourists crowd Poblet, 45 kilometres northwest of Tarragona. While Montserrat clings to its granite

This powerful Cistercian monastery was founded more than 800 years ago by the count of Barcelona, Ramón Berenguer IV, as a gesture of thanksgiving for the reconquest of Catalonia from the Moors. The royal connections brought the monastery fame, fortune and historical importance. Poblet's church, as large as a cathedral, contains the **tombs** of the kings

mountain, Poblet sprawls upon a wide-open plateau amidst fertile hillsides. Montserrat's buildings, almost totally destroyed in 1811, were replaced by undistinguished architecture. Poblet's buildings were plundered and pillaged in 1835, but lovingly restored—and they have great architectural importance, as well as beauty.

of Aragon, suspended on unique low arches in the cross vault. Here lie James I the Conqueror (Jaime I el Conquistador), Peter the Ceremonious (Pedro el Ceremonioso), John I (Juan I) and his two wives, and Alphonse the Chaste (Alfonso el Casto). (Only fragments of the original sculpture were preserved, so the pantheon of today is a skilled reproduction.) Another outstanding example of alabaster sculpture is the **altarpiece** by the 16th-century artist Damia Forment. Tourists are guided through the most historic halls making up the monastic community.

The real appreciation of a monastic mood comes in the **cloister,** with its rose bushes

Beauty and tranquillity in medieval surroundings at Poblet monastery.

and four brooding poplars, the quiet relieved only by the trickling fountain and the twitter of birds. Beauty and serenity reign in this historic quadrangle.

Santes Creus
(Barcelona, 98 km.)

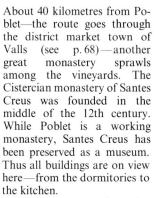

About 40 kilometres from Poblet—the route goes through the district market town of Valls (see p. 68)—another great monastery sprawls among the vineyards. The Cistercian monastery of Santes Creus was founded in the middle of the 12th century. While Poblet is a working monastery, Santes Creus has been preserved as a museum. Thus all buildings are on view here—from the dormitories to the kitchen.

The **cloister,** a pioneering work of Catalan Gothic design, dates from the beginning of the 14th century. Notice the stone carvings on the arches and in unexpected places on the walls: heraldic designs, animals, sometimes humorous faces.

The **church,** begun in 1174, is austere and powerful. The kings of Aragon and Catalonia were patrons of Santes Creus; the monastery's abbot was royal chaplain. And here, opposite the presbytery, are royal sepulchres. King Peter III the Great (Pedro el Grande) is buried here in a temple-within-in-a-church—a tall Gothic tabernacle. The royal remains **67** were interred in a Roman bath resting on four stone lions and covered by an elaborate alabaster tombstone.

In addition to several tombs of lesser grandeur, the monastery reveals its regal connections in the so-called "Royal Palace"—living quarters surrounding a perfect 14th-century patio of delicate arches and a finely sculpted staircase.

Human castle team assembles
68 *itself gingerly at breakneck speed.*

Valls

(Barcelona, 105 km.)

The busy provincial town of Valls (population about 15,000) is famous throughout Catalonia for two odd superlatives. It produces the highest-rising human castles and the most delicious onions.

The *castellers* (see FOLKLORE, page 71) of Valls—known here as the *Xiquets* (pronounced SHEE-kets)—are looked up to both figuratively and literally. No other team in Catalonia has ever managed such skyscrapers of boys balanced atop men astride giants.

As for the onions—called *calçots*—they are gently cooked when very young, dipped in a special sauce, and consumed with grilled sausage or lamb. Summer tourists miss the boat, for this feast only takes place from about December to April.

The next best treat for visitors is *Firagost*, as the festivities of the first half of August are called. Farmers from the entire district bring their finest flowers and fruits to Valls for a tribute to the bounty of the earth. It's a lively time, with folk-dancing, fireworks and, of course, personal appearances by the *Xiquets.*

Vilafranca del Penedés
(Barcelona, 54 km.)

In the year 1217 the Catalonian parliament—the Cortes Catalanes—convened for the first time. The place: Vilafranca del Penedés, on a fertile plateau midway between Barcelona and Tarragona. Since then the population has grown tenfold, to 20,000. But the city still commands more fame than its size would justify. Thousands of tourists who come here by car or coach think of Vilafranca as Wine City. This is the home of Spain's most impressive **wine museum.**

You don't have to be a connoisseur, or even a drinker, to find fascination in the exhibits. Lively three-dimensional dioramas illustrate the business and pleasure of wine through the ages. You can see the actual wine presses which were crushing the grapes 2,000 years ago. And one hall displays glasses, bottles and jugs covering centuries of thirst. There is even an art gallery devoted to the vine and its ramifications.

The wine museum shares its quarters with the **Museu Municipal** (city museum) of Vilafranca, devoted primarily to geological exhibits and pre-historic finds. The building used to be a palace of the counts of Barcelona and the kings of Aragon.

Vilafranca del Penedés has one other enthusiasm. The local team of *castellers*— human pyramids—so captivates the citizens that in 1963 a monument was unveiled in their honour. It's right there in Plaça Jaume I, an interpretation of a five-story *pilar*; locally it's claimed to be among the world's tallest modern statues.

Several wine producers in the Penedés district invite tourists to visit their premises for an explanation of the production process and a sample of the end result. An impressive establishment at Sant Sadurní d'Anoia, the Codorniu caves, attracts many excursion coaches. From January to June, this one plant turns out thousands of bottles of "sparkling cellar wine" per day.

Andorra
(Barcelona, 220 km.)

Excursion firms all along the Costa Dorada advertise gruelling one-day trips to Andorra, **69** the 188-square-mile principality huddling between mountain peaks in the Pyrenees. With well over 200 kilometres of travel in each direction, not much time is left for sightseeing in tiny Andorra itself. In fact, most of the visit is devoted to shopping. Since Andorra is free of the taxes which afflict neighbouring countries, the price of almost

are almost universally understood, while English and German are most useful in the shops.

Aside from the crass business of bargain-hunting, take time for a stroll through ANDORRA LA VELLA, the capital. Most of the principality's permanent residents live there. Visit the Casa dels Valls, a 16th-century building in which

everything comes as a refreshing surprise. After 700 years of fiercely defended independence, the country's spectacular scenery now takes second place; most of today's visitors are heading straight for the bulging shops of Carrer Meritxell.

Andorra is the only country in which the official language is Catalan. Spanish and French

Flag and escutcheon proclaim individuality of state of Andorra, protected by peaks of Pyrenees.

the country's parliament and court are housed. The nation's archives rest in a chest secured with six locks, the keys to which are held in the six parishes.

What to Do

Folklore

The stately *sardana,* the national dance of Catalonia, evokes an uncommon affection and interest among the people. The music may grate at first, because of its hints of Arabic woodwinds and the trills of Italian operetta. It also endures longer than one would have thought possible: just four lines of music repeated without mercy for up to ten minutes. This is a rugged workout for the dancers, who link hands, young and old together, friends or strangers, in an ancient type of round dance. Serious *sardana* dancers change into traditional light shoes—*alpargatas*—but anyone can join in. The musical instruments accompanying these floating but subtle exertions are a sort of oboe and a small flute and a small drum, the latter two played in tandem, one for each hand.

A dance for specialists is the *Ball dels Bastons* (dance of the sticks) which enlivens many fiestas. Highly trained young men or boys in costume perform an intricate and potentially somewhat dangerous stick-dance, reminiscent of fencing and jousting.

Castellers are the men and boys who climb upon each other's shoulders to form human towers. The sport requires the skill of the mountain climber and the tightrope walker, plus trust and teamwork to the extreme. One false move could tumble the whole pyramid.

The *castellers* will always climb barefoot. The unsung, unseen heroes are the behemoths on the bottom layer. The most pampered participant is the local boy—perhaps only six years old—who has been trained to scamper to the summit like a monkey. When he reaches the top of the pyramid, the *enxaneta* (weathercock) releases one hand for a couple of seconds to wave a victory sign. The crowd cheers. Deftly, the castle comes apart from the top down.

During religious processions and other combinations of solemnity and fireworks, many towns parade their giant effigies *(Gegants* and *Cabezudos)*. Skilled crews hidden beneath these figures, which are three times human size, balance the heavy statues and even make them dance. At some festivals, firecracker squads reminiscent of Chinese dragon impersona-

Earnest musicians set the pace for sardana *dancing in Barcelona.*

tors plough through the crowds, generating blinding glare and deafening noise. No one finds it incongruous when all this is followed by a plodding procession of little girls and old women holding lighted tapers and religious banners. The quick-changing moods are contagious.

The Bullfight

Nothing is more uniquely Spanish—or incomprehensible to the foreigner—than the *fiesta brava,* the bullfight. If you've never experienced this spectacle, you may want to seize the chance on your visit to the Coşta Dorada. Although bullfighting is not a particularly Catalonian pursuit it is extremely popular, particularly in Barcelona, which has two bullrings.

Understand from the beginning that the bullfight is not regarded as a sport. A sport is a contest between equals; in bullfighting the odds are weighted heavily against the bull. The *corrida* is a ritualistic preparation for the bull's death. Yet, every time the *torero* enters the ring, he knows his own life is in danger. (Call him a *torero,* please, and not *toreador,* which you may have picked up—erroneously—from Bizet's *Carmen.*) In the first *tercio* (third) of the fight, the matador meets the fierce bull, takes his measure and begins to tire him using the big red and yellow *capote.*

In the second *tercio* the *picador,* a mounted spearman in Sancho Panza costume, lances the bull's shoulder muscles, and the deft *banderilleros* stab darts into the animal's shoulders.

At last the matador returns to taunt the bull with the small, dark-red *muleta* cape, eventually dominating the beast. Finally, as the bull awaits the death he must now sense is inevitable, the *torero* lunges for the kill.

Flamenco

Spain's best-known entertainment, after the bullfight, is flamenco—throbbing guitars, stamping heels and songs that gush from the soul. Many of the songs resemble the wailing chants of Arab music, which may be a strong clue to flamenco's origins. Throughout the region, flamenco shows

The bull staggers to its knees, bringing the corrida to an end.

You may be upset or fascinated or simply confused by an afternoon at the *plaza de toros*. But you will have witnessed a violent act which at times contains touching beauty. With luck, you'll come to understand why this ballet of death is considered an art form in Spain.

are popular tourist attractions.

There are two main groups of songs: one, bouncier and more cheerful, is known as the *cante chico* (a light tune). The second group of songs, called *cante jondo,* deals with love, death, all the human drama, in the slow, piercing style of the great flamenco singers.

But it's the *cante chico* you'll hear at the nightclub floorshow called the *tablao flamenco.* Less dramatic and soulsearching, the *cante chico* is **73** basically lighthearted but can be philosophical and touching. It all makes for a big night out with excitement and colour. And perhaps you'll come away with a feeling for the real flamenco: an ageless beauty in a dramatic ruffle dress, clapping hands as fast as a hummingbird flaps its wings, defying an arrogant dark man chanting with his eyes half-closed.

Shopping

Shopping Hours

Along the coast most shops are open from about 9 a.m. to 2 p.m. and again from 4 to 8 or 10 p.m.

A significant exception: the big, non-stop department stores of Barcelona, which disregard the siesta tradition.

(Bars and cafés normally remain open from around 8 a.m. until midnight or later, with no afternoon break.)

Best Buys

Catalonian ceramics can be primitive or sophisticated, but they're usually quite original. Note the cheerful colours on the sleek modern bowls, which resemble Scandinavian dishware, and the subtle innovations in traditional pots and vases. Decorative tiles can be artistic or just witty with slogans in the Catalan language.

An intensive cottage industry along the coast produces leatherwork, mainly handbags and items of clothing. The quality of the leather and the workmanship is erratic and so is the style, but good buys can be found if you can spare the time to search for them.

Shoes often cost less in Spain than elsewhere in Europe but the workmanship of cheap models is unimpressive. Stylish shoes and boots can be top-class but expensive.

Embroidery, lacework and woven goods such as rugs and bedspreads are produced in coastal villages which keep alive the old patterns and skills. Notice the women of the knitting circles hiding from the hot sun; their products are often on sale in the local shops.

Jewellery, either simple modern designs or traditional styles with lots of silver or gold filigree, can include bargains for the knowledgeable.

For less expansive budgets, there are records of Catalan music—the *sardana* played by those reed bands, or emotional choral works—to remind you always of your holiday.

Or local glasswork, such as the *porróns,* from which wine is projected through the air to the consumer—or which just look intriguing on a shelf.

Or wooden candlesticks in locally carved designs.

Or vaguely snobbish miniature reproductions of Leonardo da Vinci inventions.

Among "best buys" of any trip to Spain are alcohol and tobacco. These are so cheap, by other European and American standards, that there's no need for duty-free shops. Many famous foreign drinks are bottled in Catalonia under licence, and cost the consumer a fraction of the price at home. But for a souvenir gift, buy a bottle of one of the regional liqueurs.

Souvenirs

If you insist on buying "traditional" Spanish souvenirs, there's no shortage of shops overflowing with mock bullfighter swords from Toledo, inlaid Moorish-style chess sets, imitation antique pistols, bullfight posters (with or without your own name imprinted as a star matador), statuettes of Don Quixote, and the typical Spanish *bota,* or wineskin (which is likely to be lined with plastic).

Antiques

You'll have to leave the tourist areas to find any amazing old trinkets at bargain prices. But even in a resort you may come across an appealing piece of old ironwork or hand carving at a relatively sensible price. At very least you can always take home a rusty old door

key suitable for a haunted house, or a kitchen iron of genuine pre-electric vintage.

Antique shopping is made easy in Barcelona, where many shops are concentrated in the ancient streets around the cathedral. Dealers carry antiques as well as reproductions of antiques; sometimes the dividing line becomes blurred.

Shopping Tips

Barcelona, with its fashionable shops, offers variety and quality, but no single street or neighbourhood will satisfy your window-shopping. The commercial area is so extensive that you might have to walk miles to compare quality and value.

Prices in tourist resorts almost always exceed those in the big cities or inland towns,

and they tend to vary from shop to shop, too.

Occasionally, you'll see a notice of sales—*rebajas* (or *rebaixes* in Catalan)—in shop windows. While legitimate sales do take place, usually at the end of the season, you'll have to be a bit cautious.

The Spanish government levies a value added tax (called "IVA") on most items. Tourists from abroad will be refunded the IVA they pay on purchases over a stipulated amount. To obtain the rebate, you have to fill out a form, provided by the shop. The shop keeps one copy; the three others must be presented at the customs on departure, together with the goods. The rebate will then be forwarded by the shop to your home address.

Museums

Barcelona alone counts more than 40 museums. This listing of Costa Dorada museums covers only those institutions of greatest general interest.

Most Spanish museums are open from Tuesday to Saturday from about 10 a.m. to 1.30 or 2 p.m., and 6 to 8 p.m., and Sundays from 10 a.m. to 2 p.m.; closed on Mondays and certain holidays.

Barcelona

Museu Arqueològic (Archaeological Museum). Art and relics dug up in the Barcelona area as well as elsewhere in Spain—prehistoric implements, Carthaginian necklaces, Roman mosaics (Carrer de Lleida, at the foot of Montjuïc; see also p. 35).

Museu d'Art de Catalunya (Museum of Catalonian Art). Top-priority museum, with a beautifully arranged and displayed collection of medieval religious art, all housed in a mock palace (Palau Nacional, Montjuïc; see p. 35).

Museu de Cera (Wax Museum). This one is commercial and more expensive. Three hundred wax effigies of historical, contemporary and fictional figures (Rambla).

Col·lecció Cambó (Cambó Collection). Paintings by Raphael and Titian, Goya and El Greco, Rubens and van Dyck, in an elegant palace (Palau de Pedralbes; see also p. 46).

Museu Picasso (Carrer de Montcada, 15). From early scribblings to most mature tri-

Barcelona boasts great collection of medieval art. Opposite: shops sell antiques and original pottery.

umphs, the life's work of the great Spanish painter is laid out in three noble mansions of Old Barcelona (see pp. 40–41).

Museu de l'Indumentaria (Costume Museum). More than 4,000 items showing the **77**

evolution of fashion from the 16th century to the present (Carrer de Montcada, 12).

Museu d'Art Modern (Museum of Modern Art). Nineteenth and 20th-century paintings by Catalan artists in the Parc de la Ciutadella (see also pp. 44–45).

Museu Marítim (Maritime Museum). Medieval shipyard (Drassanes) converted into repository of full-sized and miniature souvenirs from the high seas, with replica of Columbus's flagship *Santa María* in the harbour (see pp. 37–38).

Fundació Joan Miró (Joan Miró Foundation). Paintings and sculptures, mostly by Miró, exhibited in brilliant galleries and gardens in the Parc de Montjuïc (see p. 35).

Museu Frederic Marés (Federico Marés Museum). Right next to the Cathedral in Carrer Comtes, a vast collection of ancient religious sculptures.

Palau de Pedralbes (Pedralbes Palace). 1920s palace fit for a King (Alfonso XIII). See also p. 46.

Poble Espanyol (Spanish Village). Instructive, imaginary all-Spanish town without children, dogs, or characters (on Montjuïc).

Museu Militar (Military Museum). Military souvenirs —uniforms, castle maquettes, toy soldiers, real guns—in a mainly 18th-century fortress atop Montjuïc.

Museu d'Història de la Ciutat (Museum of the History of the City). Built by chance right on top of Barcelona's richest archaeological digs in Plaça del Rei, this museum's skilfully lit basement is an archaeology lover's delight (see p. 26).

Museu del Monestir de Pedralbes (Museum of the Monastery of Pedralbes). Main attraction of this museum is a collection of beautiful wall paintings by Ferrer Bassa from the 14th century (see also p. 46).

Tarragona

Museu Arqueològic (Archaeological Museum). Statues, mosaics and medaillons from Tarragona's Roman era. (Note: Adjoining **Pretori Romà** with additional ancient objects.)

Necròpoli i Museu Paleocristià (Necropolis and Paleo-Christian Museum). Tarragona's early Christians were buried here in style and grace.

Passeig Arqueològic (Archaeological promenade). City walls and watch towers amid meticulously tended gardens. Open until midnight in summer. (Roman Forum, another outdoor attraction, also operates floodlit in summer.)

For Children

Barcelona Zoo. As pleasant and instructive a zoo as you'll find anywhere in the world.

Poble Espanyol, Barcelona. Simulated Spanish town recreating architecture from all provinces in one slightly confusing ensemble. Watch a woodcarver chisel a statuette, a glassblower make a vase.

Rent-a-burro: how to make a child happy. The donkey's smiling, too.

Boat Trips. Round Barcelona harbour in a launch, for instance, for a close-up inspection of a busy port. Excursion firms also operate day-trips by bus and boat to Costa Brava.

Fun Fairs (Amusement Parks). Two big ones in Barcelona, on Montjuïc and Tibidabo. Noise and gaiety along with fine views of the city and sea.

Güell Park. Gaudí's zany whimsicality charms children, who especially admire his optical illusions. Free.

Barcelona Maritime Museum. The history of sailing, from Roman anchors to model of nuclear-propelled ship.

Santa María replica. Part of the Maritime Museum, a full-size model of Columbus's flagship is moored in the port nearby, available for boarding during the daytime.

Burro Safari. Travel agencies mobilize donkeys for tourist outings.

Tartana Excursions. A country trip in a horse-drawn cart, as devised by travel agencies.

Bloodless Bullfights. Mock *corridas* with baby bulls and audience participation. Some agencies include "champagne" and dancing.

Safari Excursion. Coach tours make a half-day outing to and through Rioleón Safari, where wild animals roam free. Near El Vendrell (Tarragona).

Festivals

Religious and civic holidays are so frequent in Spain that the odds favour your witnessing a fiesta during your holiday, wherever you may be:

Balloons and bouncing balls prove
80 *simple pleasures are usually best.*

February

L'Ametlla de Mar — *Festes de la Candelària*. Religious procession, regatta.

Vilanova i la Geltrú — *Festes de "Les Comparses"*. Folklore and "battle of sweets": 40 tons of sweets are consumed.

March or April

Montserrat Poblet — *Setmana Santa* (Holy Week) ceremonies. Processions and other observances in all towns.

April

Barcelona — *Diada de Sant Jordi*. St. George's Day, coinciding with Cervantes Day, a Book Fair, and the Day of Lovers. Animation and colour.

May

Badalona — *Festes de Primavera i Sant Anastasi*. Spring Festival and St. Anastasius' Day. Exhibition of roses.

Calella — *Festes de Primavera*. Spring Festival. Folk-dancing competition, old car parade, marching bands.

May or June

Sitges — *Festa del Corpus Christi*. Streets carpeted with flowers. Music, dancing, fireworks.

June

Calella — *"Aplec" de Sardanas*. Catalonia's most important folk-dance festival.

July

Arenys de Mar — *Festa major de Sant Zenón*. Celebrations asea and ashore. Folklore.

August

Valls — *Festes del Firagost* (Assumption). Harvest celebration, folklore, religious procession.

Vilafranca del Penedés — *Festa major de Sant Félix, mártir*. Religious procession. Folklore featuring "human castles".

September

Barcelona — *Festes de la Mercè*. Theatre, music.

Tarragona — *Festes de Santa Tecla* (St. Thecla). Religious and folkloric spectacles.

October

Sitges — *Festa de la Varema* (Grape-harvest festival). Tastings and dance.

81

Nightlife

Barcelona swings. So do the major resorts. Almost anywhere tourists alight along the Costa Dorada they find a conglomeration of bars, discothèques and *boîtes*. There's really no excuse except exhaustion for spending an evening slumped before the television in your hotel lounge.

Tour agencies along the coast run a Saturday-night excursion to Barcelona to admire the illuminated fountains of Montjuïc and see Flamenco dancers in small specialized restaurants. There are two basic kinds of Flamenco (see p. 73), and the animated *cante chico* is the version usually performed in *tablaos*. Although Flamenco is essentially an art of Southern Spain and seen to its best effect there, Barcelona attracts many of the great performers.

Another excursion by coach takes in the most elegant floorshows in Barcelona. Normally the all-inclusive price includes dinner and a quota of drinks.

Organized barbecue evenings are a popular rustic substitute for the big-city nightclub tour. Travel agencies

take coachloads of tourists from the resorts to a regional beauty spot where plenty of food, wine and music are supplied.

Big and little towns along the coast have their discothèques and flamenco shows. In fine weather it's a novelty to escape from deafening smoke-filled rooms into deafening open-air nightspots. There is something special about dancing under the moon and stars.

Concerts, Opera, Ballet

Local or visiting orchestras and choirs provide a steady diet for Barcelona music-lovers.

The city's Opera House, the Gran Teatre del Liceu, was described as the finest theatre in the world when it opened in 1857. Famous opera and ballet companies appear there every year between November and May. Most of its seats belong to subscribers, so it may be difficult for the casual ticket-hunter to obtain seats.

Major concerts also take place at the wildly *art nouveau*

Night on the Costa Dorada: bars, discos, restaurants for all tastes.

Palau de la Música Catalana.

Recitals, including occasional jazz concerts, are held in the stark surroundings of the 14th-century Església de Santa Maria del Mar.

Catalans are deeply dedicated to music, so you may chance upon a concert in any resort town—perhaps the local choir performing in the parish church or the town cinema.

Theatre, Films

Most of Barcelona's dozen theatres seem to specialize in musicals and farces, but straight plays—in Spanish or Catalan—are also presented.

Almost all the films shown commercially in Spain have been dubbed into Spanish. Depending on the location of the cinema and success of the film, the prices of seats vary (see p. 100).

Fiestas

Village fetes, which occur with great frequency, can provide rousing spectacles, music, folk dancing. But Spaniards are very casual about fireworks, so beware of the more explosive parts of town.

Wining and Dining

When in Spain, try some Spanish food. This advice is not so ludicrous as it may seem. You could easily spend a fortnight's holiday in Barcelona or on the Costa Dorada subsisting on the anonymous international food in your hotel. What a shame.

Spanish cooking varies drastically from region to region.*

To many visitors, a favourite dish is *gazpacho* (pronounced gath-PAT-cho), a chilled, highly flavoured soup to which chopped tomatoes, peppers, cucumbers, onions and sippets (croutons) are added to taste—a rousing refresher on a hot summer day.

Another classic Spanish dish, *paella* (pronounced pie-ALE-

*For a comprehensive food list, ask at your bookshop for the Berlitz Spanish-English/English-Spanish dictionary, or the Berlitz EUROPEAN MENU READER.

84

ya), originated just down the coast in Valencia. It's named after the black iron pan in which the saffron rice is cooked. To this the cook adds whatever inspires him at the moment—squid, sausage, shrimp, rabbit, chicken, mussels, onion, peppers, peas, beans, tomatoes, garlic… Authentically, *paella* is served at lunchtime, cooked to order (about half an hour). Some Spaniards consider it a first course; others dig into it for the whole meal.

Catalan Cuisine

Esqueixada (pronounced eskay-SHA-da) is a stimulating salad of cod, beans, pickled onions and tomato.

Xató (pronounced sha-TO) *de Sitges* is a related, but more complicated salad including anchovies, tunny fish or cod and a hot sauce made of olive oil, vinegar, red pepper, diced anchovies, garlic and ground almonds.

Pa amb tomàquet goes well with any salad. Peasant-style bread, in huge slices, is smeared with fresh tomato and grilled; it comes out a sort of primitive cousin of a pizza.

Escudella is considered a winter-time dish, but out of season you may come across the hearty broth containing beans, pasta, a chunk of sausage and a slice of meatloaf.

Butifarra is one of several varieties of sausage much appreciated in Catalonia. One famous species of sausage comes from the town of Vic.

Rovellons are enormous wild mushrooms which mark the start of autumn on the Costa Dorada. They're cooked with garlic and parsley, eaten with sausage or alone.

Pollo al ast (barbecued chicken) is grilled and basted on the spit, usually outside a restaurant so that the aroma lures customers inside.

Riz parellada, a Costa Do-

Rushed from the farm, fruits and vegetables temptingly displayed.

rada refinement of *paella,* is a gourmand's dream. The kitchen will have removed all the shells and bones from the seafood and meat before this feast is cooked, so it can be gulped down without mess or delay.

Fish in general makes up a substantial part of the local diet. Mostly it is just grilled and served with a salad and fried potatoes. In more sophisticated restaurants, you'll be offered elaborate variations with subtle sauces. No matter how primitive or elegant the place, the raw materials are likely to be first-rate.

Romesco is the fish sauce from Tarragona, envied and imitated in other Costa Dorada towns. This red sauce tastes right at home beside the Mediterranean in the company of fried fish and shellfish. The cooks of Tarragona are very coy when asked for the recipe, but key ingredients would appear to be red pepper, olive oil, garlic, bread crumbs and ground almonds.

Calçotada, an even more provincial dish, comes from Valls—tender baby onions in what's claimed to be the most irresistible combination of vegetables, meat and spices in all of Catalonia.

Sweets: The pastries of the Costa Dorada will destroy your diet. Just look in a bakery window; you don't have to know the names. One is more delectable than the next, crowned with nuts, custard, dried fruits, meringue, chocolate or powder sugar.

Crema Catalana, made of eggs, sugar, milk and cinnamon, is cooked to a more solid consistency than its Spanish cousin, *flan,* and it has a caramel-glaze topping.

Breakfast

In Spain breakfast is an insignificant meal—just an eye-opener to keep one alive until a huge and late lunch. A typical Costa Dorada breakfast consists of a cup of coffee and pastry. Breakfast coffee (*café con leche*) is half coffee, half hot milk. If it tastes too foreign to you, many bars and restaurants stock milder instant coffee, as well. Also in deference to foreign habits, *desayuno completo* is now available in most hotels and some cafés: orange juice, eggs, toast and coffee.

Returning to the subject of breakfast pastry, two types are worth a try. *Ensaimadas* are large fluffy sweet rolls dusted with sugar, a Balearic islands speciality also popular in Catalonia. *Churros* are fritters, often made before your eyes by a contraption which shoots the batter into boiling oil. If you *don't* dunk *churros* in your coffee, everyone will stare. (*Churros* with very thick hot chocolate is a popular afternoon snack in Spain.)

Restaurants

All Spanish restaurants are officially graded by forks, not stars. One fork is the lowest grade, five forks the élite. But ratings are awarded according to the facilities available, not the quality of the food. Many forks on the door guarantee higher prices but not necessarily better cooking.

Spanish restaurants usually offer a *menú del día* (day's special). This usually lists three courses available with bread and wine at a reasonable set price. But the *menú* is not always a bargain; in fact, it might even work out to cost more than the sum of its parts. Add up the *à la carte* prices to be certain. On the other hand, in country or working-class restaurants, the *menú* is

often the favourite of the regular clients, and cheap.

Normally, menu prices are "all-inclusive"—including all taxes and service charge. But it's still customary to leave a tip. Ten percent is acceptable, 15 percent is generous.

All restaurants, for the record, announce that an official complaints book is available to dissatisfied clients.

All that food but too busy to eat: rush hour in a Barcelona kitchen.

Meal times tend to be later than in most European countries. Restaurants serve lunch from about 1 to 3.30 p.m. and dinner from about 8.30 to 11. **87**

Resort hotels may serve dinner earlier for the convenience of foreign guests.

One hint for economy: order *vino de la casa* (house wine). It may be served in an anonymous bottle, a colourful ceramic carafe or even in a mislabelled second-hand bottle. But it's almost bound to be tolerably good and will cost less than half the price of a brand-name bottle.

Foreign Restaurants

Barcelona is reasonably well provided with restaurants featuring foreign cuisines. They include French, Italian, German and Chinese restaurants. In addition Barcelona has many fine restaurants devoted to regional cooking from the various gourmet regions of Spain.

Most resort centres also have eating places aiming at foreign palates. The restaurants enjoy varying degrees of authenticity.

Bars and Cafés

Open-air cafés are one of the pleasures of the region. A cup of coffee buys you a ringside seat for as long as you care to dawdle.

Bar and café bills include service charges, but small tips are the custom. Prices are usually 10 or 15 percent higher if you're served at a table rather than at the bar.

Bodegas are wine-cellars. In resort towns many popular tourist bars have been designed to create the atmosphere of casks and barrels.

Merenderos are beach restaurants, serving simple but tasty food.

Tapas

A *tapa* is a bite-sized morsel of food—meatballs, olives, fried-fish chunks, shellfish, seafood, vegetable salad; it can be almost anything edible. The word *tapa* means "lid" and comes from the old custom of giving a bite of food with a drink, the food being served on a saucer covering the top of the glass like a lid. Nowadays, sadly, the custom of giving away the *tapa* is all but nonexistent. But the idea of selling *tapas* is stronger than ever. Some bars, called *tascas*, specialize in the snack trade. Instead of sitting down to a formal meal in a restaurant you can wander into a *tapa* bar, point to the items you like and eat your way down the counter. One helping is called a *porción*. For a large serving of any given *tapa,* ask for a *ración*. If that's too much for you, order a *media-ración*. Caution: it's quite possible to spend more for a meal of *tapas* than for a good, conventional dinner.

Wines and Spirits

Both provinces of the Costa Dorada—Barcelona and Tarragona—produce good wine.

Priorato is a well-known red wine of the region. Tarragona wines are notable in white or rosé. Penedés can be red or white. In Sitges a dessert wine, malmsey (*malvasía* in Spanish), is produced. And the Penedés region is a major source of the world's best selling white sparkling wine, called *cava*.

Don't give a thought to "winemanship", or matching wits with the wine waiter to choose just the right vintage. When the average Spaniard sits down to a meal, he just orders *"vino"*, and it means *red* wine to the average waiter. Often served chilled, this house wine can go with fish or meat or anything. Relax and enjoy the unpretentiousness.

There is no social misdemeanour implied in diluting your wine if you wish, particularly on a hot day. The addition of *gaseosa,* a cheap fizzy lemonade, turns red wine into an imitation of *sangría*. (Real

As in all Mediterranean countries, outdoor cafés prosper in Catalonia. **89**

sangría, however, is a mixture of red wine, lemon and orange juice, brandy, mineral water, ice and slices of fruit—rather like punch and very popular in hot summer.)

If you're not in the mood for wine at all, have no qualms about ordering beer or a soft drink or mineral water. No one will turn up a snobbish nose.

You may consider Spanish brandy too heavy or sweet for your taste, compared with French cognac. But it's very cheap—often the same price as a soft drink.

A word about prices: if you insist on drinking imported Scotch or bourbon, expect to pay plenty. However, an enormous range of familiar spirits and liqueurs are available at very low prices because they are made under licence in Spain. Look around a wine shop to see just how cheap some brands are.

A last word to alert you to a non-alcoholic drink you might not have noticed. *Horchata de chufa* is a very Spanish refresher, possibly first imported by the Moors. It's made from a fruity, wrinkled little nut with a sweet taste, similar to an almond. *Horchaterías,* bars specializing in this popular cold drink, often have terraces and also serve all kinds of ice-cream.

To help you order...

Could we have a table?
Do you have a set menu?
I'd like a/an/some...

¿Nos puede dar una mesa?
¿Tiene un menú del día?
Quisiera...

beer	**una cerveza**	milk	**leche**
bread	**pan**	mineral water	**agua mineral**
coffee	**un café**	napkin	**una servilleta**
condiments	**los condimentos**	potatoes	**patatas**
cutlery	**los cubiertos**	rice	**arroz**
dessert	**un postre**	salad	**una ensalada**
fish	**pescado**	sandwich	**un bocadillo**
fruit	**fruta**	soup	**sopa**
glass	**un vaso**	sugar	**azúcar**
ice-cream	**un helado**	tea	**un té**
meat	**carne**	(iced) water	**agua (fresca)**
menu	**la carta**	wine	**vino**

...and read the menu

aceitunas	olives	**guisantes**	peas
ajo	garlic	**helado**	ice-cream
albaricoques	apricots	**higos**	figs
albóndigas	meatballs	**huevo**	eggs
almejas	baby clams	**jamón**	ham
anchoas	anchovies	**judías**	beans
anguila	eel	**langosta**	spiny lobster
arroz	rice	**langostino**	prawn
asado	roast	**lenguado**	sole
atún	tunny (tuna)	**limón**	lemon
bacalao	codfish	**lomo**	loin
besugo	sea bream	**manzana**	apple
bistec	beef steak	**mariscos**	shellfish
boquerones	fresh anchovies	**mejillones**	mussels
caballa	mackerel	**melocotón**	peach
calamares	squid	**merluza**	hake
(a la romana)	(deep fried)	**naranja**	orange
callos	tripe	**ostras**	oysters
cangrejo	crab	**pastel**	cake
caracoles	snails	**pescado**	fish
cebollas	onions	**pescadilla**	whiting
cerdo	pork	**pez espada**	swordfish
champiñones	mushrooms	**pimiento**	green pepper
chorizo	a spicy pork	**piña**	pineapple
	sausage	**plátano**	banana
chuleta	chops	**pollo**	chicken
cordero	lamb	**postre**	dessert
dorada	sea-bass	**pulpitos**	baby octopus
ensalada	salad	**queso**	cheese
entremeses	hors-d'oeuvre	**salchichón**	salami
estofado	stew	**salmonete**	red mullet
filete	fillet	**salsa**	sauce
flan	caramel mould	**sandía**	watermelon
frambuesas	raspberries	**sopa**	soup
fresas	strawberries	**ternera**	veal
frito	fried	**tortilla**	omelet
galletas	biscuits	**tostada**	toast
	(cookies)	**trucha**	trout
gambas	shrimp	**uvas**	grapes
granadas	pomegranates	**verduras**	vegetables

Sports and Other Activities

Vast sand beaches make the Costa Dorada a natural winner for holiday-makers inclined to water sports. The mild climate, moreover, extends the season for sports ashore. And if it should rain, the indoor sports provide exciting diversion, whether you play table tennis or watch Basques scoop up a bullet-fast *pelota*.

Here's a run-down of sports to choose from:

Beach Pursuits

Along much of the coast, golden sand slopes gently into a calm sea. The angle is less dependably gradual north-east of Barcelona; be alert for undercurrents. With few exceptions, lifeguards do not exist. But in many resorts first-aid stations are established on the main beaches.

Facilities vary from zero along isolated stretches to the elaborate bars and changing rooms of the big resorts.

Deck-chairs and umbrellas can be hired everywhere for a reasonable price. Air mattresses *(colchoneta),* for sunbathing and swimming, are another matter. It may well work out cheaper to buy your own for the season.

Boating and Sailing

If you arrive in your own yacht, you'll find the facilities you need at any of these boating centres: Barcelona, Garraf, Vilanova i la Geltrú, Torredembarra, Tarragona, Salou, Cambrils, Sant Carles de la Rápita, Arenys de Mar.

If you've left your yacht at home but would like to hire a boat on the spot, many resorts can come up with sailing boats. It usually depends upon local beach and sea conditions. Small fibre-glass dinghies are perfectly safe for sailing just off shore. If you plan to do much sailing on your holiday, try to negotiate a cheaper bulk rate.

of age on the coast. Equipment and instructors are available in many resorts.

For the less adventurous or less affluent, there remains the *patines* (paddle boat). This seaborne bicycle built for two can

Down to the sea in bathing suits, or all rigged up in a parachute to keep up with latest holiday sport.

Boardsailing, also known as windsurfing and windgliding —combining the speed of sailing with the thrill of tightrope walking—has come

be as unglamorous as an 1890s bathing costume, but it will take you far from the crowds. Check the prices before you embark.

Water-Skiing

Increased fuel costs have pushed this sport into the luxury class.

In some resorts, an exciting airborne variation—kite-skiing—is attracting great attention. Definitely not for the faint-hearted.

Fishing

In all resorts inexpensive rods and reels are sold.

Deep-sea-style fishing is a logistical problem; if you can organize a group you may be able to hire a boat. There are no facilities for renting equipment.

For all information and licences, consult the local office of the Instituto Nacional para la Conservación de la Naturaleza (ICONA):

Barcelona: Carrer Sabino de Arana, 22.

Tarragona: Avda. de Catalunya, 22-E.

Underwater Fishing

This increasingly popular sport requires a licence, issued by the local Comandancia de Marina (Maritime Authorities). You may use a snorkel tube and mask along with mechanical harpoon. Underwater fishing with scuba oxygen equipment or air guns is strictly not allowed. Incidentally, if you should come upon archaeological relics in your undersea travels, remember that it is forbidden to collect these specimens.

Golf

Some golf courses are open all-year-round on the Costa Dorada, mostly near Barcelona.

- Real Club de Golf El Prat,

Horse-Riding

Some resort travel agencies advertise riding excursions with transport to and from a ranch, a few hours of riding, and a country meal.

The Spanish sun is shining for the fishers on the quayside as for sedate golfers on the beautiful green near Barcelona.

in El Prat de Llobregat (near Barcelona airport). 27 holes.
- Club de Golf de San Cugat, near Sant Cugat del Vallés. 18 holes.
- Club de Golf Terramar, Sitges. Nine holes.

Hunting and Shooting

Two areas of unusual interest for hunters in the southern part of Catalonia: the Ebro Delta and the rugged mountain zone west of Tortosa.

A Sheep Dog Named Cobi Welcomes Olympic Visitors

His name is Cobi, and though he may not look it at first glance, or even tenth glance, he's a kind of Catalan sheep dog of the Pyrenees, a Gos d'Altura. He's a very special dog, because he's the mascot of the Barcelona Olympics. The COOB, on the other hand, is the Barcelona Olympics Organizing Committee which chose the Cobi design "to break with the Disney-type of 'super-cute' humanized animals like Mischa the bear and Eagle Sam used by recent Olympics.".

The Olympic emblem, also visible on Cobi's chest, consists of three brush strokes, blue, yellow and red, in the strong colours of a Miró painting, or of the Spanish sea, sun and soil. The three strokes compose a leaping figure with arms outstretched in hospitality, athletically clearing "Barcelona '92" and the five rings of the Olympic logo.

Three large luxury hotels have been totally reserved as the headquarters of the International Olympic Committee, international sports federations and national committees.

The Ebro Delta, the marshy peninsula facing Amposta, is considered one of the dozen best waterfowl spots in Spain, and Spain claims Europe's best waterfowl hunting. The season begins in October and lasts to mid-March. For information and the actual hunting licence apply to the Instituto Nacional para la Conservación de la Naturaleza (ICONA), Avda. de Catalunya, 22-E, Tarragona.

The same ICONA office can answer your questions on the national hunting reserve of the Tortosa and Beceite passes. This is one of the refuges of the Spanish mountain goat, a rare species in modern times. Hunting there is very severely controlled.

Otherwise, the Costa Dorada area is inhabited by unexceptional quantities of rabbit, hare and partridge. The small game season opens on October 12 and closes in February.

Tennis

Tennis courts open to the public are located in Pedralbes in the Can Caralleu sports centre, where there are also indoor and outdoor swimming pools. The courts are open from 8 a.m. to 11 p.m. For information on courts, phone 203-7874. Your hotel may also be able to arrange guest privileges at a Barcelona tennis club. Squash courts are available at Squash Barcelona, Av. Dr del Marañón 17, tel. 334-0258. Riding can be arranged through the Club Hípic de Barcelona, Ciutat de Balaguer 68, tel. 417-3039. Sailing in-

within a few hours of Barcelona: Núria, at 1,963 metres (6,440 ft.); La Molina, whose slopes rise to 2,537 metres (8,324 ft.); and Vallter with 12 slopes and a top station at 2,500 metres (8,203 ft.). Information on the conditions of roads and slopes can be obtained by phoning the Associació Catalana d'Estacions d'Esquí, tel. (93) 238-3135.

formation can be obtained from the Reial Club Marítim de Barcelona, tel. 315-0007.

Skiing

Skiing may be the fastest-growing sport in Catalonia. Each year brings new developments in the Pyrenees, most

Just Looking

The great spectator sport in Barcelona is football, and football means the Barça. The top-ranked team of the F.C. Barcelona has a 120,000-seat stadium, Camp Nou, in the university district. Consult a newspaper or the nearest local for dates and times of games.

BLUEPRINT for a Perfect Trip

How to Get There

If the choice of ways to get to the Costa Dorada is bewildering, the complexity of fares and regulations can be downright stupefying. A reliable travel agent, up to date on the latest zigs and zags, can suggest which plan is best for your timetable and budget.

BY AIR

Scheduled flights

Barcelona Airport (see p.102) is linked by regular flights from many European and certain overseas cities. Connecting services from cities throughout Europe and North Africa operate via Madrid's airport, which is the main point of entry to Spain for transatlantic and intercontinental travellers. The flight from London to Barcelona takes about 2 hours, from New York, approximately 8 hours.

Charter flights and package tours

From the U.K. and Ireland Many companies operate all-in package tours, which include flight, hotel and meals; check carefully to make sure that you are not liable to any surcharges. British travel agents offer guarantees in case of bankruptcy or cancellation by the hotels or airlines. Most recommend insurance, too, for tourists who are forced to cancel because of illness or accident.

If you prefer to arrange your own accommodation and do not mind having to restrict your holiday to either one or two weeks, you can take advantage of the many charter flights that are available.

From North America Most charter flights operate to Madrid or the Costa del Sol. If extensions are offered, it is possible to visit Barcelona and the Costa Dorada independently. Barcelona is often featured on package tours combining Majorca or the Costa del Sol.

BY ROAD

The main access road from France to Barcelona is at the eastern side of the Pyrenees, on the toll motorway (expressway), or via the more scenic coastal road. You could also travel via Toulouse and cross the Spanish border at Puigcerdà near Andorra and from there take the N-152 to Barcelona, or go via Pau (France) to Candanchú and Saragossa and/or Lleida (Lérida). There is a long-distance ferry service between Plymouth and Santander in northern Spain (a 24-hour trip); from Santander, follow the N-240 to Barcelona.

Express **coach services** operate between London and Barcelona, with frequent departures in summer. You can travel by coach as part of a package holiday from London.

BY RAIL

The *Barcelona-Talgo* links Paris with Barcelona in about 11½ hours. For most other connections you'll have to change trains at Port Bou. Seat and sleeper reservations are compulsory on most Spanish trains.

Both *Inter-Rail* and *Rail Europ Senior* cards are valid in Spain, as is the Eurailpass for non-European residents (sign up before you leave home).

Visitors from abroad can buy the RENFE (*Red Nacional de los Ferrocarriles Española, the Spanish National Railways*) *Tourist Card* for a reasonable price, valid for unlimited rail travel within the country for periods of 8, 15 or 22 days (lst and 2nd classes available).

When to Go

Sunbathers enjoy the beaches of the Costa Dorada for about six months of the year; the rest of the time the mild climate still provides a pleasant break for visitors from northern Europe.

The accompanying chart deals specifically with the climate of Barcelona, damper than Tarragona and intermediate beach areas.

		J	F	M	A	M	J	J	A	S	O	N	D
average daily	°F	55	57	60	65	71	78	82	82	77	69	62	56
maximum*	°C	13	14	16	18	21	25	28	28	25	21	16	13
average daily	°F	43	45	48	52	57	65	69	69	66	58	51	46
minimum*	°C	6	7	9	11	14	18	21	21	19	15	11	8
average sea	°F	55	55	55	57	60	69	70	73	70	68	60	57
temperatures	°C	13	13	13	14	16	20	22	23	22	20	16	14

*Minimum temperatures are measured just before sunrise, maximum temperatures in the afternoon.

Planning Your Budget

To give you an idea of what to expect, here's a list of average prices in Spanish pesetas. However, they must be regarded as approximate, as inflation creeps relentlessly up. Prices quoted may be subject to a VAT/sales tax (IVA) of either 6% or 12%.

Airport transfer 175 ptas (by train).

Baby-sitters 500 ptas per hour.

Camping *De luxe* 400-500 ptas per day per person, 1,500-2,000 ptas per tent or caravan (trailer); *3rd category* 300-400 ptas per day per person, 550-650 ptas per tent or caravan. Reductions for children.

Car hire *Seat Fura L* 2,750 ptas per day, 22 ptas per km, 33 ,600 ptas per week with unlimited mileage. *Ford Escort* 4,900 ptas per day, 35 ptas per km, 56,000 ptas per week with unlimited mileage. *Ford Sierra 2000* 8,200 ptas per day, 70 ptas per km, 112,000 ptas per week with unlimited mileage. Add 12% IVA.

Cigarettes Spanish brands 60-115 ptas per packet of 20, imported brands 175 ptas and up.

Entertainment Cinema in Barcelona 500 ptas, in resorts 200-300 ptas. Theatre 500-1,200 ptas. Flamenco nightclub 2,500–3,000 ptas and up. Discotheque 600–1,500 ptas and up. Museums 50-400 ptas.

Hairdressers *Woman's* shampoo and set or blow-dry 700-1,500 ptas. *Man's* haircut 500-1,500 ptas.

Hotels (double room with bath per night) 5-star 24,000–44,000 ptas, 4-star 15,000-25,000 ptas, 3-star 10,000–19,000 ptas, 2-star 8,000 ptas, 1-star 5,800 ptas. Add 12% (for luxury hotels) or 6% (for other hotels) IVA.

Meals and drinks Continental breakfast 500–1,000 ptas, three-course menu 600–1,500 ptas including wine, lunch/dinner in a good restaurant 2,000–4,000 ptas, beer 100 ptas, coffee 90 ptas (with milk 125 ptas), Spanish brandy 300 ptas, soft drinks 100–160 ptas.

Metro (or bus) 75 ptas (80 ptas on Sundays and daily after 10p.m).

Shopping bag Bread (half kg) 80 ptas, 250g of butter 250 ptas, dozen eggs 200 ptas, 1kg of veal 1,300-1,800 ptas, 250g of coffee 225 ptas, 1 l. of fruit juice 155 ptas, 1 l. of milk 110 ptas, bottle of wine from 200 ptas.

Taxi Initial charge 225 ptas (including the first 6 minutes or the first 2km), from 55 ptas per km, 75 ptas per piece of luggage.

An A-Z Summary of Practical Information and Facts

A star (*) following an entry indicates that relevant prices are to be found on p.101.

Listed after some basic entries is the appropriate Spanish translation, usually in the singular, plus a number of phrases that should help you when seeking assistance.

A **AIRPORT** (*aeropuerto*) Barcelona's modern international airport, along the sea at El Prat de Llobregat, is only about 15km (9 miles) from the centre of the city. Porters are available to carry your bags to the taxi rank or bus stop; free baggage trolleys also are at passengers' disposal. A tourist information office, car hire agencies, souvenir shops, a currency exchange office and a duty-free shop operate here.

The Spanish Railways operate a link between the airport and Central-Sants station in western Barcelona. Trains run every 30 minutes, and the trip takes only 15-20 minutes.

Charter flights for resorts near Tarragona often use the military airfield at Reus. Tour operators provide ground transportation.

B **BABY-SITTERS*** This service can usually be arranged with your hotel. Rates can vary considerably but are generally lower in the quieter resort areas; in most places they go up after midnight.

Can you get me a baby-sitter for tonight?	**¿Puede conseguirme una niñera (or una "canguro") para esta noche?**

BICYCLE and MOTORSCOOTER HIRE (*bicicletas/motos de alquiler*) In a few resorts bicycles—including tandem models—can be hired by the hour or by the day. You may also be able to find a garage which will rent you a moped by the day or week. However, these 49-cc machines are a less-than-carefree mode of transport on resort-area roads, especially in season when traffic is extremely heavy.

Motorscooters of 125 to 175-cc, powerful enough for a driver and a
passenger, cost almost as much to hire as a car. Be prepared to lay out a
deposit. Use of crash helmets is compulsory whatever the capacity of the
engine.

I'd like to hire a bicycle.	**Quisiera alquilar una bicicleta.**
What's the charge per day/week?	**¿Cuánto cuesta por día/semana?**

CAMPING* *(camping)* The Costa Dorada has more officially approved
campsites than any other resort area in Spain. Apply to any tourist information service or:

Federació Catalana de Campings, Diputació 279, Barcelona; tel. 317 4416

Camping grounds are divided into four categories (luxury, 1st, 2nd and
3rd class), and rates and facilities vary accordingly. All sites, however,
have electricity, drinking water, toilets and showers, and are under surveil-
lance night and day.

For a complete list of campsites throughout Spain, consult any Spanish
National Tourist Office (see Tourist Information Offices).

May we camp here?	**¿Podemos acampar aquí?**
We have a tent/caravan (trailer).	**Tenemos una tienda de camping/una caravana.**

CAR HIRE* *(coches de alquiler).* See also DRIVING. There are car hire
firms in the main towns and tourist resorts. You'll find many types of cars
for hire, but the most common one is the Seat. Ask for any available sea-
sonal deals.

A deposit, as well as advance payment of the estimated rental charge, is
generally required, although holders of major credit cards are normally
exempt from this. A VAT (sales tax) is added to the total; third-party
insurance is automatically included, but taking out additional full collision
coverage is advisable.

To rent a car, drivers must be over 21 years old and have held a licence
for at least one year.

I'd like to rent a car (tomorrow).	**Quisiera alquilar un coche (para mañana).**
for one day/a week	**por un día/una semana**

C **CIGARETTES, CIGARS TOBACCO*** *(cigarrillos, puros, tabaco)*
Spanish cigarettes can be made of strong, black tobacco *(negro)* or light
tobacco *(rubio)*. Imported foreign brands are up to three times the price of
local makes, though foreign brands produced in Spain under licence can
be cheaper than when bought at home. Locally made cigars are cheap and
reasonably good. Canary Island cigars are excellent and Cuban cigars are
readily available. Pipe smokers find the local tobacco somewhat rough.

Tabacalera S.A. is the government tobacco monopoly: they supply their
official shops, *tabacos*, who supply everybody else. Cigarette shops sell
postage stamps, too.

A packet of…/A box of matches, please	**Un paquete de…/Una caja de cerillas, por favor.**
filter-tipped	**con filtro**
without filter	**sin filtro**

CLOTHING Whatever you wear for hot north European summers will be
fine for Barcelona and the Costa Dorada. By day between July and early
September you'll be very unlucky to need a wrap, but have one handy in
the evenings. In other months, especially between November and March,
winds can sometimes blow cold, so always carry a jacket or coat. Even in
August you'll need a warm covering in the mountains. When visiting
churches women no longer *have* to cover their heads, but decent dress is
certainly expected.

COMMUNICATIONS Post offices *(correos)* are for mail and telegrams;
you can't usually make telephone calls from them.

Post office hours 9a.m. to 1 or 2p.m. and 4 or 5 to 6 or 7p.m. Monday to
Friday, mornings only on Saturdays. Barcelona's main post office, on
Plaça d'Antonio Lopez in the port area, is open from 9a.m. to 9p.m.
Monday to Friday, 9a.m. to 2p.m. Saturday.

Mail If you don't know in advance where you'll be staying, you can have
your mail addressed to the *Lista de Coreos* (poste restante or general
delivery) in the nearest town. Take your passport to the post office as
identification and be prepared to pay a small fee for each letter received.

Postage stamps are also on sale at tobacconists *(tabacos)* and often at
hotel desks.

104   Mail boxes are yellow.

Telegrams *(telegrama)* Telegram and post office counter services work
independent hours and usually overlap. Times vary from town to town,
too, but you can always send telegrams by phone—dial 322 2000.

The telegraph section in the main post offices of major cities stays open
24 hours a day. If you are staying at a hotel, the receptionist can take telegrams. Telex service is also available in principal post offices.

Telephone *(teléfono)*. You can make local and international calls from
public telephone booths in the street, from most hotels (often with heavy
surcharges) and from some post offices. Area codes for different countries
are given in the telephone directory. You'll need a supply of small change.
For international direct dialling, pick up the receiver, wait for the dial
tone, then dial 07, wait for a second sound and dial the country code (U.K
44, Canada/U.S.A 1), city code and number.

To reverse the charges, ask for *cobro revertido*. For a personal (person-
to-person) call, specify *persona a persona* (only valid for international
calls).

Can you get me this number in…?	**¿Puede comunicarme con este número en…?**
Have you received any mail for…?	**¿Ha recibido correo para…?**
A stamp for this letter/postcard, please.	**Por favor, un sello para esta carta/postal.**
express (special delivery)	**urgente**
airmail	**vía aérea**
registered	**certificado**
I want to send a telegram to…	**Quisiera mandar un telegrama a…**

COMPLAINTS By law, all hotels, campsites and restaurants must have
official complaint forms *(Libro Oficial de Reclamaciónes/Llibre Oficial de
Reclamacions)* and produce them on demand. The original of this tripli-
cate document should be sent to the regional office of the Ministry of
Tourism, one copy remains with the establishment complained against and
you keep the third sheet. Merely asking for a complaint form is usually
enough to resolve most matters since tourism authorities take a serious
view of complaints and your host wants to keep both his reputation and his
licence.

C   In the rare event of major obstruction, when it is not possible to call in the police, write directly to the Secretaría de Estado de Turismo, Sección de Inspección y Reclamaciones, Turespaña, Maria de Molina, 28006 Madrid.

New legislation has been introduced that greatly strengthens the consumer's hand. Public information offices are being set up, controls carried out, and fallacious information made punishable by law. For a tourist's needs, however, the tourist office, or in really serious cases, the police would normally be able to handle or, at least, to advise where to go.

CONSULATES *(consulado)* Almost all Western European countries have consulates in Barcelona. All embassies are located in Madrid. If you run into trouble with authorities or the police, ask your consulate for advice.

Canada Via Augusta 125, Barcelona; tel. 209 0634

Eire 10th floor, Gran Via Carles III 94, Barcelona; tel. 330 9652

South Africa Gran Via de les Corts Catalanes 634, Barcelona; tel. 301 55 85

U.K (also for citizens of Commonwealth countries) Avinguda Diagonal 477, Barcelona; tel. 419 9044; Real 33, Tarragona; tel. 32 08 12

U.S.A Via Laietana 33, Barcelona; tel. 319 9550

CONVERTER CHARTS For fluid and distance measures see p.109. Spain uses the metric system.

Temperature

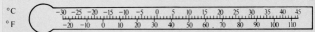

Weight

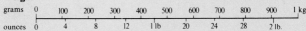

Length

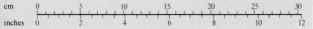

cm

inches

metres

ft./yd.

CRIME and THEFT Spain's crime rate has caught up with the rest of the world. Thefts and break-ins are now common occurences. Hang on to purses and wallets, especially in busy places—the bullfight, open-air markets, fiestas. Don't take valuables to the beach. Lock cars and never leave cases, cameras, etc., on view. In Barcelona, tourists are a target for bag snatchers and the like—especially along the Ramblas and in the notorious Barri Chino—so be on your guard. If you suffer a theft or break-in, report it to the Guardia Urbana. In Barcelona, go to your consulate where you will fill in a form that you then present at the police station (comisaría).

I want to report a theft.   **Quiero denunciar un robo.**

My ticket/wallet/passport has   **Me han robado mi billete/**
  been stolen.   **mi cartera/mi pasaporte.**

DRIVING IN SPAIN To take your car into Spain, you should have:

● an International Driving Permit (not obligatory for citizens of most Western European countries—ask your automobile association—but recommended in case of difficulties with the police as it carries a text in Spanish) or a legalized and certified translation of your driving licence

● car registration papers

● Green Card (an exctension to your regular insurance policy, making it valid for foreign countries)

Also recommended: With your certificate of insurance, you should carry a bail bond. If you injure somebody in an accident in Spain, you can be imprisoned while the accident is under investigation. This bond will bail you out. Apply to your automobile association or insurance company.

  A nationality sticker must be prominently displayed on the back of your car. Seat belts are compulsory. Not using them outside towns makes you liable to a stiff fine. A red reflecting warning triangle is compulsory when

D driving on motorways (expressways). Motorcycle riders and their passengers must wear crash helmets.

Driving conditions Drive on the right, pass on the left. Yield right of way to all traffic coming from the right. Spanish drivers tend to use their horn (daytime) or lights (night) when passing other vehicles.

Main roads are adequate to very good and improving all the time. Secondary roads can be bumpy. The main danger of driving in Spain comes from impatience, especially on busy roads. A large percentage of accidents in Spain occur when passing, so take it easy.

Spanish truck and lorry drivers will often wave you on (by hand or by flashing their right directional signal) if it's clear ahead.

Parking and driving in Barcelona, as in most major cities unless you really know your way about, are not much fun. Streams of heavy traffic roar down long, straight avenues, carrying all before them (including you, probably). And beware of horrendous traffic jams on Sunday evenings as the crowds return from the beach.

Beware, too, of that delicious but oh-so-heavy Spanish wine: the drinking and driving laws have been tightened up considerably, and fines are truly horrible!

Note that on motorways in Catalonia the word for exit is *sortida*, while in the rest of Spain it is *salida*.

Speed limits 120kph (75mph) on motorways, 100kph (62mph) or 90kph (56mph) on other roads, 60kph (36mph) in towns and built-up areas. Cars towing caravans (trailers) are restricted to 80kph (50mph) on the open road.

Traffic Police The Traffic Civil Guard (*Guardia Civil de Tráfico*) patrols the highways on powerful black motorcycles. Always in pairs, these capable-looking characters are courteous, good mechanics and will stop to help anyone in trouble.

The police are, however, severe on lawbreakers. The most frequent offences include:

- speeding

- travelling too close to the car in front

- overtaking (passing) without flashing your direction indicator lights

- travelling at night with a burnt-out light (Spanish law requires you to carry a complete set of spare bulbs at all times)

- failing to come to a complete halt at a STOP sign

108 Fines are payable on the spot.

Parking Many towns charge a token fee for parking during working hours; the cities more. The attendants are often disabled, and it's usual to round off the price of the ticket upwards.

Fuel and oil Fuel is theoretically available in super (97 octane), normal (96 octane), unleaded (still rare; 95 octane) and diesel. But not every petrol station carries the full range. It is customary to give the attendant a coin or two as a tip.

Fluid measures

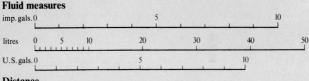

Distance

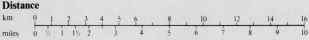

Breakdowns Spanish garages are as efficient as any, and a breakdown will probably be cheaper to repair in Spain than in your home country. Spare parts are readily available for all major makes of cars.

Road signs Most road signs are the standard pictographs used throughout Europe. However, you may encounter these written signs:

Aparcamiento	Parking
Autopista (de peaje/peatge)	(Toll) motorway (expressway)
Ceda el paso	Give way (Yield)
Cruce peligroso	Dangerous crossroads
Cuidado	Caution
Despacio	Slow
Desvió	Diversion (Detour)
Peligro	Danger
Prohibido adelantar	No overtaking (passing)
Prohibido aparcar	No parking
Puesto de socorro	First-aid post

(International) Driving Licence	**Carnet de conducir (internacional)**
Car registration papers	**Permiso de circulación**
Green Card	**Carta verde**

D Are we on the right road for ...?	**¿Es ésta la carretera hacia ...?**
Full tank, please.	**Llene el depósito, por favor.**
normal	**normal**
super	**super**
leadfree	**sin plomo**
Check the oil/tires/battery.	**Por favor, mire el aceite/los neumáticos/la batería.**
I've had a breakdown.	**Mi coche se ha estropeado.**
There's been an accident.	**Ha habido un accidente.**

DRUGS Until the 1980s, Spain had some of the strictest drug laws in Europe. Then possession of small quantities for personal use was legalized. Now the pendulum has swung back in the other direction: possession and sale of drugs is once again a criminal offense in Spain.

E **ELECTRIC CURRENT** (*corriente eléctrica*) Today 220-volt A.C. is becoming standard, but older installations of 125 volts can still be found. Check before plugging in. If the voltage is 125, American appliances (e.g. razors) built for 60 cycles will run on 5O-cycle European current but more slowly.

If you have trouble with any of your appliances, ask your hotel receptionist to recommend an *electricista*.

What's the voltage—125 or 220?	**¿Que voltaje es—ciento veinticinco (125) o doscientos veinte (220)?**
an adaptor/a battery	**un transformador/una pila**

EMERGENCIES

National police (crimes) 091

Traffic police (car accidents, Barcelona area) 092

Fire (Barcelona area) 080

You can always visit the local Municipal Police or the Guardia Civil. If possible take a Spanish speaker with you. Depending on the nature of the emergency, refer to the separate entries in this book, such as CONSULATES, MEDICAL CARE, POLICE, etc.

Though we hope you'll never need them, here are a few key words you might like to learn in advance:

Careful	**Cuidado**	Police	**Policía**
Fire	**Fuego**	Stop	**Deténgase**
Help	**Socorro**	Stop thief	**Al ladrón**

ENTRY and CUSTOMS FORMALITIES *(aduana)* Most visitors require only a valid passport to visit Spain, and even this requirement is waived for the British, who may enter on the simplified Visitor's Passport. Though residents of Europe and North America aren't subject to any health requirements, visitors from further afield should check with a travel agent before departure in case inoculation certificates are called for.

The following chart shows customs allowances for certain items of personal use.

Into:	Cigarettes		Cigars		Tobacco	Spirits		Wine
Spain 1)	300	or	75	or	400g	1.5 l.	and	5 l.
2)	200	or	50	or	250g	1 l.	or	2 l.
Australia	200	or	250 g.	or	250 g.	1 l.	or	1 l.
Canada	200	and	50	and	900g	1.1 l.	or	1.1 l.
Eire	200	or	50	or	250g	1 l.	and	2 l.
N. Zealand	200	or	50	or	250g	1.1 l.	and	4.5 l.
S. Africa	400	and	50	and	250g	1 l.	and	2 l.
U.K	200	or	50	or	250g	1 l.	and	2 l.
U.S.A	200	and	100	and	3)	1 l.	or	1 l.

1) Visitors arriving from EEC countries.
2) Visitors arriving from other countries.
3) A reasonable quantity.

Currency restrictions Tourists may bring an unlimited amount of Spanish or foreign currency into the country. Departing, though, the limit is 100,000 ptas and the equivalent of 500,000 ptas in foreign currency. If you intend to bring in and take out again larger sums, declare this on arrival and departure.

FIRE *(incendio)* Forest fires are a real menace during the scorching summers in Catalonia, so be very careful where you throw your cigarette butts. If you are camping, make sure your fire is extinguished before you move.

G GUIDES *(guía)* Local tourist offices, hotels and travel agencies can put you in touch with qualified guides and interpreters if you want a personally directed tour or help in business negotiations.

We'd like an English-speaking guide	**Queremos un guía que hable inglés.**
I need an English interpreter.	**Necesito un intérprete de inglés.**

H HAIRDRESSERS *(peluquería)* and **BARBERS** *(barbería)*. Many hotels have their own salons, and the standard is generally good. Prices vary widely according to the class of establishment, but rates are often displayed in the window.

Not too much off (here).	**No corte mucho (aquí).**
A little more off (here).	**Un poco más (aquí).**
haircut	**corte**
shampoo and set	**lavado y marcado**
blow-dry	**modelado**
permanent wave	**permanente**
a colour rinse/hair-dye	**champú colorante/tinte**
a colour chart	**un muestrario de tintes**

HITCH-HIKING *(auto-stop)* In Spain hitch-hiking is permitted everywhere and is on the whole safe—which does not mean that it is necessarily easy! Waiting under that unblinking sun can be a thirsty business, interspersed with moments of despair…

If you sleep out in the open, don't bed down close to camping and caravan (trailer) sites. Police passing the campsite may awaken you to check your identity.

Can you give me/us a lift to ...?	**¿Puede llevarme/llevarnos a ...?**

HOTELS and ACCOMMODATION* *(hotel; alojamiento)* Spanish hotel prices are no longer government-controlled. Accommodation ranges from simple rooms in a pensión (boarding house) to the luxurious surroundings of a five-star hotel. Before taking a room, guests have to sign a

form indicating the hotel category, the room number and its price. **H**
Breakfast is normally included in the room rate.

When you check into your hotel you might have to leave your passport
at the desk. Don't worry, you'll get it back in the morning.

Other accommodation:

Hostal and **Hotel-Residencia** Modest hotels, often family concerns, also
graded by stars.

Pensión Boarding house, few amenities.

Fonda Village inn, clean and unpretentious.

Parador State-run inns, often in beautifully restored old buildings and
often in isolated or little-developed areas.

Albergue de Juventud There are youth hostels in Arenys de Mar,
Barcelona and Tarragona. During the tourist season it is wise to book in
advance.

a single/double room	**una habitación individual/doble**
with bath/shower	**con baño/ducha**
What's the rate per night?	**¿Cuál es el precio por noche?**

HOURS In Barcelona, the big department stores, some main bank
branches and shops remain open all day. Other than this, very few shops
open all day without interruption; usual hours are 9.30a.m. to 1.30p.m. and
4.30 to 8p.m., Monday to Saturday. Restaurants start serving lunch about
1p.m. until 3p.m., and dinner around 8–9p.m. to 11p.m. or later.

LANGUAGE The official language of Spain, Castilian, is understood in **L**
Barcelona and on the Costa Dorada. However, a related Romance language, Catalan, is the native language of the people of Catalonia. Since the
death of General Franco, there has been an immense increase in the use of
Catalan and many Catalans express themselves more freely—and more
willingly—in Catalan than in Spanish. On a brief visit to Barcelona and
the Costa Dorada, your elementary Spanish will suffice, even if a few
words of Catalan will always be appreciated.

For geographical reasons, the French language is widely understood and
admired in Catalonia. In tourist areas, English and German are spoken as
well. See also MAPS AND STREET NAMES. **113**

L

	Catalan	Castilian
Good morning	*Bon dia*	*Buenos días*
Good afternoon	*Bona tarda*	*Buenas tardes*
Good night	*Bona nit*	*Buenas noches*
Thank you	*Gràcies*	*Gracias*
You're welcome	*De res*	*De nada*
Please	*Si us plau*	*Por favor*
Goodbye	*Adéu*	*Adiós*

The Berlitz phrase book Spanish for Travellers covers most situations you are likely to encounter during your travels in Spain. The Berlitz Spanish-English/English-Spanish pocket dictionary contains 12,500 concepts, plus a menu-reader supplement.

Do you speak English?	**¿Habla usted inglés?**
I don't speak Spanish.	**No hablo español.**

LAUNDRY *(lavandería)* and **DRY-CLEANING** *(tintorería).* Most hotels will handle laundry and dry-cleaning, but they'll usually charge more than a laundry or a dry-cleaners. For still greater savings, you can try a quick service.

Where's the nearest laundry/dry-cleaners?	**¿Dónde está la lavandería/ tintoreria más cercana?**
When will it be ready?	**¿Cuándo estará listo?**
I must have this for tomorrow morning.	**Lo necesito para mañana por la mañana.**

LOST PROPERTY The first thing to do when you discover you've lost something is, obviously, to retrace your steps. If nothing comes to light report the loss to the Municipal Police or the Guardia Civil.

I've lost my wallet/handbag/ passport.	**He perdido mi cartera/ bolso/pasaporte.**

M **MAPS and STREET NAMES** Spain has been undergoing a formidable upheaval in many domains since 1975. One manifestation is in the names of streets, many of which are being re-baptised, causing a tourist considerable confusion.

Place and street names in Catalonia are mostly met with today in their Catalan version: former San Carlos is now seen as Sant Carles, Lérida as Lleida, Gerona as Girona, etc.

A tip to help recognize Catalan street signs:

Catalan	English	Castilian
Avenida	Avenue	*Avinguda*
Calle	Street	*Carrer*
Iglesia	Church	*Església*
Palacio	Palace	*Palau*
Paseo	Boulevard	*Passeig*
Pasaje	Passageway	*Passatge*
Plaza	Square	*Plaça*

The maps in this book were prepared by Falk-Verlag, Hamburg, that also publish a detailed map of Barcelona.

Id like a street plan of…	**Quisiera un plano de la ciudad de ...**
a road map of this region	**un mapa de carreteras de esta comarca**

MEDICAL CARE By far the best solution, to be completely at ease, is to take out a special health insurance policy to cover the risk of illness and accident while on holiday. Your travel agent can also fix you up with Spanish tourist insurance (ASTES), but it is a slow-moving process. ASTES covers doctors' fees and clinical care.

Health care in the resort areas and in the major cities is good but expensive, hence the need for adequate insurance. Most of the major resort towns have private clinics; the cities and rural areas are served by municipal or provincial hospitals.

For minor ailments, visit the local first-aid post *(casa de socorro or dispensario)*. Away from your hotel, don't hesitate to ask the police or a tourist information office for help. At your hotel, ask the staff to help you.

Pharmacies *(farmacia)* are usually open during normal shopping hours. After hours, at least one per town remains open all night, the *farmacia de guardia*. Its location is posted in the window of all other *farmacias*.

Where's the nearest (all-night) pharmacy?	**¿Dónde está la farmacia (de guardia) más cercana?**
I need a doctor/dentist.	**Necesito un médico/dentista.**
I've a pain here.	**Me duele aquí.**
a fever/sunburn	**fiebre/quemadura del sol**
an upset stomach	**molestias de estómago**

M **MEETING PEOPLE** Politeness and simple courtesies still matter in Spain. A handshake on greeting and leaving is normal. Always begin any conversation whether with a friend, shop girl, taxi-driver, policeman or telephone operator, with a *buenos días* (good morning) or *buenas tardes* (good afternoon). Always say *adiós* (good-bye) or, at night, *buenas noches* when leaving. *Por favor* (please) should begin all requests.

Incidentally, if anyone should say *adiós* to you when seeing you in the street, it's not that they don't want to have anything to do with you—it's a familiar greeting, meaning roughly "hello".

The Spanish have their own pace. Not only is it bad manners to try to rush them, but unproductive as well.

MONEY MATTERS

Currency The monetary unit of Spain is the *peseta* (abbreviated *pta*).

Coins: 1, 5, 10, 25, 50, 100, 200, 500 ptas.

Banknotes: 1,000, 2,000, 5,000, 10,000 ptas.

A 5-peseta coin is traditionally called a *duro*, so if someone should quote a price as 10 duros. he means 50 pesetas. For currency restrictions, see ENTRY AND CUSTOMS FORMALITIES.

Banking hours are from 9a.m. to 2p.m. Monday to Friday, till 1p.m. on Saturdays (closed Saturday during the summer).

Banks are closed on Sundays and holidays—watch out, too, for those local holidays which always seem to crop up in Spain! Outside normal banking hours, many travel agencies and other businesses displaying a *cambio* sign will change foreign currency into pesetas. In Barcelona, there are exchange offices open in the afternoon and at weekends at the Estació Central-Sants, Estació de França and at the airport. Both banks and exchange offices pay slightly more for traveller's cheques than for cash. Always take your passport with you when you go to exchange money.

Credit cards All the internationally recognized cards are accepted by hotels, restaurants and businesses in Spain.

Eurocheques You'll have no problem settling bills or paying for purchases with Eurocheques.

Traveller's cheques In tourist areas, shops and all banks, hotels and travel
116 agencies accept them, though you're likely to get a better exchange rate at

a national or regional bank. Remember always to take your passport with
you if you expect to cash a traveller's cheque.

Paying cash Although many shops and bars will accept payment in sterling or dollars, you're better off paying in pesetas. Shops will invariably give you less than the bank rate for foreign currency.

Prices Although Spain has by no means escaped the scourge of inflation, the Costa Dorada remains quite competitive with the other tourist regions of Europe. An exciting night on the town—either at a discotheque or a flamenco nightclub—won't completely ruin you. In the realm of eating, drinking and smoking, Spain still provides indisputable value for money.

Certain rates are listed on p.101 to give you an idea of what things cost.

Where's the nearest bank/ currency exchange office?	**¿Dónde está el banco/la oficina de cambio más cercana?**
I want to change some pounds/ dollars.	**Quiero cambiar libras/dólares.**
Do you accept traveller's cheques?	**¿Acepta usted cheques de viaje?**
Can I pay with this credit card?	**¿Puedo pagar con esta tarjeta de crédito?**
How much is that?	**¿Cuánto es?**

MOSQUITOES With the occasional exception there are rarely more than a few mosquitoes at a given time, but they survive the year round, and just one can ruin a night's sleep. Few hotels, flats or villas—anywhere on the Mediterranean—have mosquito-proofed windows. Bring your own anti-mosquito devices, whether nets, buzzers, lotions, sprays or incense-type coils.

NEWSPAPERS and MAGAZINES *(periódico; revista)* At the height of the tourist season, all major British and Continental newspapers are on sale up and down the coast on their publication day. U.S magazines and the Paris-based *International Herald Tribune* are also available.

Have you any English-language newspapers/magazines?	**¿Tienen periódicos/revistas en inglés?**

P **PHOTOGRAPHY** There's tremendous scope for the keen photographer, but beware of the light. For beaches, whitewashed houses and other strongly lit scenes, use incidental readings stopped down i.e. reduced by one-third or one-half stop; or follow the instructions with the film. If in doubt, bracket your exposures—expose above and below the selected exposure—especially with transparency film. For good results don't shoot between 11a.m. and 3p.m. unless there's light cloud to soften the sun.

All popular brands of film are on sale. Customs regulations limit importing film to 10 rolls per camera. Spanish-made film is much less expensive and of a reasonable quality. To get best results from the black-and-white *Negra* and *Valca*, you'll need to experiment, especially with processing. The colour negative film *Negracolor* is fine for family shots. All transparency film is imported.

Shops in Barcelona and major resorts can develop and print black-and-white or colour film in a few days, and some specialize in l-hour service. If possible always keep film—exposed and unexposed—in a refrigerator.

Photos shops sell lead-coated plastic bags which protect films from X-rays at airport security checkpoints.

I'd like a film for this camera.	**Quisiera un carrete para esta máquina.**
a black-and-white film	**un carrete en blanco y negro**
a colour-slide film	**un carrete de diapositivas**
a film for colour-pictures	**un carrete para película en color**
35-mm film	**un carrete treinta y cinco**
super-8	**super ocho**
How long will it take to develop (and print) this film?	**¿Cuánto tardará en revelar (y sacar copias de) este carrete?**

POLICE *(policía)* There are three police forces in Spain: the *Policía Municipal*, who are attached to the local town hall and usually wear a blue uniform; the *Cuerpo Nacional de Policía*, a national anti-crime unit recognized by their brown uniforms; and the *Guardia Civil*, the national police force patrolling highways and rural areas.

If you need police assistance, you can call on any one of the three.

Where's the nearest police station?	**¿Dónde está la comisaría más cercana?**

January 1	*Ano Nuevo*	New Year's Day
January 6	*Epifanía*	Epiphany
March 19	*San José*	St Joseph's Day
May 1	*Día del Trabajo*	Labour Day
July 25	*Santiago Apóstol*	St James's Day
August 15	*Asunción*	Assumption
October 12	*Día de la Hispanidad*	Discovery of America Day (Columbus Day)
November 1	*Todos los Santos*	All Saints' Day
December 6	*Día de la Constitución Española*	Constitution Day
December 25	*Navidad*	Christmas Day
Movable dates:	*Jueves Santo*	Maundy Thursday
	Viernes Santo	Good Friday
	Lunes de Pascua	Easter Monday (Catalonia only)
	Corpus Christi	Corpus Christi
	Inmaculada Concepción	Immaculate Conception (normally December 8)

These are only the national holidays of Spain. There are many special holidays for different branches of the economy or different regions. Consult the tourist office where you are staying.

Are you open tomorrow?   **¿Está abierto mañana?**

RADIO and TV (*radio; televisión*) A short-wave set of reasonable quality   R
will pick up all European capitals. Reception of Britain's BBC World
Service usually rates from good to excellent, either direct or through their
eastern Mediterranean relay station. In the winter, especially mornings and
evenings, a good set will pull in the BBC medium and long wave "home"
programmes. The Voice of America usually comes through loud and clear,
though in Spain the programme is not received 24 hours a day. The
Spanish music programme, *segundo programa*, jazz to Bach but mostly
classical, is excellent. It's FM only, around 88UKW on the band.

R   Most hotels and bars have television, usually tuned in to sports—including international soccer and rugby—bull fighting, variety or nature programmes.

RELIGIOUS SERVICES *(servicio religioso)* The national religion of Spain is Roman Catholicism. Masses are said regularly in almost all churches, including those of outstanding artistic or historical interest.

In Barcelona, Catholic and Protestant services are held in foreign languages, and there is also a synagogue and a mosque. In Barcelona Cathedral, confessions are heard each Sunday in English.

T   **TIME DIFFERENCES** Spanish time coincides with most of Western Europe—Greenwich Mean Time plus one hour. In spring, another hour is added for Daylight Saving Time (Summer Time).

Summer Time chart:

New York	London	**Spain**	Jo'burg	Sydney	Auckland
6a.m.	11a.m.	**noon**	noon	8p.m.	10p.m.

What time is it?   **¿Qué hora es?**

TIPPING Since a service charge is included in hotel and restaurant bills, tipping is not obligatory. However, it's appropriate to tip porters, bellboys, etc, for their efforts. Rough guidelines are:

Hotel porter, per bag	50ptas
Maid, for extra services	100-200ptas
Waiter	10% (optional)
Taxi driver	10%
Tourist guide	10%
Hairdresser	10%
Lavatory attendant	25-50ptas

TOILETS There are many expressions for "toilets" in Spanish: a*seos, servicios, W.C., water* and *rereles.* The first terms are the more common.

Public toilets are to be found in most large towns, but rarely in villages. However, just about every bar and restaurant has a toilet available for

public use. It's considered polite to buy a coffee or a glass of wine if you
drop in specifically to use the conveniences.

Where are the toilets?   **¿Donde están los servicios?**

TOURIST INFORMATION OFFICES *(oficinas de turismo)* Spanish
National Tourist Offices are maintained in many countries throughout the
world:

Canada 102 Bloor Street West, 14th floor, Toronto, Ont. M5S 1MB; tel.
(416) 961-3131

U.K 57-58 St James's Street, London SWlA lLD; tel. (071) 499 1169

U.S.A 845 N. Michigan Avenue, Chicago, IL 60611; tel. (312) 944 0216;
8383 Wilshire Boulevard, Suite 960, Beverly Hills, CA 90211; tel.
(213) 658 7188/93;
665 5th Avenue, New York, NY 10022; tel. (212) 7598822;
1221 Brickell Avenue, Miami, FL 33131; tel (305) 358 1992

These offices will supply you with a wide range of brochures and maps in
English on the various towns and regions in Spain. You can also consult a
copy of the master directory of hotels in Spain, listing all facilities and
prices.

All major cities and leading resorts in Spain have their own tourist
information offices, with information and brochures on local tourist attractions.

Barcelona At the airport, the central railway station *(Estació Central-
Sants)*, the *Estació de França* (in the harbour), in *Plaça de Sant Jaume*
(Gothic Quarter), in Palau de la Virreina at *Rambla 99* and in *Gran Via de
les Corts Catalanes 658*.

Barcelona's tourist authority is the Patronat de Turisme, Passeig de
Gràcia 35, 08007 Barcelona.

While in Barcelona, you can dial 010 for tourist and other information
about the city.

Sitges Plaça d'Eduard Maristany

Tarragona Rambla Nova 46

Where is the tourist office?   **¿Dónde está la oficina de turismo?**   121

T TRANSPORT

Buses More than 50 bus lines cover Barcelona. As in many cities, the rush hours are best avoided.

Buses are boarded from the front, and tickets are issued by the driver. Take out a multiple-journey ticket valid for bus and Metro if it looks likely you're going to travel around and sightsee a lot in Barcelona. A simple and excellent way to sightsee is to hop on—or off, as many times and wherever you like—bus No.100—all on the same ticket. The route followed in a 1½ hour tour takes in the most interesting highspots of a Barcelona visit. Departure from Pla del Palau every 45 minutes.

To reach the resorts from Barcelona, trains are more frequent and practical than the bus services.

Metro* Barcelona's underground railway, consisting of five main lines, crisscrosses the city more rapidly than other forms of public transport.

"Metro" signs with a red diamond-shaped insignia mark the entrances, where detailed maps of all lines are displayed. Trains run from 5a.m. to 11p.m.

Taxis* You can recognize taxis by the letters 'SP' *(servicio público)* on the front and rear bumpers. Some also have a green light on the roof and a *libre* (free) sign on the windscreen. Each town has its own type of car and colour scheme (Barcelona's taxis are all painted yellow and black). In smaller towns, there are fixed fares instead of meters: in major cities, the meter clicks relentlessly as you go. The figure displayed at the end of your trip probably is not the full fare— the driver carries an official list giving the correct total, adjusted upwards for inflation. Additional charges are legitimately made for any number of circumstances—such as nights and holidays, or picking you up at a railway station, airport theatre or bullring. Whatever the total, it usually still costs less than a comparable journey in many other European countries.

Ferries From Barcelona, there are regular ferry services (with cabin or deck seating) to Palma de Mallorca, Menorca and Ibiza. For information and booking, contact any local travel agency.

Trains From Barcelona, main line trains reach to most corners of Spain. Local trains are slow, stopping at most stations. Long-distance services are fast and punctual. Tickets can be purchased at travel agencies as well as at the stations *(estació[n] de ferrocarril)*. For bargain rail tickets, see p.100.

Trains to resorts north east of Barcelona use the Cercanías station, a separate installation behind the Estació de França in the harbour. Suburban trains to the south-east run from the Passeig de Gràcia station in the centre of town and from the central station—Estació de Sants—in western Barcelona.

EuroCity (EC)	International express, first and second classes
Talgo, Intercity, Electrotren, Ter, Tren Estrella	Luxury, first and second classes; supplementary charge over regular fare
Expreso, Rápido	Long-distance expresses, stopping at main stations only; supplementary charge
Tranvía	Local trains, with frequent stops, usually second class only
Auto Expreso	Car train
coche cama	Sleeping-car with 1-, 2- or 3-bed compartments, washing facilities
coche restaurante	Dining-car
litera	Sleeping-berth car (couchette) with blankets, sheets and pillows
furgón de equipajes	Luggage van (baggage car); only registered luggage permitted

When's the next bus/train to ...? **¿Cuándo sale el próximo autobús/tren para ...?**

single (one-way) **ida**
return (round-trip) **ida y vuelta**

What's the fare to ...? **¿Cuánto es la tarifa a ...?**
first/second class **primera/segunda clase**
I'd like to make seat reservations. **Quiero reservar asientos.**

Where can I get a taxi? **¿Dónde puedo coger un taxi?**

W **WATER** If you're particularly sensitive to a change in water, you may want to order the bottled variety. Both still (non-carbonated) and fizzy (carbonated) water are available.

a bottle of mineral water	**una botella de agua mineral**
fizzy	**con gas**
still	**sin gas**
Is this drinking water?	**¿El agua es potable?**

DAYS OF THE WEEK

Sunday	*domingo*	Thursday	*jueves*
Monday	*lunes*	Friday	*viernes*
Tuesday	*martes*	Saturday	*sábado*
Wednesday	*miércoles*		

NUMBERS

0	**cero**	19	**diecinueve**
1	**uno**	20	**veinte**
2	**dos**	21	**veintiuno**
3	**tres**	22	**veintidós**
4	**cuatro**	30	**treinta**
5	**cinco**	31	**treinta y uno**
6	**seis**	32	**treinta y dos**
7	**siete**	40	**cuarenta**
8	**ocho**	50	**cincuenta**
9	**nueve**	60	**sesenta**
10	**diez**	70	**setenta**
11	**once**	80	**ochenta**
12	**doce**	90	**noventa**
13	**trece**	100	**cien**
14	**catorce**	101	**cientouno**
15	**quince**	500	**quinientos**
16	**dieciséis**	1,000	**mil**
17	**diecisiete**		
18	**dieciocho**		

SOME USEFUL EXPRESSIONS

yes/no	**sí/no**
please/thank you	**por favor/gracias**
excuse me/you're welcome	**perdone/de nada**
where/when/how	**dónde/cuándo/cómo**
how long/how far	**cuánto tiempo/a qué distancia**
yesterday/today/tomorrow	**ayer/hoy/mañana**
day/week/month/year	**día/semana/mes/año**
left/right	**izquierda/derecha**
up/down	**arriba/abajo**
good/bad	**bueno/malo**
big/small	**grande/pequeño**
cheap/expensive	**barato/caro**
hot/cold	**caliente/frío**
old/new	**viejo/nuevo**
open/closed	**abierto/cerrado**
here/there	**aquí/allí**
free (vacant)/occupied	**libre/ocupado**
early/late	**temprano/tarde**
easy/difficult	**fácil/diffcil**

Does anyone here speak English?	**¿Hay alguien aquí que hable inglés?**
What does this mean?	**¿Qué quiere decir esto?**
I dont understand.	**No comprendo.**
Please write it down.	**Escríbamelo, por favor.**
Is there an admission charge?	**¿Se debe pagar la entrada?**
Waiter!/Waitress!	**¡Camarero!/¡Camarera!**
I'd like ...	**Quisiera ...**
How much is that?	**¿Cuánto es?**
Have you something less expensive?	**¿Tiene algo más barato?**
Just a minute.	**Un momento.**
Help me, please	**Ayúdeme, por favor.**
Get a doctor, quickly.	**¡Llamen a un médico, rápidamente!**

INDEX

An asterisk (*) next to a page number indicates a map reference.

126

Selection of Barcelona Hotels and Restaurants

plus a section on Points of Excursion

Where do you start? Choosing a hotel or restaurant in a place you're not familiar with can be daunting. To help you find your way in and around Barcelona, we have made a selection from the *Red Guide to Spain and Portugal* published by Michelin, the recognized authority on gastronomy and accommodation throughout Europe.

Our own Berlitz criteria have been price and location. In the hotel section, for a double room with bath but without breakfast, "Higher-priced" means above 10,000 ptas, "Medium-priced" 6,000-10,000 ptas, "Lower-priced" below 6,000 ptas. The number of stars for each hotel are those awarded under the Spanish system of grading hotels. As to restaurants, for a meal consisting of a starter, a main course and a dessert, "Higher-priced" means above 3,500 ptas, "Medium-priced" 2,300-3,500 ptas, "Lower-priced" below 2,300 ptas. For Costa Dorada resorts, however, to avoid confusion of detail, we have used the symbol $$$ for Higher-priced, $$ for Medium-priced and $ for Lower-priced.

Special features where applicable, plus regular closing days are also given. As a general rule many Barcelona restaurants are closed in August. Hotels at Costa Dorada resorts often close during the winter season. For hotels and restaurants, check that they are open; reservations are advisable. In Spain, hotel and restaurant prices include a service charge, but 6-12% tax will be added to the bill.

For a wider choice of hotels and restaurants, we recommend you obtain the authoritative Michelin *Red Guide to Spain and Portugal*, which gives a comprehensive picture of the situation throughout these countries.

Barcelona

HOTELS

HIGHER PRICED
(above 10,000 ptas)

Alexandra ****
Mallorca 251, 08008 Barcelona.
Tel. 487 0505, fax 216 0606
Situated in the centre of the
Eixample area.

Avenida Palace *****
Gran Via de les Corts Catalanes
605, 08007 Barcelona. Tel. 301
9600, fax 318 1234
Deluxe hotel, with standard of
service to match.

Diplomatic *****
Pau Claris 122, 08009
Barcelona. Tel. 317 3100, fax
318 6531
Outdoor swimming pool. La
Salsa restaurant.

Gran Derby ****
Loreto 28, 08029 Barcelona. Tel
322 2062, fax 419 6820
Exceptionally pleasant small
hotel.

Gran Hotel Calderón ****
Rambla de Catalunya 26, 08007
Barcelona. Tel. 301 0000, fax
317 3157
On the main rambla. Indoor and
outdoor swimming pools.

Hilton *****
Avenida Diagonal 589-591,
08014 Barcelona. Tel. 419 2233,
fax 322 5291
Modern hotel on the main
upmarket shopping street.

Majéstic ****
Passeig de Gràcia 70, 08007
Barcelona. Tel. 215 4512, fax
215 7773
Picturesque, central location.
Swimming pool, terrace.

Melià Barcelona Sarrià *****
Avenida de Sarrià 50, 08029
Barcelona. Tel. 410 6060, fax
321 5179
Modern hotel. Picturesque setting
in Sarrià.

Presidente *****
avenida Diagonal 570, 08021
Barcelona. Tel. 200 2111, fax
209 5106
Modern hotel with luxury
facilities. Outdoor swimming
pool.

Princess Sofia *****
Plaça Pius XII s/n, 08028
Barcelona. Tel. 330 7111, fax
330 7621
Luxury hotel in a picturesque
setting. Terrace, swimming pool.

Ramada Renaissance *****
Rambla 111, 08002 Barcelona.
Tel. 318 6200, fax 301 7776
Central location.

Ritz *****
*Gran Vía de les Corts Catalanes
668, 08010 Barcelona.
Tel. 318 5200, fax 318 0148*
The most elegant of Barcelona's
luxury hotels. Outdoor dining.

MEDIUM-PRICED
(6,000-10,000 ptas)

Aragón ***
*Aragó 569bis, 08026 Barcelona.
Tel. 245 8905, fax 447 0923*

Arenas ****
*Capità Arenas 20, 08034
Barcelona. Tel. 280 0303,
fax 280 3392*
Close to Pedralbes.

Barcelona ****
*Casp 1-13, 08010 Barcelona.
Tel. 302 5858, fax 301 8674*
Central location.

Colón ****
*Avenida Catedral 7, 08002
Barcelona. Tel. 301 1404,
fax 317 2915*
Opposite the cathedral.

Condes de Barcelona ****
*Passeig de Gràcia 75, 08008
Barcelona. Tel. 487 3737,
fax 287 1442*
Modern, centrally located hotel
in beautiful setting. Impeccable
facilities and service.

Cristal ****
*Diputació 257, 08007 Barcelona.
Tel. 301 6600, fax 317 5979*
In the centre of the Eixample.

Gótico ***
*Jaime I 14, 08002 Barcelona.
Tel. 315 2211, fax 315 3819*
Picturesque, central location.

Gran Hotel Cristina ****
*Avenida Diagonal 458, 08036
Barcelona. Tel. 217 6800,
fax 217 6900*
At the heart of the elegant
shopping area.

Numáncia ***
*Numáncia 74, 08029 Barcelona.
Tel. 322 4451, fax 410 7642*
Cafeteria only.

Rallye ***
*Travessera de les Corts 150,
08028 Barcelona. Tel. 339 9050,
fax 411 0790*
Swimming pool.

Regente ****
*Rambla de Catalunya 76, 08007
Barcelona. Tel. 215 2570,
fax 487 3227*
Outdoor swimming pool.

Royal ****
*Rambla 117, 08002 Barcelona.
Tel. 301 9400, fax 317 3179*
Central location. Picturesque
setting.

Suizo ***
Plaça de l'Angel 12, 08002 Barcelona. Tel. 315 4111, fax 315 3819.
Central location.

Terminal ***
Provença 1, 08029 Barcelona. Tel. 321 5350
Close to Estacio Sants.

Tres Torres ***
Calatrava 32-34, 08017 Barcelona. Tel. 417 7300, fax 418 9834
In Sevria and Bonanova.

LOWER-PRICED
(below 6,000 ptas)

Bonanova Park **
Capità Arenas 51, 08034 Barcelona. Tel. 204 09 O0, fax 204 5014
Close to Pedalbes.

Cortés **
Santa Ana 25, 08002 Barcelona. Tel. 317 9212, fax 302 7870
Just off the Ramblas.

Covadonga ***
Avenida Diagonal 596, 08021 Barcelona. Tel. 209 5511, fax 209 5833
No restaurant, but snacks available.

España **
Sant Pau 9-11, 08001 Barcelona. Tel. 318 1758
Beautiful modernist dining-rooms.

Gaudí ***
Nou de la Rambla 12, 08001 Barcelona. Tel. 317 9032, fax 412 2636
Central location.

Ginebra *
Rambla de Catalunya 1, 08007 Barcelona. Tel. 317 1063
Central location.

Gran Via ***
Gran Via de les Corts, Catalanes 642, 08007 Barcelona. Tel 318 1900, fax 318 9997
Picturesque, central location. Historic building.

Lleó **
Pelai 24, 08001 Barcelona. Tel.318 1312, fax 412 2657
Central location.

Park Hotel ***
Avenida Marquès de l'Argentera 11, 08003 Barcelona. Tel 319 6000, fax 319 4519

Regencia Colón ***
Sagristans 13-17, 08002 Barcelona. Tel. 318 9858, fax 317 2822
Central location. Historic building.

San Agustin **

plaça de Sant Agustí 3, 08001
Barcelona. Tel. 317 2882,
fax 317 2928
Picturesque, central location.

Toledano *

Rambla 138, 08002 Barcelona.
Tel. 301 0872, fax 412 3142.
Central location.

Via Augusta **

Via Augusta 63, 08006
Barcelona. Tel. 217 9250,
fax 237 7714

RESTAURANTS

HIGHER-PRICED

(above 3,500 ptas)

Ara-Cata

Dr. Ferràn 33, 08034 Barcelona.
Tel.204 1053
Notably good French and Catalan
cuisine. Discreetly elegant.
Closed Saturday.

Azulete

vía Augusta 281, 08017
Barcelona. Tel.203 5943
Excellent Mediterranean
cooking. Outdoor dining.
Flowered terrace. Closed
Saturday lunchtime, Sunday and
public holidays.

Bel Air

Córcega 286, 08008 Barcelona.
Tel. 237 7588
Rice specialities and market
cuisine. Closed Sunday.

Botafumeiro

Gran de Grácia 81, 08012
Barcelona. Tel.218 4230
Excellent Galician seafood
specialities. Closed Sunday
evening and Monday.

La Cúpula

Teodora Roviralta 37, 08022
Barcelona.
Tel. 212 4888/418 5141
Market cuisine. Ancient tower.
Spacious garden-terrace.

Eldorado Petit

Dolors Monserdà 51, 08017
Barcelona. Tel. 204 5153
Top rate Catalan cuisine in
pleasant surroundings. Outdoor
dining. Closed Sunday and for
two weeks in August.

Neichel

Avenida de Pedralbes 16 bis,
08034 Barcelona. Tel. 203 8408
Imaginative French cooking with
seafood specialities. Closed
Sunday and public holidays.

Reno

Tuset 27, 08006 Barcelona.
Tel. 200 9129
Excellent French and Catalan
cuisine in elegant surroundings.

Vía Veneto
Ganduxer 10,
08021 Barcelona.
Tel. 200 7044
Considered the best restaurant in Barcelona. Belle Epoque decor. Closed Saturday lunch and all day Sunday.

MEDIUM-PRICED
(2,300-3,500 ptas)

Agut d'Avignon
Trinidad 3 (Avinyó 8),
08002 Barcelona.
Tel. 302 6034
Catalan cuisine.
Typical local decor.

Aitor
Carbonnell 5, 08003 Barcelona.
Tel. 319 9488
Basque cuisine. Closed Sunday, and from mid-August to mid-September.

Alt Berlin
Sabina de Arana 54,
08028 Barcelona.
Tel. 339 0166
German cuisine.

Brasserie Flo
Jonqueres 10, 08003 Barcelona.
Tel. 317 8037
Excellent quality French and Catalan cuisine.

Can Majó
Almirall Aixada 23
(Barceloneta), 08003 Barcelona.
Tel. 310 1455/319 5096
Rice and seafood specialities. Closed Monday.

Can Solé
San Carlos 4, 08003 Barcelona.
Tel. 319 5012
Seafood specialities. Closed Saturday evening, all day Sunday.

Los Caracoles
Escudellers 14, 08002
Barcelona. Tel. 301 2041
Regional country style decor.

La Cuineta
Paradís 4, 08002 Barcelona.
Tel. 315 0111
Tastefully installed in a 17th-century "bodega". Regional specialities.

Gorria
Diputació 421, 08013 Barcelona.
Tel. 245 1164
Excellent Basque-Navarre cuisine. Reservations essential. Closed Sunday.

El Gran Café
Avinyó 9, 08002 Barcelona.
Tel. 318 7986
French and Catalan cuisine. Turn-of-the-century decor. Piano music in the evening. Closed Sunday.

Hostal del Sol
piso 1 (1st floor), passeig de Gràcia 44, 08007 Barcelona.
Tel. 215 6225
Catalan and seafood specialities.
Piano music in the evening.

Hostal Sant Jordi
Travessera de Dalt 121, 08024 Barcelona. Tel. 213 1037
Catalan-French cuisine. Closed Sunday evening.

Jaume de Provença
Provença 88, 08029 Barcelona.
Tel. 430 0029
Catalan and French cuisine.
Modern restaurant.
Closed Sunday evening and Monday.

Lagunak
Berlín 19, 08014 Barcelona.
Tel. 490 5911
Basque-Navarre cuisine. Closed Sunday.

A la Menta
passeig Manuel Girona 50, 08034 Barcelona. Tel.204 1549
Specializes in meat and fish dishes on the grill. Reservation essential. Closed Sunday evening.

Network Cafe
Diagonal 616, 08021 Barcelona.
Tel. 201 7238
Designer decor.

La Odisea
Copons 7, 08002 Barcelona.
Tel. 302 3692
Good French/Catalan cuisine.
Classically tasteful decor.
Closed Saturday lunchtime and Sunday.

Pá i Trago
Parlamento 41, 08015 Barcelona. Tel. 441 1320
Typical local restaurant,
Catalan cuisine. Closed Monday.

A'Palloza
Casanova 42, 08011 Barcelona.
Tel. 453 1786
Seafood specialities, meat and fish on the grill. Closed Sunday.

La Perla Nera
Via Layetano 32-34, 08003 Barcelona.
Tel. 310 5646
Italian cuisine. Excellent pizzas.

La Senyora Grill
Bori i Fontesta 45, 08017 Barcelona.
Tel. 201 2577
Outdoor dining.

El Trapio
Esperanza 25, 08017 Barcelona.
Tel. 211 5817
Covered terrace and magnificent garden. International cuisine.
Closed Sunday evening and Monday.

La Venta
*plaça Dr. Andreu, 08022
Barcelona. Tel. 212 6455*
Old café, market cuisine.
Outdoor dining. Closed Sunday.

Outskirts of Barcelona

Casa Quirze
*Laureano Miró 202, 08950
Esplugues de Llobregat.
Tel. 371 1084*
Good Catalan and market
cuisine. Closed Sunday evening
and Monday .

La Masía
*Avenida Paisos Catalans 58,
08950 Esplugues de Llobregat.
Tel. 371 3742*
Outdoor dining on terrace
beneath the pines.

LOWER-PRICED
(below 2,300 ptas)

Bel Cavalletto
*Santaló 125, 08021 Barcelona.
Tel. 201 79 11*
Italian cuisine.

Can Culleretes
*Quintana 5, 08002 Barcelona.
Tel. 317 6485*
One of the oldest restaurants in
Barcelona. Typical local
restaurant, excellent value.
Closed Sunday evening and
Monday.

Can Punyetes
*Mariano Cubi 189, 08030
Barcelona. Tel. 200 9159*
Excellent grilled Catalan food.
Reservation advisable.

Egipte
*Jerusalem 3, 08001 Barcelona.
Tel. 317 7480*
Large old house behind the
Boqueria serves good Catalan
market food. Popular. Closed
Sunday.

La Garduña
*Morena 17, 08001 Barcelona.
Tel. 302 4323*
Popular Catalan and market food
situated at the back of the
Boqueria. Theatre haunt.

Julivert Meu
*Jorge Girona Salgado 12, 08034
Barcelona. Tel. 204 1196*
Catalan cuisine.

L'Olivé
*Muntaner 171, 08036 Barcelona.
Tel. 430 9027*
Outdoor dining. Typical local
restaurant. Reservation essential.
Closed Sunday.

El Patí Blau
*Jorge Girona Salgado 14, 08034
Barcelona. Tel. 204 2215*
Catalan cuisine.

7 Puertas
*passeig d'Isabel 11-14, 08003
Barcelona. Tel. 319 3033*
Good Catalan food. Over 100
years old and still popular.

Outskirts of Barcelona

Can Cortés
*Urbanización Ciudad Condal
Tibidabo, on Sant Cugat del
Vallés highway,
08023 Barcelona.
Tel. 674 1704*
View. Outdoor dining.
Catalan wine bar. Old "masía".
Outdoor swimming pool
(small fee) .

Costa Dorada and Inland Resorts

CALAFELL

HOTELS

Canadá $
*Avenida Mosén Jaime Soler 44,
43820 Calafell.
Tel. (977) 69 15 00*
Outdoor dining. Outdoor
swimming pool. Hotel tennis
court.

Kursaal $$
*Avenida San Juan de Dios 119,
43820 Calafell.
Tel. (977) 69 23 00*
Quiet hotel. View. Outdoor
dining.

RESTAURANTS

La Barca Ca L'Ardet $$
*Avenida San Juan de Dios 79,
43820 Calafell.
Tel. (977) 69 15 59*
Outdoor dining. Seafood
specialties.

O Braseiro Galaico $
*Marta Moraga 29, 43882
Segur de Calafell.
Tel. (977) 69 2O 33*
Seafood specialities. Closed
Tuesday.

CAMBRILS

HOTELS

Can Solé $
*Ramón Llull 19, 43850 Cambrils.
Tel. (977) 36 O2 36*
Outdoor dining.

Mónica H. $
*Galcerán Marquet 3,
43850 Cambrils.
Tel. (977) 36 01 16*
Lawn with palm trees. Garden.

Rovira $
*Avenida Diputación 6, 43850
Cambrils. Tel. (977) 36 09 00*
View. Outdoor dining.

Tropicana $
Avenida Diputación, 43850
Cambrils. Tel. (977) 36 01 l2
Outdoor dining. Outdoor
swimming pool. Garden.

RESTAURANTS

El Caliu $$
Pau Casals 22, 43850 Cambrils.
Tel. (977) 36 01 08
Country-style decor. Outdoor
dining. Meat prepared on a grill.
Closed Sunday evening and
Monday.

Can Bosch $$
Rambla Jaime 1-19, 43850
Cambrils. Tel. (977) 36 00 19
Notably good cuisine. Seafood
specialities. Outdoor dining.
Closed Sunday evening and
Monday.

Can Gatell $$
Paseo Miramar 27, 43850
Cambrils. Tel. (977) 36 01 06
Notably good cuisine. Seafood
specialities. Outdoor dining.
View. Closed Monday evening,
Tuesday all day out of season
and Tuesday and Wednesday
lunchtime in summer.

Casa Gallau $$
Pescadores 25, 43850 Cambrils.
Tel. (977) 36 02 61
Outdoor dining. Seafood
specialities. Closed Wednesday
evening and Thursday.

Casa Gatell $$$
Paseo Miramar 26, 43850
Cambrils. Tel. (977) 36 00 57
Notably good cuisine. Seafood
specialities. Outdoor dining.
View. Closed Sunday evening
and Monday.

Eugenia $$
Consolat de Mar 80, 43850
Cambrils. Tel. (977) 36 01 68
Notably good cuisine. Seafood
specialities. Outdoor dining.
Terrace with flowers. Closed
Tuesday evening and
Wednesday.

Marina $$
Paseo Miramar 42, 43850
Cambrils. Tel. (977) 36 04 32
View. Outdoor dining. Closed
Thursday.

Mas Gallau $$
on highway N340, apartado 129,
Cambrils. Tel. (977) 36 05 88
Country-style decor.

CASTELLDEFELS

HOTELS

Luna $$
Paseo de la Marina 155, 08860
Castelldefels. Tel. (93) 665 2150,
fax (93) 665 2212
Outdoor swimming pool.
Garden.

Mediterráneo $
Paseo Marítimo 294, 08860
Castelldefels. Tel. (93) 665 2l00,
fax (93) 665 2250
Outdoor swimming pool.

G. H. Rey Don Jaime $$$
Torre Barona, 08860
Castelldefels. Tel. (93) 665 1300,
fax (93) 665 1801
Quiet hotel. Outdoor dining.
Outdoor swimming pool.
Garden. Hotel tennis court.

Riviera $
on highway C 246, 08860
Castelldefels. Tel. (93) 665 1400,
fax (93) 665 1404

RESTAURANTS

Las Botas $$
on highway C 246, 08860
Castelldefels. Tel. (93) 665 1824
Outdoor dining. Typical decor.
Closed Sunday evening.

La Canasta $$
Plaça del Mar 3, 08860
Castelldefels. Tel. (93) 665 6857
Outdoor dining. Closed Tuesday.

COMARRUGA

HOTELS

Casa Martí $
Vilafranca 8, 43880 Comarruga.
Tel. (977) 68 01 11,
fax (977) 68 22 77
Quiet hotel. View. Outdoor
swimming pool. Tennis court.

G. H. Europe $$
Vía Palfuriana 107,
43880 Comarruga.
Tel. (977) 68 04 11,
fax (977) 68 01 89
View. Outdoor dining. Heated
outdoor swimming pool. Hotel
tennis court.

HOSPITALET DEL INFANTE

HOTELS

Infante $
Del Mar 24, 43890
Hospitalet del Infante.
Tel. (977) 82 30 00,
fax (977) 82 32 75
Quiet hotel. View. Outdoor
dining. Outdoor swimming pool.
Hotel tennis court.

Tropicana $
Carretera N 340,
43892 Miami Playa.
Tel. (977) 81 03 40,
fax (977) 81 05 18
Outdoor swimming pool.

RESTAURANTS

Les Barques $$
Comandante Gimeno 21, 43890
Hospitalet del Infante.
Tel. (977) 82 39 61
View. Seafood specialities.

MONTSERRAT
HOTELS

Albat Cisneros $
*plaça Monasterio, 08691
Montserrat. Tel. (93) 835 0201,
fax (93) 828 4006*
Quiet hotel.

RESTAURANTS

Montserrat $$
*plaça Apostols, 08691
Montserrat. Tel. (93) 835 O251
(ext. 165)*
View. Lunch only.

Santa Cecilia $
*on Casa Masana highway, 08691
Montserrat. Tel. (93) 835 0309*
View. Outdoor dining. Closed
Thursday except July and August.

SALOU
HOTELS

Carabela Roc $
*Pau Casals 108, 43840 Salou.
Tel. (977) 37 01 66,
fax (977) 37 07 62*
Beneath the pine trees. View. No
restaurant.

Planas $
*plaça Bonet 3, 43840 Salou. Tel.
(977) 38 01 08*
Outdoor dining. Terrace.

RESTAURANTS

Casa Font $$
*Colón 17, Edificio Els
Pilons, 43840 Salou.
Tel. (977) 38 57 45*
International cuisine. View.
Outdoor dining. Closed
Mondays.

Casa Soler $$
*Virgen del Carmen, 43840 Salou.
Tel. (977) 38 04 63*
Outdoor dining. International
cuisine.

La Goleta $$
*Gavina — playa Capellans,
43840 Salou. Tel. (977) 38 35 66*
Seafood specialities. View.
Outdoor dining.

Macarrilla $$
*Paseo Jaime I 24, 43840 Salou.
Tel. (977) 38 54 15*
Outdoor dining. International
cuisine.

SITGES
HOTELS

Antemare $$
*Verge de Montserrat 48, 08870
Sitges. Tel. (93) 894 06 00,
fax (93) 894 6301*
Quiet hotel. Outdoor dining.
Outdoor swimming pool.

Calípolis $$
Passeig Maritim, 08870 Sitges.
Tel. (93) 894 1500
View. Outdoor dining. La Brasa
grill.

Galeón $
San Francisco 44, 08870 Sitges.
Tel. (93) 894 0612,
fax (93) 894 6335
Outdoor swimming pool.

Subur Maritim $$
Passeig Maritim, 08870 Sitges.
Tel. (93) 894 1550,
fax (93) 894 0427
View . Outdoor swimming pool.

Platjador $
Passeig de la Ribera 35,
08870 Sitges.
Tel. (93) 894 5054,
fax (93) 894 6335

Romantic y la Renaixença $
Sant Isidre 33, 08870 Sitges.
Tel. (93) 894 0643,
fax (93) 894 8167
No restaurant. Patio-garden
planted with trees.

Terramar $$
Passeig Maritim 30,
08870 Sitges. Tel. (93) 894 0050,
fax (93) 894 5604
Quiet hotel. View.
Outdoor dining. Outdoor
swimming pool. Garden. Tennis
court.

RESTAURANTS

Els 4 Gats $
San Pablo 13, 08870 Sitges. Tel.
(93) 894 1915
Closed Wednesday.

Mare Nostrum $$
Passeig de la Ribera 60, 08870
Sitges. Tel. (93) 894 3393
Outdoor dining. Closed
Wednesday.

La Masía $$
Paseo Vilanova 164, 08870
Sitges. Tel. (93) 894 1076
Outdoor dining. Catalan cuisines
and country-style regional decor.

Ródenas $$
Isla de Cuba 8, 08870 Sitges.
Tel. (93) 894 4401
Closed Wednesday.

Vivero $$
Passeig Balmins, 08870 Sitges.
Tel. (93) 894 2149
View. Outdoor dining. Seafood
specialities. Closed Tuesday
December to May.

TARRAGONA

HOTELS

Astari $
Via Augusta 95, 43003
Tarragona. Tel. (977) 23 69 00,
fax (977) 23 69 11
View. Outdoor dining. Outdoor
swimming pool. Garden.

Lauria $
*Rambla Nova 20, 43004
Tarragona. Tel. (977) 13 67 12,
fax (977) 23 6700*
No restaurant. Outdoor
swimming pool.

Paris $
*Maragall 4, 43003 Tarragona.
Tel. (977) 23 60 12,
fax (977) 23 86 54*
No restaurant.

Urbis $
*Reding 20 bis, 43001 Tarragona.
Tel. (977) 24 01 16, fax
(977) 24 36 54*
No restaurant.

RESTAURANTS

La Puda $$
*Muelle Pescadores 25, 43004
Tarragona. Tel. (977) 21 15 11*
Seafood specialities.

La Rambla $$
*Rambla Nova 10, 43004
Tarragona. Tel. (977) 23 87 29*
International cuisine. Outdoor
dining.

Sol Ric $$
*via Augusta 227, 43007
Tarragona. Tel. (977) 23 20 32*
Excellent and original cuisine
with emphasis on seafood.
Outdoor dining. Country-style
decor. Terrace planted with trees.
Closed Sunday evening and
Monday.

TORTOSA

HOTELS

Berenguer IV $
*Cervantes 23, 43500 Tortosa.
Tel. (977) 44 08 16, fax (977) 44
55 13*
Cafeteria only.

**Parador Nacional
Castillo de la Zuda** $$
*43500 Tortosa Tel. (977) 44 44
50, fax (977) 44 44 58*
Quiet hotel. View . Outdoor
swimming pool. Garden.

Tortosa Parc $
*Conde de Bañuelos 10, 43500
Tortosa. Tel. (977) 44 61 12*
No restaurant.

VILLANUEVA Y
GELTRU

HOTELS

César $
*Isaac Peral 4, 08800 Villanueva
y Geltrú. Tel. (93) 81511 25, fax
(93) 815 6719*
Quiet hotel. Terrace planted with
trees. La Fitorra restaurant.

Solvi 70 $
*Paseo Ribes Roges 1, 08800
Villanueva y Geltrú. Tel. (93)
81512 45*
View.

RESTAURANTS

Chez Bernard et Marguerite $$
*Ramón Llull 4, 08800 Villanueva
y Geltrú. Tel. (93) 815 56 04*
French cuisine. Outdoor dining.

Cossetania $$
*Passeig Maritim 92, 08800
Villanueva y Geltrú. Tel. (93)
815 55 59*
Outdoor dining. Seafood
specialities. Closed Wednesday.

Peixerot $$
*Passeig Maritim 56, 08800
Villanueva y Geltrú. Tel. (93)
815 06 25*
Outdoor dining. Seafood
specialities. Closed Sunday
evening except in summer.

Pere Peral $$
*Isaac Peral 15, 08800 Villanueva
y Geltrú. Tel. (93) 815 2996*
Outdoor dining. Terrace beneath
the pine trees. Closed Monday
evening.

El Pescador $
*Passeig del Carme 45, 08800
Villanueva y Geltrú. Tel. (93)
815 31 42*
Outdoor dining. Seafood
specialities.